Law and Risk Management in Dental Practice

Law and Risk Management in Dental Practice

Burton R. Pollack, DDS, MPH, JD

Professor and Dean Emeritus
School of Dental Medicine
State University of New York at Stony Brook
Stony Brook, New York

Quintessence Publishing Co, Inc

Chicago, Berlin, Tokyo, Copenhagen, London, Paris, Milan,
Barcelona, Istanbul, São Paulo, New Delhi, Moscow, Prague, and Warsaw

Library of Congress Cataloging-in-Publication Data

Pollack, Burton R., 1923-
  Law and risk management in dental practice / Burton R. Pollack.
      p. ; cm.
Includes bibliographical references and index.
  ISBN 0-86715-416-0 (pbk.)
  1. Dentistry--Practice. 2. Risk management. 3.
Dentists--Malpractice.
  [DNLM: 1. Dentistry--United States. 2. Jurisprudence--United States.
3. Legislation, Dental--United States. 4. Risk Management--United
States. W 705 P771L 2002] I. Title.
  RK58 .P65 2002
  617.6'0068--dc21

                                          2002002549

Quintessence Publishing Co, Inc
551 Kimberly Drive
Carol Stream, IL 60188
www.quintpub.com

Disclaimer: The purpose of the information contained in this book is to present legal trends that relate to dental practice. It is not intended to provide the reader with legal advice. For personal legal advice related to any subject presented in this book, the reader is advised to consult an attorney.

Photo credits:

Photographs on pages 1, 39, 81, 103, and 133 were originally published in: Wolfgang Bengel. *Mastering Dental Photography.* Berlin: Quintessenz, 2002.

Photographs on pages 51, 67, 89, and 201 were originally published in: Antonella Tani Botticelli. *Experience Is the Best Teacher: Manual of Dental Hygiene.* London: Quintessence, 2002.

Photograph on page 117 courtesy of Dr Rodney Phoenix.

Partial support for the book was received from the National Society of Dental Practitioners and the Redwoods Group Dentists Insurance Program.

Editor: Kathryn O'Malley
Production: Patrick L. Penney
Internal Design: Sue Robinson
Cover Design: Dawn Hartman

Printed in Canada

To my wife, Barbara, without whose patience and encouragement this book could never have been written; to my children and grandchildren whom I neglected during the writing; and to Louis J. P. Calisti, educator and dear friend, who during his brilliant life served as my role model, personally and professionally. Thanks, Lou, for sharing part of your life with me.

Table of Contents

Preface

The idea for this text came shortly after I entered law school in 1955, 9 years after I had graduated from dental school. During those 9 years I was in a part-time solo dental practice and on the faculty of the dental school at the University of Maryland. What surprised me most during my first year in law school was the realization of how little I knew about how the practice of my profession was regulated and how much less I knew about the legal risks associated with practice. As I searched the literature and the material being taught in the dental schools, I began to realize that there was nothing available to guide a practicing dentist through the turbulent waters of litigation and the regulation of dentists and dental practice. However, the book had to wait—my practice, teaching, and my young family were naturally my first priorities.

About 15 years later, in the 1970s and early 1980s, the profession underwent some dramatic changes when the public and its attorneys were awakened to the risks of treatment. Patients began to bring malpractice cases against dentists in rapidly increasing numbers. The malpractice crisis had arrived. During that time period and for many years that followed, pressure from consumer groups resulted in the enactment of new laws to regulate dentists and dental practice. Cases brought against dentists by government agencies for violations of the laws showed a similar increase. Dentists were at risk; their professional reputation, standing, and financial resources were being attacked.

The increase in litigation, regulation, and legislation over the years has been of such proportion that the busy practitioner finds it difficult, if not impossible, to keep current on the laws affecting dental practice. Court decisions and the statutes and rules and regulations of each state as well as those of the federal government are scattered throughout the official publications of each jurisdiction, and there is no national central depository in which all decisions related to dental malpractice cases and dental regulatory laws are available. Finding all of this information is therefore a difficult task for all but the most experienced attorneys, and is impossible for a dentist without an education in law.

For 30 years, I have been collecting almost everything available in legal texts and case reports related to dental litigation; the result is the publication of this book. It describes how dentists can protect themselves from unfounded claims of malpractice, excessive jury awards, and allegations of violations of the regulatory laws. Its primary goal is to educate members of the dental profession, including students, in the principles and practices of risk management. The book is designed for use by students, in preparation for their entrance into the dental profession, and by practitioners, including general dentists, dental specialists, dental hygienists, and dental assistants. It is intended as a relatively quick reference guide to legal decisions that directly impact dental practitioners.

There are four caveats to keep in mind when reading the text: *(1)* The laws are all state specific, ie, they differ in each state; New York is used as a model from which the reader can learn the general parameters of state regulation; *(2)* the statutes relating to dental practice may change at each meeting of the legislative body, and the rules and regulations relating to dental practice may change at each meeting of an administrative agency; *(3)* courts have been known to reverse prior decisions and to make "new law"; and *(4)* in legal practice there are two sides to every argument.

Finally, I would like to call attention to the treatment of gender in the text. To avoid the awkward use of *he/she, s/he,* or *him/her,* I alternately use *he* and *she* as the personal pronouns. In any given situation, therefore, the use of either personal pronoun is not intended to convey the sense of gender alone but rather is intended to be generic.

A work of this magnitude, covering over a century of health professional litigation in the United States, could not have been completed without the assistance of many individuals, and to them I owe much of the credit (but not the blame) for the contents of this book. Many debates on legal issues were held with Robert Himmelfarb, DDS, an "expert" expert witness in many malpractice trials, and with Lawrence Jerrold, DDS, JD, who questioned my legal opinions more often than I might have wished. A debt of gratitude is also owed to Richard Breitweiser, Esq, who contributed the chapter on insurance and who pointed out to me cases I had overlooked. Another to whom I owe appreciation is James Nemeth, DDS, who in his professional capacity has listened to hundreds of phone calls from dentists reporting potential problems with the law and was kind enough to pass the information on to me. A very special acknowledgment goes to the late Louis J. P. Calisti, DDS, MPH, who always reminded me what the book should be about. I also extend thanks to Mort Glick and Virginia Verduin, who were tolerant of my missed deadlines on other assignments during the writing of this book, and to Ann Joachim and Italia Mazzullo, who provided expert secretarial and computer assistance with patience and tolerance of my obsession for getting things done as soon as possible. I am also grateful to the staff of Quintessence Publishing Co, Inc for their assistance in completing this project. And finally I would like to thank Dean Barry R. Rifkin, DDS, PhD, who provided me with the resources I needed and, equally important, took over my position as dean of the School of Dental Medicine at Stony Brook, which left me with the time to complete the book.

CHAPTER ONE

Introduction to the Judicial System of the United States

1.1 The Court System

Introduction

1.1.1 Anyone who wants to know what the law is must first understand how the United States court system is organized. The decision of one court, for example, may establish procedures for obtaining patient consent that the decision of another court explicitly rules unnecessary. It is impossible to know what the law is in such a case without knowing the jurisdiction of the two courts and their impact upon precedent law (see chapter 9). Or, a certain court may not hold a defendant dentist responsible for the negligent act of a dental hygienist, while you believe a dentist *should be* responsible. You can understand if the court made "new law" only if you understand the powers of that court (see section 1.5). This chapter provides a brief description of the courts, their organization, their jurisdiction, and their overall effect on regulating dental practice.

Types of Courts

1.1.2 Courts may be classified in many ways: as having jurisdiction over a certain region or subject matter, as criminal or civil, as trial or appellate. This book focuses on the decisions of trial courts and appellate courts.

Trial courts, also known as lower courts, are the courts of original jurisdiction, the first to hear and decide a case brought against a dentist in which a patient alleges negligence or malpractice (see chapter 4). Such courts may hold either jury trials, heard by a jury, or bench trials, heard by a judge alone. In most jurisdictions, the litigants choose between the two. In New York, a bench trial is held unless either party claims a jury. Almost all malpractice cases are decided by a jury. The number of jurors in a civil case is governed by local trial procedure. In New York, six are required, five of which must agree to declare the defendant guilty of the alleged act. The defendant's guilt must be established by a preponderance of the evidence (more than 50%) in a civil case; "beyond a reasonable doubt" (95% to 100%) in a criminal case.

Decisions made in a lower court may be appealed to a higher, or appellate, court should the losing party feel that either:

1. The lower court violated procedure as established by an appellate court or by court procedural rules.
2. The judge, in instructions to the jury, applied the wrong law to guide the jury in arriving at a decision in the case.

Juries decide the facts; the judge applies the law to the facts decided by the jury. In a bench trial, the judge both decides the facts and applies the law.

The legal rule of *stare decisis*, meaning "to abide by higher decisions," requires lower courts to abide by decisions of the appellate court in whose jurisdiction they sit. Thus, appellate courts make what is known as *precedent law*. But whether or not the lower court applies precedent law, if the case is not taken to appeal its decision stands undisturbed.

Appellate courts hear appeals from decisions made in the lower courts; they are the upper courts. In some states cases are so plentiful that two levels of appellate courts are established: intermediate appellate courts and a single higher court of last resort. Cases taken to appeal are heard by judges without juries, because juries decide only facts, and facts are established in the lower court on the basis of the testimony of witnesses whose credibility can be judged only by direct observation. Appellate courts simply accept these facts (with a few exceptions that have no bearing on the subject of this book), then decide whether the wrong law was applied by the lower court, or an error was made during the trial. The appeal court may:

1. Affirm the decision of the lower court
2. Declare that a procedural error was made in the lower court, vacate the decision, and remand the case for retrial
3. Reverse the decision based upon the fact that the wrong law was applied by the judge in the lower court's decision
4. Modify the decision as it relates to damages: reduce it, increase it, or nullify it

Names of Courts

1.1.3   Each state names its courts, as does the federal government. For example, in New York, the lower court of original jurisdiction, the first to hear an action brought against a dentist by a patient alleging negligence, malpractice, or breach of contract, is called the Supreme Court. There is one Supreme Court in each county. The state is divided geographically into four appellate jurisdictions, and in each is an Appellate Division of the Supreme Court. The Appellate Divisions hear and decide appeals brought to them from the lower courts within their geographic jurisdiction. The highest court in the state, the court of last resort whose decisions are binding on all courts in the state, is called the New York Court of Appeals.

By contrast, in New Jersey, the court of original jurisdiction is called the Superior Court, of which there is one for each county. The intermediate appellate court is called the Superior Court, Appellate Division, and the court of last resort the Supreme Court. In Illinois, the court of original jurisdiction is called the Circuit Court, the intermediate appellate court the Appellate Court of Illinois (District and Division), and the court of last resort the Supreme Court.

In the federal system, the United States is divided into 88 districts, each with at least one District Court. The federal intermediate court is the US Court of Appeals, at least one for each of the 11 Judicial Circuits. The highest court of the land, the court of last resort, is the US Supreme Court, which consists of eight justices and a Chief Justice. Any seven can hear a case, but five must agree to take any case. Decisions of the US Supreme Court are binding on all courts in the United States.

1.2   Common Law, Case Law, and Black Letter Law

Common Law and Case Law

1.2.1   The English Common Law was adopted in the United States at the time of its independence. It is based upon principles of justice, reason, and common sense rather than on set laws. When applied to specific situations by a judicial body, it becomes case law. Except for cases decided in federal courts, case law is state-specific. Only the jurisdiction in which the appellate court sits is affected by its case law.

The decisions of appellate courts are published officially by their jurisdictions. They are published within hours of the decision because each one may change case law, and they are made available to all law libraries and to the electronic databases of legal publishing companies such as Westlaw and Lexis. States publish what are called *Reports*. Westlaw publishes the *Reporter System*, which contains the report of the case and its editorial comments. Both are widely distributed and available in all law libraries throughout the country. Attorneys must remain current on changes in case law that affect their field of practice or a particular case for which they are retained by a client.

While appellate decisions are officially published as *Reports*, decisions of the lower trial courts are recorded in the court in which the case was heard. Because thousands of trial courts are scattered throughout the country, there is no simple way to collect national data on what takes place in them. It is therefore impossible to know just what is happening in the field of malpractice litigation. Only the insurance companies collect this information, and they share only what suits them. Further, their knowledge is limited to cases in which a dentist defendant is insured for malpractice, and, surprisingly, some practice without it (see chapters 17 and 19).

Black Letter Law

1.2.2   Black letter law (BLL) is law written in black ink on white paper. While common law is *discovered,* black letter law is *promulgated*: that is, effective as of a certain date. Such law comes from several sources: elected officials serving in some form of formal organization, such as a congress, a state legislature, a city council, etc, or from administrative agencies established by the elected body of a jurisdiction. Laws enacted by elected bodies are called by various names: the US Congress enacts acts of congress, called public laws; a state legislatures enact statutes; lower jurisdictions enact codes, ordinances, etc. Except for that of the federal government, BLL is state specific: the BLL regulating dental practice in Vermont has no impact on dental practice in Ohio. Laws adopted specifically to regulate the practice of dentistry are known in most states as the Dental Practice Act (DPA). The DPA includes the statutes of the state and the rules or regulations of the agencies responsible for dental practice. However, many other statutes and regulations, scattered throughout the laws of states and not included in the DPA, affect dental practice.

Black letter law is, again, promulgated to be effective as of a certain date. Suppose that the current law in a state prohibits a dental hygienist from administering a local anesthetic, and that in June of the year 1997, the state legislature passes and the governor signs legislation, effective as of July 1, 1998, permitting a dental hygienist to administer a local anesthetic. A dental hygienist who administered a local anesthetic June 30, 1998 was in violation of the law, despite the fact that the same act committed on the following day was legal. By contrast, case law is said to be present long before it is applied by the court; it has been discovered, not promulgated (see section 1.4).

Criminal and Civil Law

1.3   Violations of the law fall into one of two major categories: criminal or civil. Cases against dentists may fall into either; and a single act performed by a dentist may result in both a criminal and a civil suit. For example, a state, applying BLL, may prosecute for professional misconduct a dentist who fails to obtain the consent of a patient before beginning treatment while the patient sues the same dentist for negligence or malpractice for not obtaining consent.

Criminal Law

1.3.1   A crime may be a violation of an act of congress, the statute of a state, one of the rules or regulations of an administrative agency, or the local law of a smaller jurisdiction. It is a crime against the people, or in the case of an administrative agency, a crime against the agency or its head. It may lead to a variety of penalties, including fines, loss or suspension of the license to practice, mandatory continuing education, counseling, community service, mandatory supervision, etc. Violating the rule or regulation of an administrative agency is termed a quasi-crime, and loss of freedom is never one of its penalties. In recent years, public interest groups have brought greater pressure on licensing agencies to intensify the policing of health practitioners in general. As a result, violations of the Dental Practice Act have become a major concern to dentists. Many states have made available on the Internet lists of health practitioners, including dentists, who have been found in violation of the licensing laws. For example, in New York the web site address is: http://www.op.nysed.gov/ramthy. For examples of cases reported on the Internet, see chapter 16.

Several states are scheduled to maintain a malpractice history of all licensed health practitioners, and there is considerable public pressure to make such information available on the Internet.

Civil Law

1.3.2 Civil law protects personal or civil rights. These rights may derive from common law or from contracts between parties. A violation of common law is called a tort; a violation of contract is called a breach of contract. Torts may be intentional or unintentional. Intentional torts include defamation, libel and slander, misrepresentation, deceit, trespass to the person, assault and battery, and false imprisonment. The unintentional tort of greatest concern to dentists is professional negligence or malpractice, in which an injury is a result of the treatment.

Victims of a civil wrong are compensated through money damages assessed against the person who committed the tort or breached the contract. Damages that mitigate the injury are known as *special damages*; damages for pain and suffering are known as *general damages*. In rare cases *punitive damages* may be assessed against the wrongdoer as punishment.

Professional liability insurance covers *special* and *general damages*. *Punitive damages* are not covered by any insurance policy (see chapter 19).

Legal Precedents, Stare Decisis, and Appeals

1.4 When an appellate court decides a case, *precedent law* is established that, as noted above, binds lower courts in its jurisdiction by the rule of *stare decisis*. If a judge's instructions to the jury do not apply the precedent established by the appellate court within the jurisdiction of the trial court, and the case is appealed by the losing party, the decision of the lower court may be reversed by the appellate court. However, decisions of the lower court may be appealed for other reasons as well. If an appellate court decides that a trial judge committed an error during the trial, the case may be remanded for retrial by the trial court. For example, a trial court judge may rule that the testimony of an expert should not be entered into evidence because the expert was not of the same specialty as the defendant dentist, and the defendant may appeal on the ground that this testimony should have been allowed. If the appellate court agrees, the case will be remanded for another trial in which the testimony of the expert is allowed.

In summary, appeals may be taken either for substantive errors, such as applying the wrong law, or for procedural errors, such as not allowing appropriate evidence. But whatever the trial court's errors, its decision is binding if the case is not appealed. This may lead to confusion. For example, one may falsely conclude, after hearing of a case in which the jury exonerated a dentist from liability for the negligent act of a hygienist, that dentists are not legally responsible for their hygienists' negligence. If the case was decided by a jury and not taken to appeal, the decision stands; and yet that decision may nonetheless have misapplied the law, which remains unaffected by it.

Flexibility in Law

1.5   How then is new law made and old law changed? Clearly Congress and state legislatures can enact new BLL and change current law as they wish. Before November 1996, there was no law in New York recognizing dental assistants as members of a profession. In that year, the state legislature enacted legislation creating a dental assistant profession with permitted duties and an official title: certified dental assistant.

Case law changes in a more complex manner. Appellate courts, in establishing precedent law, recognize the changing needs of society, advances in technology and science, new public policy issues, etc, all of which reach them through trial court decisions. Some of these are "cases of first impression," involving an issue that has never been faced by a court in the jurisdiction. Such a case arose in New York, for example, when a trial court was asked to decide if a nurse in a physician's office could obtain a valid consent to a surgical procedure performed by the physician. The appellate court in rendering its decision stated that "no New York case has directly addressed the issue" and that "a review of case law from other states revealed only one case directly on point," a Pennsylvania case in which the dentist's assistant, his wife, obtained the consent of the patient. The New York court ultimately concluded "that a nurse trained in obtaining informed consent to a particular procedure could act as an agent for the treating physician," thereby establishing a precedent and creating new case law.[1] (For details about informed consent law, see chapter 17.)

Some decisions of appellate courts are called *landmark decisions*, or *landmark cases*. These are cases of extreme importance that set precedents that are recognized as new law.

[1] 543 NYS2d 242 (1989).

Legal Terms

1.6   One of the major characteristics of the law is its precision: words used in law have precise meanings. It is when they are combined into phrases and sentences that interpretations may vary. Punctuation may change the meaning of a sentence; an unintended or misplaced comma may have a major effect upon the outcome of a case.

The Words *Shall* and *May*

1.6.1   First let's deal with some simple words used in written law: *shall* and *may*. If the law states that you, "*Shall* register your license triennially," you are given no choice but to comply, or else suffer the penalty imposed by the licensing agency. The word *may* provides for the exercise of an option. If the law states that you *may* report a case of suspected child abuse, you have the option of reporting or not reporting. If you fail to report, there is no penalty. The word *must* is not generally used in law, but it is synonymous with *shall*. When reading the law, whether case law or BLL, pay careful attention to the *shalls* and *mays*.

The Words *Medical*, *Dental*, *Physician*, and *Dentist*

1.6.2   In deciding cases that involve legislation, courts must by necessity decide on the exact meaning of the words contained in the legislation and determine the intent of the lawmakers. This is not always easy. In 1974, for example, as the result of a so-called malpractice crisis, the legislature in New York adopted what came to be known as "malpractice legislation." This was designed to change current law so as to make it more difficult for patients injured through the negligence of physicians and hospitals to be compensated. For example, the statute of limitations for initiating malpractice suits was reduced from 3 years to $2^1/_2$ years (see chapter 5).

In writing the new laws the legislature used the terms *medical* and *hospital*, and the question soon arose whether the new laws applied equally to dentists. Several court cases addressed this issue. However, in the defining case, cited by others that followed, the court stated:

> The primary definition of the word "medical" refers to physicians and the practice of medicine. The definition of the practice of medicine (Education Law, §6521) and the definition of the practice of dentistry (Education Law, §6601) are amazingly similar. The practice of dentistry is limited to the human mouth while the practice of medicine involves the entire human body. However, the practice of medicine and use of the title "physician" is limited to those having a degree of doctor of medicine or doctor of osteopathy (Education Law, §6522 and §6524).[2]
>
> It seems therefore, that the practice of dentistry does not come within the usual and ordinary meaning of the word "medical" and the defendant is not protected by CPLR [New York Civil Practice Laws and Rules] 3017(c).

[2] 413 NYS2d 99 (1979). See also: 443 NYS2d 758 (1981); 437 NYS2d 641 (1981); and 97 Misc2d 972 (1979).

The dentists in the state thus found themselves governed by the old, and less favorable, laws; and so the lobbying began: it was not until several years later that the legislature adopted the "dental catch-up bills," providing dentists the same advantages as physicians.

Particularly confusing here is that, while the courts interpret the words *physician* and *medical* in BLL as excluding dentists, they interpret the same words in case law as including dentists. In an early case decided in New York, the court described a certain standard of care for physicians and then stated, "These same standards apply equally to dentists in the treatment of their

[3]226 NYS2d 576 (1962).

patients."[3] Similar definitions are found in other states, so that the entire body of case law involving physicians applies, for the most part, to dentists, whereas BLL involving physicians usually does not.

Special Characteristics of the Law

1.7   Those not educated in the legal profession often find law confusing and illogical—and understandably so. Law is commonly (*1*) complex, and (*2*) unpredictable. Legal procedure in federal, state, and local courts may, and often does, vary, and most lawyers in practice complain bitterly about this lack of uniformity.

The law is fundamentally unpredictable because no one, not even the most experienced lawyer, can be certain what a judge or jury will do. Two lawyers or sets of lawyers, on opposite sides of a dispute, argue a case as if winning were the most important thing in their lives. They enter the trial believing in the merits of the side they represent, and their arguments during the trial reflect their conviction. Yet one side prevails and the other loses. The best a lawyer can promise is a 50% chance of winning, not a very good chance for health practitioners and their patients.

Moreover, a single set of facts may lead to two completely different rulings in different jurisdictions, or in the same jurisdiction at different times. For example, for years the Supreme Court of the United States, in several cases brought before it, ruled that "separate but equal" education was constitutional. Then one day the court ruled that it was unconstitutional. What appeared to be a reversal was in fact the result of the court's decision to take into account the testimony of psychologists.

You should therefore be wary in dealing with the law. In reading articles or attending lectures on the subject, determine the credibility of the author or speaker. Does a dentist lecturing or writing about legal issues or risk management have the same level of credibility as an attorney? Does an attorney, however experienced with cases involving the dental profession, understand the practice of dentistry?

Legal Research: How to Find a Case

1.8   The success of any law practice depends to a large degree on its access to information. Most law firms have a library of their own, but these are usually limited to the state in which they practice and their area of special interest. Law schools and courts have everything available: legal texts, law review journals, and the BLL and case law of all states and the federal government. Their law libraries represent a major annual expenditure and occupy considerable space. Looking up the BLL in such libraries is relatively simple. Statute books and the books of administrative agencies have extensive indexes. Suppose you want to determine what duties dental hygienists are permitted to perform. First, look up *dental hygienist* in the index of the statutes in the jurisdiction of interest to you. Then go to the book it references and read the statutes. Next consult the rules and regulations of the dental board or the appropriate agency within the state that is responsible for regulating dental hygiene practice.

The index will lead you to the section on the regulation of dental hygienists. The annotated versions of these books will provide the dates on which specific laws and regulations became effective and list the cases in which the courts have interpreted them.

Finding case law on a given subject is considerably more difficult. If you have access to one of the computerized law databases, Westlaw or Lexis, the task is considerably simplified. You may type in a key word or phrase to start a search in a jurisdiction in which you are interested. For example, if you wish to find all cases in the state of Pennsylvania in which a dentist was sued by a patient alleging that the dentist was negligent in the extraction of a tooth, you identify Pennsylvania as the state you wish to explore, and then key the words *dentist, malpractice, tooth extraction* into the search. You may also search cases by the names of litigants. In fact, the possibilities of search are limitless. However, there is no database available for cases decided in lower courts because these cases, although *recorded*, are not *reported*. Lower court decisions are rarely included in Westlaw or Lexis.

Using the law library is considerably more difficult than using a database: entire law school courses are devoted to it. It is not of much practical use to one not educated in the law.

To find information about a lower court case, you must go to the records of the court in which the case was tried. Companies in many states publish books under the title *Jury Trial Reports* or something similar. These are limited to civil trials. Moran Publishing Company in New York publishes the *New York Jury Verdict Reporter*. This includes approximately 90% of all jury trials held in the state. Another of its publications is limited to medical and dental malpractice cases and is published each month: *New York Medical Malpractice: Verdicts, Settlements, and Appeals*. The report lists the court in which the trial was conducted; the date; the name of the sitting judge; the makeup of the jury as to sex; the decision and the amount of the award if any; the vote of the jury; the length of the trial; the length of the jury deliberation; the names of the experts and their specialties; whether an appeal was taken; the physical evidence (demonstrative evidence) produced at the trial; the subject of the case; whether there was an offer and demand for settlement and the amount of each; and a description of what took place at the trial. This publication is of major importance to attorneys that represent clients who claim an injury as a result of treatment provided by a health practitioner, and to professional liability companies.

For an example of a series of cases reported in *New York Medical Malpractice: Verdicts, Settlements, and Appeals,* see chapter 16.

Case Citations

1.9   Each case decided by a court is recorded using a uniform system of descriptors that enable an interested party to locate the case; together these make up the case citation. The first descriptor is the number of the volume in which the case is recorded; the second is the name of the volume or jurisdiction; and the third is the page on which the report begins. Each state and the federal government has its own set of volumes. For example, 414 Mass 105 indicates a case decided in Massachusetts that begins on page 105 of volume 414 of the *Massachusetts Reporter*. The notation 12 US 576, or 12 S Ct 576, indicates a case decided by the US Supreme Court and beginning on page 576 of volume 12 of its reports. This citation system is used by the major publisher of reported cases, which also publishes cases in geographically grouped volumes: the *Atlantic Reporter*, for example, includes cases decided in New York, the New England states, New Jersey, Maryland, Pennsylvania, Delaware, and the District of Columbia. Other states are grouped as Pacific (P), South West (SW), North West (NW), North East (NE), South (S), and South East (SE). A decision reached by a court in Illinois might be reported as 119 Ill 937 in the *Illinois Reporter* and at the same time as 690 NE 1021 in the *North East Reporter*. At times in the regional reports, the state in which the case is decided follows the citation, as may the year, thus: 143 NE 123 (Ind), or 143 NE 123 (1996). All law school libraries contain the entire set of reporters, as do most law courts, especially all appellate and federal courts. Official citations begin with the names of litigants, and often conclude with the date the case was decided, eg, Smith v Jones, 128 NYS2d 128 (1999).

In this book, case citations are located in the margins near where the case is discussed in the text.

A Sample Case Report

1.10

Appellate court case reports generally follow the following format. The heading includes the plaintiff and the defendant, the name of the appellate court deciding the case and its location, and the date of the decision. The court first describes how the case found its way to the appellate level, then sets out the facts as determined by the lower court, then repeats the arguments presented by each side. Next, the court discusses the arguments and presents its opinion on those arguments. Finally, the court renders its decision. It may affirm, modify, or reverse the decision of the lower court, or remand the case for a new trial in whole or in part. On the following pages is a reprint of an actual case decided by an appellate court in New York.[4] (Some inessential details were omitted; the case will be discussed in more detail in chapter 4.)

[4]189 AD 827: 179 NYS 281.

Case Report 1

[C.R.]

v

[C.N.]

Supreme Court, Appellate Division, Second Department.
December, 1919

Appeal from Trial term, Kings County.

Action by [C.R.] against [C.N.]. From a judgment for plaintiff, and from an order denying his motion to set aside the verdict and for a new trial, made on the minutes, defendant appeals. Reversed, and complaint dismissed.

The plaintiff went to the defendant's office and informed him that she had some trouble with her tooth—that it was "bothering" her. It was a crowned tooth, with another false tooth supported by this crown. The defendant removed the crown, bored into the tooth, and found that the tooth was not fully filled and that it emitted an offensive odor. He thereupon took an X-ray photograph, which confirmed his diagnosis that the root was not entirely filled and contained decomposing organic matter. He then told the plaintiff that the tooth should be extracted, and it was extracted. The plaintiff desired to have gas administered, and gas was administered. It was found difficult to bring about complete unconsciousness in the patient by the administration of gas. Two attempts made by the defendant were unsuccessful, and then the plaintiff's husband came to the dentist's office, and the operation was continued with his assistance. With the aid of the plaintiff's husband and a nurse employed by the defendant, the dentist was able to administer sufficient gas to bring about sufficient unconsciousness, and the tooth was removed.

The plaintiff claims that in the removal of the tooth it was broken off, and that the doctor made repeated efforts to extract the root; that in the course of these efforts he administered cocaine, and that in the administration of cocaine the needle of the instrument used by the dentist either came out or broke off, and that the defendant removed it from the gum with forceps. After the operation the plaintiff fainted, but soon recovered and went to the house of a friend, where she spent the day and returned home with her husband. That night her mouth was very sore, and she claims that pieces of bone and pieces of flesh were subsequently cut away by a dentist who later treated her. She was treated by this dentist, and also by a physician, and was for a time in a sanitarium. Undoubtedly she had a very sore mouth and jaw as a result of this extraction.

It seems to me that this case necessarily involves a holding that if a person has a tooth extracted, and thereafter his mouth is sore or he is ill, the dentist is responsible. This is not the law. The court [the trial court judge], correctly charged the jury:

> The defendant was not a guarantor of his work, or the result that would follow; he is not an insurer as to the result. In other words, in this case, he was required to use the ordinary care of such a man having the ordinary skill in this locality; and, if he does not, the mere fact that there is a bad result is not enough, but you have got to trace it to his lack of skill, or his negligence.

More to the same effect could be quoted from the charge, but I think the quotation sufficiently shows that the court correctly instructed the jury that an untoward result of an operation did not make the defendant liable, unless the result was brought about by his lack of the ordinary skill of dentists in his locality, or his negligence.

Applying that rule, what facts are there upon which to base a finding of the defendant's liability? The defendant extracted the plaintiff's tooth, but there is not a hint or claim that it was not necessary. He

Case Report 1 (cont)

administered gas, and had some difficulty in doing so. The plaintiff desired it, and there is no proof that it was improper to do so, that too much was administered, or that it could have been done by any better method. Her mouth bled, but this is usual, ordinary, and unavoidable. The cavity looked large to the plaintiff. Again this was the usual and ordinary result. No one else having special knowledge upon the subject confirmed her opinion. She had difficulty in talking. Two teeth had been removed—one natural tooth and an artificial tooth attached to it. This difficulty was disagreeable, natural, and temporary. Small pieces of the alveolar process, commonly called bone, came out.

Again, however, there is an absolute dearth of testimony that this was the result of any lack of skill, or anything more than frequently happened. The plaintiff claimed, at the time of the trial, that her gum was so sunken at the place of this extraction as to necessitate her having artificial teeth of an unusually large size. The only purpose of this that I can think of was to give the jury the impression that too much alveolar process was removed by this extraction. Of this there is no testimony. The testimony, on the contrary, is to the effect that such alveolar process as remains in the vicinity of an extraction is absorbed and disappears. This is also a fact of common and general knowledge. Plaintiff claims her lips were cut and bleeding. When plaintiff struggled, so that even with the help of a nurse defendant was unable to administer gas, and was only able to do so with the added assistance of plaintiff's husband, this result cannot be attributed to any lack of skill or negligence upon the part of the defendant. These are all of the immediate physical effects of the operation. It is true that the plaintiff was ill afterward, and that illness may have been attributable to the extraction of this tooth, but that does not warrant holding the defendant liable, as he does not, under the law, guarantee the result.

If the treatment of the defendant was unskillful or negligent, it was incumbent upon the plaintiff to show it by those qualified to testify to the proper method of performing such an operation; and if the untoward results present here might have been avoided by due care, the duty of showing that was also on the plaintiff.

I am not unmindful of the fact that in some cases the lack of skill or want of care is so obvious that expert testimony is unnecessary. This, however, is not such a case, and the counsel for the respondent in his brief fails to point out anything which the defendant did or omitted to do that indicated absence of skill or lack of care. He merely refers to results, and claims from these a want of care may be inferred. But these, as previously stated, are not of such a character as to warrant that inference without the aid of medical testimony.

The judgment and order should be reversed, and the complaint dismissed, with costs. All concur.

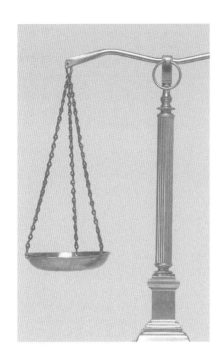

CHAPTER TWO

The Regulation of Dental Practice

History

2.1   The right of a state to regulate the practice of medicine was first confirmed by the courts in the late 1880s. A resident of West Virginia, refused a license to practice medicine after the legislature passed a law setting out requirements for a medical license, sued the state, demanding a license and questioning the state's right to regulate the profession. The case found its way to the US Supreme Court, which rejected the plaintiff's claim, stating:

> Few professions require more careful preparation by one who seeks to enter it than that of medicine. It has to deal with all those subtle and mysterious influences upon which health and life depend, and requires not only a knowledge of the properties of vegetable and mineral substances, but of the human body in all its complicated parts, and their relation to each other, as well as their influence upon the mind. The physician must be able to detect readily the presence of disease, and prescribe appropriate remedies for its removal. Every one may have occasion to consult him, but comparatively few can judge of the qualifications of learning and skill which he possesses. Reliance must be placed upon the assurance given by his license, issued by an authority competent to judge in that respect, that he possesses the requisite qualifications. Due consideration, therefore, for the protection of society may well induce the state to exclude from practice those who have not such a license, or who are found upon examination not to be fully qualified.

The court concluded, "The power of the state to provide for the general welfare of its people authorizes it to prescribe all such regulations as in its judgment will secure or tend to secure them against the consequences of ignorance and incapacity, as well as of deception and fraud."[1]

[1]129 US 114 (1889).

[2]213 NYS2d 92 (1914).

A New York court confirmed the power of the state to regulate dentists.[2] A dentist in Minnesota brought a similar case to the US Supreme Court, which stated, "It is well settled that a state may, consistently with the Fourteenth Amendment, prescribe that only persons possessing the reasonably necessary qualifications of learning and skill shall practice medicine or dentistry."[3]

[3]272 US 425 (1926).

Caveats in the Regulation of Dental Practice

2.2 Fifty-four different jurisdictions—the fifty states, Puerto Rico, the Virgin Islands, the District of Columbia, and the federal government—have exercised their right to regulate the health professions, including dentistry. Only federal laws apply to all US health practitioners. State laws apply only in the state in which they are adopted; however, some legal principles apply nationwide. For example, the legal principle of the statute of limitations is the same in all jurisdictions, though the statute may begin to run at different times and run for different lengths of time in each state (see chapter 5).

Dentists should know local as well as applicable federal law. The same act may be legal in one state and illegal in another. For example, a dentist in New York who sends a patient to a dental laboratory to select a shade for a crown is not in violation of the law, while a dentist who does the same thing in Massachusetts is.

Regulation by the State: The Dental Practice Act

2.3 The "Dental Practice Act" is the common, but not the official, title of a collection of laws and regulations enacted by states to regulate dental practice. It includes the statutes of the state and the rules or regulations of the agency responsible for dental practice. However, many other statutes and regulations scattered throughout the laws of the state also affect dental practice.

Though statutes and regulations differ among states, some general relations between legislatures and regulating agencies are the same in all. Statutes adopted by the legislature of a state can only be changed by the legislature; but the rules and regulations of an administrative agency can be changed by the agency without the legislature, though not without a public hearing. An administrative agency is not permitted to expand upon a statute adopted by the legislature. For example, if a statute forbids a dental hygienist to provide an irreversible service, an administrative agency regulating dental practice cannot permit a dental hygienist to prepare a tooth for a restoration. The rules and regulations of the administrative agency must comply with but not expand upon the statutes.

An abbreviated and edited version of the Dental Practice Act of New York follows. It is included as an example of how dentistry is regulated in one state. The reader should keep in mind that, although many of the laws of New York may be found in the laws of other states, many also may not, and these differences may be significant. Dentists should obtain a copy of the Dental Practice Act from the state in which they practice, and those dentists who practice in New York should request of the New York State Education Department a copy of the latest statutes and rules and regulations that govern the practice of dentistry.

Regulation of Dental Practice in New York

2.4 As stated above, 54 elected bodies have enacted legislation designed to regulate the health professional. Because the members of these bodies have neither the time nor the expertise to control the daily activities of the profession and the details of practice, they have enacted additional legislation (enabling legislation and statutory authority) establishing administrative agencies and granting that agency the power to adopt administrative laws (rules and regulations) to carry out its mission.

These administrative agencies may vary in name and other details, but their general regulatory structures are, for the most part, similar. In New York several administrative agencies regulate dentists and other health professionals. However, two are directly charged with this task: the State Education Department, the Commissioner of which is empowered to adopt regulations; and the Board of Regents, which is empowered to adopt rules. The State Board for Dentistry adopts neither rules nor regulations; it is charged instead with three responsibilities: *(1)* to serve as an examining body recommending licensure as dentists to the State Education Department; *(2)* to advise the state legislature, the Commissioner of Education, and the Board of Regents on dental matters, eg proposed changes and additions to the Dental Practice Act; and *(3)* to serve as an administrative body to hear violations of rules and regulations and to report its findings to the Board of Regents. In New Jersey, as in most other states, one administrative agency regulates the practice of dentistry: the New Jersey State Board of Dentistry. That Board combines most of the duties assigned to the three agencies in New York.

The statutes and the rules and regulations of the administrative agency make up the body of black letter law (BLL): the Dental Practice Act of the state. However, dentists in all jurisdictions should not forget that many other laws may affect their practice: federal laws, public health laws, sanitary codes, education laws, etc.

New York Statutes—Legislation

2.4.1 A statute may be changed or added only after an act of the legislature is signed into law by the governor. In contrast, a regulation may be changed or added by the State Education Department, or a rule by the Board of Regents, following a public announcement of the proposed change or addition and a public hearing. Again, however, neither a regulation nor a rule may be inconsistent with, or expand upon, a statute.

The statutes that relate to dental practice are included in Title VIII of the Education Law.

Article 130

2.4.1.1 This, the first of several articles on professional practice, contains the general provisions that regulate the admission to and the practice of certain professions, including dentistry, dental hygiene, and dental assisting. The latter was the last occupation to be added to the list of dental professionals and regulated by the State Education Department.

Subarticle 1. Section 6502 states that the license is valid during the life of the holder, but must be registered with the State Education Department at a fee and for an interval determined by the department. Dentists and dental hygienists are required to register their licenses every 3 years.

Section 6503 states that admission *(1)* entitles the licensee to practice the profession, *(2)* entitles the licensee to use the professional title (dentist or dental hygienist), and *(3)* subjects the licensee to a set of laws and to penalties for their violation.

Therefore, a graduate of a dental school is not a *dentist* until licensed and may not engage in dental practice until both licensed and registered. On graduation from a dental school, the graduate is a *doctor*, a title conferred by the university, but not a *dentist,* a title conferred by the state.

Subarticle 2. This part provides for the Board of Regents' supervision, and the Commissioner of the State Education Department's administration, of the professions. It permits the Board of Regents to adopt rules and the Commissioner to adopt regulations. It also describes the educational requirements for licensure, and in general terms, the examination for licensure. For example, it states that candidates for licensure as a dentist must be at least 21 years of age to take the examination.

Section 6507 enables the State Education Department to conduct investigations. A recently added provision requires each licensee to complete, before the next registration period, a 2-hour course in the recognition and reporting of child abuse and maltreatment (see Commissioner's Regulations, 59.12 below).

Section 6508 establishes various state boards to assist the Board of Regents and the State Education Department in carrying out their functions. It provides for the Board of Regents to appoint members to these boards on the recommendation of the Commissioner of Education, and further describes the general composition of the boards (the composition of the State Board for Dentistry will be found below). It lists the functions of the boards: *(1)* to assist the Board of Regents and the State Education Department; *(2)* to conduct examinations for licensure; and *(3)* to conduct a disciplinary hearing when there is an alleged violation by a licensed dental professional of the practice act.

Subarticle 3. Section 6509 is perhaps the most important to all practicing dentists. It defines *professional misconduct* for which a license to practice may be revoked or suspended, or for which a dentist may be fined or otherwise penalized, in some cases by jail. The following are some of the more important definitions of professional misconduct in dentistry it lists:

> 2. Practicing the profession fraudulently, beyond its authorized scope, with gross incompetence, with gross negligence on a particular occasion, or with negligence or incompetence on more than one occasion

3. Practicing the profession while the ability to practice is impaired by alcohol, drugs, physical disability, or mental disability
4. Being habitually drunk, or dependent on, or a habitual user of, narcotics, barbiturates, amphetamines, hallucinogens, or other drugs with similar effects
5a. Being convicted of committing an act constituting a crime under New York law, or federal law, or the law of another jurisdiction and which, if committed within the state, would have constituted a crime under New York law
5b. Having been found by the commissioner of health to be in violation of article 33 of the public health law (see below)
6. Refusing to provide professional service to a person because of such person's race, creed, color, or national origin (disabilities are treated in another section)
7. Permitting, aiding, or abetting an unlicensed person to perform activities requiring a license
9. Committing *unprofessional conduct*, as defined by the Board of Regents

Note that by incorporating "*unprofessional conduct* as defined by the Board of Regents," Section 9 brings a section of the Rules of the Board directly into the statutes. The Board's definition of *unprofessional conduct* is found below in the section Rules of the Board of Regents.

Section 6510 defines an additional act of *professional misconduct* for which there is a penalty: fee-splitting, rebates, etc.

Section 6510a describes in detail the proceedings that follow when a dentist or hygienist is accused of professional misconduct. A complaint may be made by any person to the State Education Department. This sets in motion an investigation by the Office of Professional Discipline (OPD), which may then lead to a charge against a practitioner. If a charge is brought, the Board for Dentistry holds a hearing, the outcome of which is reviewed by a Board of Regents' Review Committee, which then makes a recommendation to the State Education Department. The accused dentist may appeal the decision to the courts.

Section 6510b allows a practitioner to surrender license and registration voluntarily without penalty because of incapacity due to drug or alcohol abuse, provided there has been no harm to a patient. A surrendered license may be restored to the practitioner under specified conditions.

Section 6511 lists the penalties that may be imposed by the State Education Department against a licensee found guilty of professional misconduct. These include:

1. Censure and reprimand
2. Suspension of license
   a. Wholly, for a fixed period of time
   b. Partially, until the licensee successfully completes a course of retraining in the area to which the suspension applies
   c. Wholly, until the licensee successfully completes a course of therapy or treatment prescribed by the regents
3. Revocation of license
4. Annulment of license or registration
5. Limitation on registration or issuance of any further license

6. A fine not to exceed $10,000 upon each specification of charges of which the respondent is determined to be guilty
7. A requirement that a licensee pursue a course of education or training
8. A requirement that a licensee perform up to 100 hours of public service

Subarticle 4 Sections 6512 and 6513 define the "unauthorized acts" punishable as crimes by up to a year in jail. These include the unauthorized use of a professional title, or aiding or abetting an unlicensed person to perform an act not permitted by law.

Section 6514 describes the criminal procedure.

Section 6515 permits the attorney general to obtain an order from a court to restrain a practitioner from practice during a judicial process if it is determined that by continuing practice the accused dentist or hygienist may cause irreparable damage—a rare provision in law in that the accused is prohibited from engaging in practice before a judicial determination of guilt is proven. It is designed to protect patients during a judicial process that may extend for many months.

Article 133

2.4.1.2   This article deals specifically with dentists and dental hygienists. Its first section, 6600 incorporates all of Article 130.

Section 6601 defines the practice of dentistry, thus:

> The practice of the profession of dentistry is defined as diagnosing, treating, operating, or prescribing for any disease, pain, injury, deficiency, deformity, or physical condition of the human mouth, including the teeth, alveolar process, gums, or jaws, and adjacent tissues; or except by the use of impressions or casts made by a licensed dentist and on his written dental laboratory prescription, furnishing, supplying, constructing, reproducing, or repairing prosthetic dentures, bridges, appliances or other structures to be used and worn as substitutes for natural teeth, or, in the treatment of abnormal conditions of the teeth or jaws or adjacent tissues; or placing such devices in the mouth or adjusting the same. The practice of dentistry may include performing physical evaluations in conjunction with the provision of dental treatment.

Section 6602 limits the use of the title *dentist* to those who are licensed.

Section 6603 restates the duties of the State Board for Dentistry, setting the membership at no less than 13 dentists and 2 hygienists, each having practiced for at least 5 years in the state.

Section 6508 requires that each board have 2 consumer representatives.

Section 6604 lists the requirements for a license as a dentist, including an examination, age at least 21, good moral character, etc.

Section 6604a (effective January, 1997) describes mandatory continuing education for dentists: a minimum of 45 hours during each triennial period, a maximum of 15 of which may be self-instructional course work as approved by the department.

Section 6605a prescribes that to employ general anesthesia or parenteral sedation outside a hospital, a dentist must have a dental anesthesia certificate issued by the department. It requires that the Commissioner set standards for such certificates that include specific training in the use of general anesthesia or parenteral sedation. (See Commissioner's Regulations below).

Section 6604a requires continuing education for dentists: during each triennial period they must complete at least 45 hours of acceptable formal continuing education, a maximum of 15 of which may be self-instructional course work as approved by the department.

Section 6606 defines the practice of dental hygiene. Violation of this section, and of 61.9 of the Regulations of the Commissioner of Education noted below, is one of the most frequent causes of allegations of professional misconduct brought against dentists. Section 6606 presents a long list of activities that dental hygienists may perform. The list has three significant effects: *(1)* it represents what constitutes the practice of dental hygiene; *(2)* it sets specific limits on the Commissioner's authority to "promulgate regulations defining the functions a dental hygienist may perform," and *(3)* it precludes the performance of these duties by any other person, except those whose license permits the performance of such duties, ie a licensed dentist; therefore, a dental assistant who performs any of the listed duties commits a criminal act as described in Subarticle 4, above. The complete list of permitted duties is presented below as part of the Commissioner's Regulations.

Section 6607 restricts the use of the title *dental hygienist* to those who are appropriately licensed.

Section 6608, effective February 1, 1996 is one of several recent addition to the statutes defining the practice of certified dental assistants. Dental assistants may, under the "direct personal supervision" of a dentist, provide patient education, take preliminary medical histories and vital signs to be reviewed by the dentist, place and remove rubber dams, select and prefit provisional crowns and orthodontic bands, remove orthodontic arch wires and ligature ties, place and remove matrix bands, take impressions for study casts or diagnostic casts, remove periodontal dressing, and perform "such other dental services authorized in regulations promulgated by the [education] commissioner." Dental hygienists are also permitted to perform these services.

Section 6608a limits the use of the title "certified dental assistant" to those certified under Section 6608b.

Section 6608b requires those who seek certification as dental assistants to file an application, to be 17 years old, to pay certain fees, to have a high school diploma or its equivalent, to have completed an approved 1-year course with 200 hours of clinical experience or an acceptable alternative that includes 1000 hours of work experience, and to pass an examination.

Section 6609 sets out the requirement for a license in dental hygiene. It states, among other things, that a hygienist must be at least 17 years of age.

Section 6609a prescribes mandatory continuing education for dental hygienists of at least 24 hours per triennial period, including currently mandated training in child-abuse reporting and infection control. No more than 10 hours can be in self-instructional course work

Section 6611 contains "Special Provisions." It is a catchall for what is not conveniently included in other sections of the law.

Subsections 1 and 2 deal with dental laboratory prescriptions. They must be made out in duplicate; the dentist and laboratory must each keep a copy for 1 year. The subsections authorize the Commissioner to adopt regulations detailing what the prescriptions shall include (see section 61.5 of the Regulations of the Commissioner below). They also give the Education Department to access to dentist's offices and laboratories for the purpose of inspecting prescriptions.

Subsection 6 is the Good Samaritan Law applied to dentists. It precludes the victim of an accident from entering suit for negligence against a dentist who comes to his or her aid. However, there are some exceptions: the aid must have been given without the expectation of a fee, and not in a medical or dental office or a hospital or in the normal course of practice; and no protection is provided for acts that constitute gross negligence.

Subsection 7 requires dentists and hygienists to apply appropriate lead shields on the patient when exposing him or her to X rays. Oddly, although others are permitted to expose a patient to dental X rays, they are not required to use any shielding device.

Subsection 8 has caused controversy within the dental profession and been interpreted by attorneys of the OPD in a manner contrary to the apparent intent of those who initiated and supported the change in the law. It permits an unlicensed person to provide "supportive services" to a dentist. Because of the controversy surrounding this provision, it is best not to rely upon it in the delegation of questionable duties to one acting as a dental assistant.

Section 6612 requires a dentist to offer to have the patient's name or initials imprinted on a prosthetic appliance. If such imprinting is not practical, the offer may be omitted. The commissioner is empowered to adopt regulations to carry out the provisions of the statute.

With the end of Section 6612 the statutes relating to dental, dental hygiene, and dental assisting practice ends, and the Regulations of the Commissioner of Education and the Rules of the Board of Regents begin.

2.4.2   Regulations of the Commissioner

Part 59: General Provisions

2.4.2.1   Sections 59.1 to 59.4 describe the educational requirements for a license and provide some general information about professional licensure examinations.

Section 59.7 and 59.8 require that each licensee register the license every 3 years, that the license be displayed in the office in which the licensee practices; and that if the practice is conducted in more than one office, a registration certificate be obtained for each location. It also lists the dates that dentists and hygienists are required to register.

Section 59.12 requires all dentists and dental hygienists to complete 2 hours of training in child-abuse reporting, unless they can show that their practice excludes children.

Section 59.13 requires dentists and dental hygienists to complete approved training in infection control, unless exempt.

Part 61: Dentistry and Dental Hygiene

2.4.2.2   Section 61.3 describes how a "limited permit" to practice in "a hospital or dental facility approved by an appropriate agency" may be obtained. It requires that the services provided by the holder of a limited permit be supervised by a licensed dentist who is present on the premises at all times.

Section 61.5 carries out the authority granted the Commissioner under Subsection 1 of Section 6611 related to laboratory prescriptions. It requires that the prescription include the name of the laboratory; the date on which it was written; a clear description of the work to be done; a clear specification of the character of the materials to be used; and the signature and license number of the dentist.

Section 61.9 lists the services that a dental hygienist is permitted to perform. The section is reproduced in its entirety because its violation remains one of the most frequent allegations brought against dentists.

> The practice of dental hygiene, in accordance with section 6606 of the Education Law, shall be performed under the supervision of a licensed dentist.
> a. The degrees of supervision by the dentist are defined as follows:
>   1. General supervision shall mean that a supervising dentist is available for consultation, diagnosis and evaluation, has authorized the dental hygienist to perform the services, and exercises that degree of supervision appropriate to the circumstances.
>   2. Personal supervision shall mean that the dentist is in the dental office or facility, personally diagnoses the condition to be treated, personally authorized the procedure and, before dismissal of the patient, personally examines the condition after treatment is completed.
> b. The following services may be performed under the general supervision of a licensed dentist:
>   1. Removing calcareous deposits, accretions, and stains, including scaling and planing of exposed root surfaces indicated for a complete prophylaxis
>   2. Applying topical agents indicated for a complete dental prophylaxis
>   3. Removing excess cement from surfaces of the teeth
>   4. Providing patient education
>   5. Placing and exposing X-ray films
>   6. Performing topical fluoride applications and topical anesthetic applications
>   7. Polishing teeth, including existing restorations
>   8. Taking medical history including the measuring and recording of vital signs
>   9. Charting caries and periodontal conditions as an aid to diagnosis by the dentist
>   10. Applying pit and fissure sealants
> c. The following services may be performed only under the personal supervision of a licensed dentist:
>   1. Placing or removing rubber dam.
>   2. Removing sutures.
>   3. Taking impressions for study casts. Study casts shall mean only such casts as will be used for purposes of diagnosis and treatment planning by the dentist and for the purposes of patient education.
>   4. Placing or removing matrix bands.
>   5. Applying a topical medication not related to a complete dental prophylaxis.
>   6. Placing and removing temporary restorations. Temporary restorations shall include only nonmetallic substances generally used for temporary intracoronal filling materials. Placing and removing tem-

porary restorations shall not include cutting or excising hard or soft tissue or the use of mechanical instrumentation.
7. Placing and removing periodontal dressings.

Section 61.10 regulates general anesthesia and parenteral sedation. It defines these procedures specifically and forbids any dentist to provide them without certification, which requires 1 year of acceptable training in anesthesiology, or specialty certification in oral and maxillofacial surgery, or 2 years of post-doctoral education that includes training in anesthesiology. It permits dentists to provide parenteral conscious sedation if they have 60 hours of relevant post-doctoral education, 20 in parenteral conscious sedation specifically (or else a combination of 40 hours of post-doctoral education and at least 2 years of clinical experience involving at least 50 patients between 1987 and 1990). It requires that dentists who use anesthesia be certified, that they use it on only one patient at a time, that they and see that the patient's recovery is monitored by a qualified dentist, physician, or nurse, that they be "responsible for all aspects of the procedure, including life-support procedures, monitoring, recovery and record keeping," that they use the procedure only in properly equipped facilities, allowing for the handling of emergencies according to posted procedures, and that they report mortality resulting from anesthesia within 30 days.

2.4.3   Rules of the Board of Regents

Part 17

2.4.3.1   Sections 17.1 through Section 17.9 detail the disciplinary proceedings in the professions.

Part 28

2.4.3.2   Section 28.8 provides that a Committee on the Professions may require that a dentist or hygienist whose license has been revoked or suspended obtain grades on a proficiency examination satisfactory to the department prior to the issuance of a license or limited permit.

Part 29

2.4.3.3   Section 29.1 lists acts that constitute *unprofessional conduct* for all professions. The following, which are relevant to dentistry, are important enough to be quoted at length:

8. Revealing of personally identifiable facts, data, or information obtained in a professional capacity without the prior consent of the patient or client, except as authorized or required by law
9. Practicing or offering to practice beyond the scope permitted by law, or accepting and performing professional responsibilities which the licensee knows or has reason to know that he or she is not competent to perform, or performing without adequate supervision professional services which the licensee is authorized to perform only under the

supervision of a licensed professional, except in an emergency situation where a person's life or health is in danger

10. Delegating professional responsibilities to a person when the licensee delegating such responsibilities knows or has reason to know that such person is not qualified, by training, by experience or by licensure to perform them

11. Performing professional services which have not been duly authorized by the patient or his legal representative

12. Advertising or soliciting for patronage that is not in the public interest:

    i. Advertising or soliciting not in the public interest shall include but not be limited to advertising or soliciting that:
        a. Is false, fraudulent, deceptive, misleading, sensational, or flamboyant
        b. Represents intimidation or undue pressure
        c. Uses testimonials
        d. Guarantees any service
        e. Makes any claim relating to professional services or products or cost or price therefore which cannot be substantiated by the licensee, who shall have the burden of proof
        f. Makes claims of professional superiority which cannot be substantiated by the licensee, who shall have the burden of proof
        g. Offers bonuses or inducements in any form other than a discount or reduction in an established fee or price for a professional service or product

    ii. The following shall be deemed appropriate means of informing the public of the availability of professional services:
        a. Informational advertising not contrary to the foregoing prohibitions
        b. The advertising in a newspaper, periodical, or professional directory or on radio or television of fixed prices, or a stated range of prices, for specified routine professional services, provided that there is an additional charge for related services which are an integral part of the overall service being provided by the licensee and the advertisement shall so state, and provided further that the advertisement indicates the period of time for which the advertised prices shall be in effect.

    iii.a. All licensees placing advertisements shall maintain, or cause to be maintained, an exact copy of each advertisement, transcript, or videotape thereof as appropriate for the medium used, for a period of one year after its last appearance. This copy shall be made available for inspection upon demand of the Education Department or in the case of physicians, physician's and specialist's assistants, the Department of Health.
        b. A licensee shall not compensate or give anything of value to representatives of the press, radio, television, or other communications media in anticipation of or in return for professional publicity in a news item.

Section 29.2 lists more types of unprofessional conduct:

a. Unprofessional conduct shall also include, (in the professions of dentistry and dental hygiene):

1. Abandoning or neglecting a patient or client under and in need of immediate professional care, without making reasonable arrangements for the continuation of such care, or abandoning a professional employment by a group practice, hospital, clinic, or other health

care facility, without reasonable notice and under circumstances which seriously impair the delivery of professional care to patients or clients.

2. Willfully harassing, abusing, or intimidating a patient either physically or verbally.

3. Failing to maintain a record for each patient which accurately reflects the evaluation and treatment of the patient. Unless otherwise provided by law, all patient records must be retained for at least six years. Obstetrical records and records of minor patients must be retained for six years, and until one year after the minor patient reaches the age of 21 years.

4. Using the word "Doctor" in offering to perform professional services without also including the profession in which the licensee holds a doctorate.

5. Failing to exercise appropriate supervision over persons who are authorized to practice only under the supervision of the licensed professional.

6. Guaranteeing that satisfaction or a cure will result from the performance of professional services.

7. Ordering of excessive tests, treatment, or use of treatment facilities not warranted by the condition of the patient.

8. Claiming or using any secret or special method of treatment which the licensee refuses to divulge to the State Board for the profession.

9. Failing to wear an identifying badge, which shall be conspicuously displayed and legible, indicating the practitioner's name and professional title authorized pursuant to the Education Law, while practicing as an employee or operator of a hospital, clinic, group practice, or multiprofessional facility, or at a commercial establishment offering health services to the public.

10. Entering into an arrangement with the pharmacy for the compounding and/or dispensing of coded or specially marked prescriptions.

11. With respect to all professional practices conduct under an assumed name, other than facilities licensed pursuant to article 28 of the Public Health Law or article 13 of the Mental Hygiene Law, failing to post conspicuously at the site of such practice the names and licensure field of all of the principal professional licensees engaged in practice at that site (ie, principal partners, officers, or principal shareholders).

12. Issuing prescriptions for drugs and devices which do not contain the following information: the date written; the prescriber's name, address, telephone number, profession, and registration number; the patient's name, address, and age; the name, strength, and quantity of the prescribed drug or device; as well as the directions for use by the patient. In addition, all prescriptions for controlled substances shall meet the requirements of Article 33 of the Public Health Law. [Effective September 13, 1991]

13. Failing to use scientifically accepted infection prevention techniques appropriate to each profession for the cleaning and sterilization or disinfection of instruments, devices, materials, and work surfaces; utilization of protective garb, use of covers for contamination-prone equipment, and the handling of sharp instruments. Such techniques shall include but not be limited to: [Note this last catchall phrase— trouble!]
[Effective March 13, 1992]

a. Wearing of appropriate protective gloves at all times when touching blood, saliva, other body fluids or secretions, mucous membranes, non-intact skin, blood-soiled items or bodily fluid-soiled items, contaminated surfaces, and sterile body areas, and during instrument cleaning and decontamination procedures

b. Discarding gloves used following treatment of a patient and changing to new gloves if torn or damaged during treatment of a patient; washing hands and other skin surfaces immediately if contaminated with blood or other body fluids

c. Wearing of appropriate masks, gowns, or aprons, and protective eyewear or chin-length plastic face shields whenever splashing or spattering of blood or other body fluids is likely to occur

d. Sterilizing equipment and devices that enter the patient's vascular system or other normally sterile areas of the body

e. Sterilizing equipment and devices that touch intact mucous membranes but do not penetrate the patient's body and using high-level disinfection for equipment and devices which cannot be sterilized prior to use for a patient

f. Using appropriate agents including but not limited to detergents for cleaning all equipment and devices prior to sterilization or disinfection

g. Cleaning, by the use of appropriate agents including but not limited to detergents, equipment and devices which do not touch the patient or that only touch the intact skin of the patient

h. Maintaining equipment and devices used for sterilization according to the manufacturer's instructions

i. Adequately monitoring the performance of all personnel, licensed or unlicensed, for whom the licensee is responsible regarding infection control techniques

j. Placing disposable used syringes, needles, scalpel blades, and other sharp instruments in appropriate puncture-resistant containers for disposal; and placing reusable needles, scalpel blades, and other sharp instruments in appropriate puncture-resistant containers until appropriately cleaned and sterilized

k. Maintaining appropriate ventilation devices to minimize the need for emergency mouth-to-mouth resuscitation

l. Refraining from all direct patient care and handling of patient-care equipment when the health care professional has exudative lesions or weeping dermatitis and the condition has not been medically evaluated and determined to be safe or capable of being safely protected against in providing direct patient care or in handling patient care equipment

m. Placing all specimens of blood and body fluids in well-constructed containers with secure lids to prevent leaking; and cleaning any spill of blood or other body fluid with an appropriate detergent and appropriate chemical germicide

b. Unprofessional conduct shall also include, in those professions specified in section 18 of the Public Health Law and in the professions of acupuncture and massage, failing to provide access by qualified persons to patient information in accordance with the standards set forth in section 18 of the Public Health Law (see below). In the professions of acupuncture and massage, qualified persons may appeal the denial of access to patient information in the manner set forth in section 18 of the Public Health Law to a record-access committee appointed by the executive secretary of the appropriate State Board. Such record-access review committees shall consist of not fewer than three nor more than five members of the appropriate state board.

Section 29.5 lists yet more types of unprofessional conduct:

> Unprofessional conduct in the practice of dentistry and dental hygiene shall include all conduct prohibited by sections 29.1 and 29.2 of this Part except as provided in this section, and shall also include the following:
> b. Claiming professional superiority or special professional abilities, attainments, methods, or resources, except that a practitioner who has completed a program of specialty training approved by the Board of Regents in a specialty recognized as such by the Board of Regents, or who can demonstrate to the satisfaction of the department the completion of the substantial equivalent of such a program, may advertise or otherwise indicate the specialty. A practitioner who has completed all of the requirements for specialty qualification except an examination may advertise or otherwise indicate the additional training which has been acquired. The phrase *practice limited to* shall be deemed a claim of special professional abilities, and may be used only by dentists who have completed specialty training satisfactory to the department or dentists who have restricted their practice to a dental specialty prior to January 1, 1979.

It is important to note that the above statutes and rules and regulations may change at each session of the state's legislature and at each meeting of the state's education department and board of regents.

2.5   Other Laws That Affect Dental Practice in New York

Prescription Writing

2.5.1   Public Health Law, Article 33, Section 3331 states that dentists can prescribe or dispense drugs only in the course of their practice

Radiographs

2.5.2   The taking of radiographs is regulated in Section 3515 of the Public Health Law. Subarticle 4 exempts students working under the "adequate" supervision of a dentist, or "a dental assistant who, under the supervision of a licensed dentist, operates only such radiographic dental equipment as may be prescribed by the commissioner in rules and regulations for the sole purpose of oral radiography and limits the beam to the face."

Elsewhere, the Commissioner of Health has limited X-ray exposure in oral radiography to a diameter of no more than 3 inches on the surface of the skin. Thus, a person acting as a *dental assistant* may take periapical films, a panographic film, or an occlusal film, but may not take a cephalometric film. A hygienist is permitted to take all dental films.

Reporting Physicians Suspected of Professional Misconduct

2.5.3   Section 230 11 of the Public Health Law *(a)* requires dentists, hygienists, certified dental assistants, and a list of other licensed health care workers to report to the Board of Health a physician who appears to be guilty of professional misconduct, and *(b)* provides legal protection for the person submitting the report, assuming good faith and no malice.

Reporting Dentists Suspected of Professional Misconduct

2.5.4   The only state law relating to a requirement to report dentists who are impaired or incompetent is found in Public Health Law Section 2805k. The requirement to report is limited to hospitals, public health facilities that contain a dental clinic, and dental school appointments of clinical faculty.

A federal law establishing the National Practitioner Data Bank mandates that specified health institutions, including professional associations, report to the National Practitioners Data Bank dentists who are found guilty of professional misconduct or negligence, or refused an appointment in a health facility, or dismissed from a professional appointment in a health facility. For additional detains about the Data Bank see section 2.11.

Patient Access to Treatment Records

2.5.5   The text of the Dental Practice Act includes as unprofessional conduct, in 29.2 (b), failing to provide qualified persons access to patient information. However, the section does not indicate who is qualified for such access, what conditions have to be met for access to be provided, or how access is defined. For this information the dentist is referred to Section 18 of the Public Health Law. This section is long and detailed. It states that upon the patient's written request, the health practitioner is to give the patient, or one designated by the patient, access to a copy of the patient's treatment record. The practitioner is allowed to charge a reasonable fee for the production of copies, but if the patient is unable to pay for the copies, they must be provided without charge. This section also describes information the practitioner is not required to release, including "personal notes and observations," and information about treatment received by the patient from another practitioner. This section also details the process by which a person denied access may appeal the practitioner's refusal to the health department. (For more information on this topic, see chapter 12.)

Privileged Communications

2.5.6   Section 4504 of the Civil Practice Laws and Rules (CPLR) deals with privileged communications. It states that unless the patient waives the privilege, a dentist must not disclose information gathered in attending that patient professionally; however, a dentist must disclose information necessary for the identification of a patient, or indicating that a patient under 16 has been the victim of a crime.

Consent Law

2.5.7   The consent law is contained in Section 2805d of the Public Health Law and applies to dentistry. It requires that a dentist inform the patient of alternatives to treatment and such foreseeable risks and benefits as a reasonable practitioner would disclose under similar circumstances. The law applies to non-emergency treatment, procedures, or surgery, and to diagnostic procedures that involve invasion or disruption of the integrity of the body.

Risks do not have to be disclosed if they are commonly known, if the patient waives the right to be advised of them, if the patient is unable to grant consent, or if in the opinion of the practitioner informing the patient of the risks would adversely affect the patient's condition.

Case law has superimposed upon consent law additional requirements for informed consent. For a detailed listing of these see chapter 9.

The Statute of Limitations

2.5.8   Section 214a of the CPLR limits an action alleging dental malpractice to 2 ½ years from the time of the "act, omission or failure complained of." However, in cases of continuous treatment, and so in most cases of dental care, it does not begin to run until the last treatment is performed; in cases involving a foreign object accidentally left in the body (such as a broken file or reamer in a root canal), it begins to run only upon discovery of the object; in cases of fraudulent concealment of adverse conditions in the course of treatment (such as root tips remaining in the bone after an extraction), it begins to run only upon discovery of those conditions.

Section 208 limits the statute as it applies to minors to 10 years, or 2 ½ years after the minor reaches majority (18 years of age), whichever comes first. (For more information on this topic, see chapter 5.)

HIV Testing

2.5.9   Section 2781 of the Public Health Law describes the conditions under which a person may be subjected to HIV testing. The law is further detailed by the administrative rules and regulations of the health commissioner in Section 63.1. In general they state that:

1. Informed consent must be obtained in writing from the subject before the test is to be performed.
2. The test must be explained to the subject, including its purpose, the meaning of the results, and the benefits of an early diagnosis.
3. The test is voluntary, and consent may be withdrawn at any time; anonymous testing must be available.
4. The results are to remain confidential, except as provided by law.

(For more information on this topic, see chapter 8.)

Discrimination in Patient Selection/Treatment

2.5.10   In July of 1990 President Bush signed the Americans with Disabilities Act (ADA), which declared health providers' offices "places of public accommodation." This change in the status of a dentist's private office has had wide-ranging effects. It clearly indicates that a dentist who refuses to provide dental services to any person declared disabled, such as a person suffering from AIDS, or who is HIV-positive, solely as a result of the disability, is in violation of the law and subject to severe penalties. There are 900 conditions listed by the federal government as disabling. Disabled persons must be afforded treatment identical to all other persons. This section of the law took effect January 1, 1992.

The law also affects employment and physical facilities in places of public accommodation. In effect, the law subjects the private dental office to the jurisdiction of the Attorney General, and on a local level to the Human Rights Commission. For a detailed discussion of discrimination by dentists in patient selection, see chapter 3.

A dentist is permitted to request information on the health history form about the HIV status of a patient, provided that the same request is made of all patients, and a positive response is not used to discriminate in any manner against the patient. When referring a patient who is HIV-positive or suffers from AIDS, one may inform the practitioner to whom the patient is referred of the patient's HIV status, provided the referring dentist believes the information is needed in the provision of care or consultation by the practitioner.

Section 6705 of the Education Law states that any licensed dentist may provide dental services to an animal upon the request and under the direct supervision of a licensed veterinarian. (For more information on this topic, see chapter 8.)

Dental Hygienists and the Administration of Nitrous Oxide

2.5.11 All licensed and currently registered dentists are permitted, without anesthesia certification, to use nitrous oxide for conscious sedation (analgesia). They may not delegate the use of nitrous oxide or the monitoring of a patient to whom nitrous oxide gas is administered. The administering dentist must be present in the operatory until the administration of the gas has ceased and the patient has recovered.

Local Zoning

2.5.12 Dentists are subject to local zoning laws. These primarily affect the physical office: its location, its size, hours of practice, parking requirements, etc. They can be more important than they seem. For example, in one case known personally to the author, a dental school graduate accepted a position as an employee of a dentist who had practiced in an office for 20 years part as of his home in a residential zone in a small village. Their professional relationship was ideal, but after 5 years, the neighbors, annoyed by the patients' cars crowding the residential street on which the home-office was located, discovered that the local village zoning law limited the use of a professional home-office in the zone to a single practitioner. They notified the local authorities, who demanded that the employee cease and desist her practice in the house. She asked the dentist to relocate to an area in the village that would permit her to continue to practice with him; but he declined, despite his personal and professional attachment to her, unwilling to move from the office in which he had spent his career. The employee was forced to leave the practice, and an ideal professional relationship was destroyed because of insufficient research into local zoning laws.

Jury Duty

2.5.13   A recent change in the law places dentists, physicians, attorneys, and other professionals, previously exempt from jury duty, on the list to serve.

Exemption from the Physician Practice Act

2.5.14   Section 6526(9) of the State Education Law provides for exemption from the laws regulating the practice of medicine to "any dentist or dental school graduate eligible for licensure in the state which administers anesthesia as part of a hospital residency program established for the purpose of training dentists in anesthesiology."

Autopsies

2.5.15   Section 4209d of the Public Health Law permits a student in a registered dental school while under the supervision of a "professor or teacher," to "make any incision preparatory to or during an autopsy." And 4209f provides the same for "a dental resident or licensed dentist while under the supervision of a physician."

Disposal of Hazardous Wastes

2.5.16   Dentists in the course of their practice are classified as "conditionally exempt generators" of "hazardous wastes." The United States Environmental Protection Agency (EPA), in response to revised federal legislation, adopted regulations applicable to conditionally exempt generators in 1986. To comply with these regulations, New York State adopted its own regulations, allowing these to be further defined by local municipalities, so long as they are at least as restrictive as either the federal or state regulations. Following is a digest of the state's regulations, which are administered by the New York State Department of Environmental Conservation, Division of Hazardous Substances Regulation. The major applicable statutes are contained in the State's Environmental Conservation Law, and the Administrative Rules and Regulations of the Commissioner of Environmental Conservation. Other related laws are contained in the Public Health Law, and the Administrative Rules And Regulations of the Commissioner of Health.

    Listed hazardous wastes include X-ray solutions and amalgam fragments. X-ray solutions are to be contained in leak-proof drums. Amalgam fragments are to be stored as described below for "Medical Wastes".

    Regulation 364.9 of the Department of Environmental Conservation, the "Standard for the Tracking and Management of Medical Waste," lists substances that are included as medical wastes. Those a dental office might generate include blood-soaked gauze or cotton; gauze or cotton encrusted with blood; needles and syringes; scalpels; body parts (gingival tissue, bone, teeth, etc).

    As to storage and disposal, the regulations require that all medical wastes be collected in red containers clearly labeled "HAZARDOUS WASTE." These may be stored for up to 180 days, after which arrangements must be made with a transporter authorized to transport the wastes. The New York State Department of Environmental Conservation maintains a hotline: (800) 462-6553.

Large-group practices may fall in other categories of generators based upon the amount of hazardous waste they generate. For the rules that apply to them, they are advised to contact the New York State Department Of Environmental Conservation, Bureau of Pollution Prevention, 50 Wolf Road, Room 231, Albany, New York 12233-7253, (518) 485-8400, or any of the regional offices.

Affidavits

2.5.17   An affidavit is a written document completed by a party swearing under oath the truth of the statements contained therein. It must follow the form set out by the courts, and it must be notarized. However, according to Section R 2106 of the CPLR, "The statement of . . . [a] dentist, authorized by law to practice in the state, who is not a party to an action, when subscribed by him to be true under the penalties of perjury, may be served or filed in lieu of and with the same force and effect as an affidavit." Therefore, neither the legal form nor notarization is required.

Use of Radiographs for Dental Services

2.5.18   Section 3515a of the Public Health Law forbids a dentist from taking radiographs of a patient simply because the third-party payer demands them as a condition of payment for dental services, either to the patient or the dentist. Only if the radiographs are essential to the treatment of a patient are they permitted.

How to Find the Law

2.6   "Ignorance of the law," as the old adage goes, "is no excuse." However, finding the laws regulating dental practice is difficult even for attorneys. On request, the agency charged with licensure of health professions will supply a set of laws regulating dental practice that includes the statutes adopted by the legislature of the state and the rules and regulations of the administrative agency or agencies created by the legislature. As mentioned above, these make up the Dental Practice Act. However, there are a multitude of regulatory laws contained in other sections of the statutes and rules and regulations of additional administrative agencies that directly affect the practice of dentistry, such as the State's Health Code, etc. Further, many sections of the Dental Practice Act have been interpreted by the courts over the years in cases that are not easy for those not educated in law to locate because the reports in which they are collected number in the hundreds for each state.

Given the complexity of the law and its spread through a multitude of law books and court decisions, how are you to remain current in it? You should read texts on the subject, attend relevant presentations at dental meetings, and participate in continuing dental education. However, before you place any reliance on what is written or said, make certain the author or speaker is credible by both education and experience. There are far too many self-styled amateur lawyers; it seems everyone knows the law, even dentists. The most credible authors and speakers are dentist-attorneys. If in doubt about the law, however, your best bet is to seek the services of an attorney. As an alternative, you can write to the licensing agency requesting an answer to a particular question. (For more information on this topic, see chapter 1.)

Regulation by Hospitals and Health Centers

2.7   In all states the license to practice dentistry is a general license. The holder of the license is permitted to provide all dental services that fall within the scope of the license as defined by state law. Without additional training a licensed dentist is permitted to provide endodontic therapy, periodontics, orthodontics, oral and maxillofacial surgery, implantology, etc. However, once the general dentist applies to be admitted to the staff of a hospital or health center, restrictions may be placed upon the scope of practice the dentist may engage in within the facility. Such restrictions may be applied by the administration of the institution upon the recommendation of the professional staff, usually the chief or director of the dental service. This process is called the "delineation of privileges." First the practitioner indicates, on a form listing all the services provided by the dental department of the institution, the services he wishes to perform while on the staff. The list is then reviewed by the chief or director of the dental department, usually in consultation with the heads of the divisions within the department representing the specialty areas of dental practice. If, for example, the applicant wishes to provide endodontic therapy on patients of the institution, and the chief or director of the dental department decides that the applicant is not sufficiently trained or experienced in endodontic therapy, the director may deny the applicant the right to engage in this activity, despite the fact that the applicant has a license to provide the service to patients in his office practice.

The legal mechanism though which hospitals and health facilities are able to limit the scope of a dentist's practice originated in the courts' determination that a hospital can be held liable for the professional services provided by the doctors who are permitted to practice within that hospital. The courts based this determination on the hospital's approval of its doctors' professional credentials. A landmark case was decided in New York in 1914:

> It is said that this relation [between doctor and the hospital] is not one of master and servant, but that the physician occupies the position, so to speak, of an independent contractor, following a separate calling, liable, of course, for his own wrongs to the patient whom he undertakes to serve, but involving the hospital in no liability, *if due care has been taken in his selection.*[4] (Emphasis added.)

[4]211 NY 125 (1914).

"Due care" has been taken to mean that the credentials of those doctors (physicians, dentists, etc) who provide care to patients have been subject to review by their peers on the staff of the institution, and that patients who enter the institution for treatment can therefore rely on the professional ability of those attending to them. Should one of them be guilty of negligence in the care of a patient, both doctor and institution may be held personally liable. A court in Ohio stated:

A license from the State of Ohio to practice medicine does not grant such licensed physician the right to practice all types of medicine in Barberton Citizens Hospital that such licensee may desire. Barberton Citizens, like all hospitals, recognizes that some duly qualified doctors are orthopedics, internal medicine specialists, and many other specialists. The privilege to use any hospital is determined by its Board of Trustees upon recommendation of the medical committee or group of staff doctors who pass upon the speciality which the applicant doctor seeks to practice. It is to that purpose that rules, regulations, and delineations of privileges are established for the specialities. The principal aim of this or any hospital should be the welfare of its consumers, the patients who need hospital care. To that end, competent users of its facilities are a necessity.[5]

Regulation by Third-Party Payers

2.8 Dentists are given the opportunity to provide services on behalf of an organization that enrolls or identifies a population entitled to receive dental care such as an insurance company or, in a case like Medicaid, the government. Having agreed to provide the service, either through a contractual relationship with the third-party payer, or through registration as with Medicaid, the dentist becomes bound by the rules of the third party, which identifies eligible services and sets fees. For example, a third-party payer may not reimburse the dentist for endodontic care. In this way, reimbursement indirectly regulates the scope of practice permitted the dentist. As managed care expands further into dentistry, additional limitations are to be expected.

OSHA and Infection Control

2.9 Several events in the 1980s resulted in major changes in the way dentistry is practiced. Today's dentist and dental assistant wear gloves and change them before caring for each patient; they wear masks, protective eyewear, and a modified operating room scrub suit; they sterilize the hand piece before using it on each patient; etc. These changes were caused by the following, apparently unrelated, events:

1. The public, through the media and professional publications, learned that AIDS is a disease that is fatal and spreading rapidly throughout the population.
2. The public learned that the disease is transmitted through contaminated blood and other body fluids, including saliva.
3. Because of the perceived risk to themselves, their employees and their families, some health providers who are exposed to the patient's blood and/or saliva (medical surgeons and dentists) refused to treat AIDS and HIV-positive patients.
4. Professional associations (the ADA and AMA) declared the refusal of practitioners to treat AIDS and HIV-positive patients unethical. The decisions had no major effect—some practitioners continued to refuse to treat patients with AIDS.

5. A person in Florida died from AIDS and the Centers for Disease Control and Prevention (CDC), an agency of the federal government, linked the transmission of the disease to a visit to a dentist. The event was highly publicized by the media. Dental offices became the target of public attention as a source of possible transmission of AIDS.

6. The CDC issued a set of guidelines designed to prevent the spread of contagious infectious diseases during the treatment of all patients. The rationale was that the practitioner may not know that a patient is infected because that patient either does not know or fears to tell. However, the guidelines are simply "recommendations" and not legal requirements; therefore, they had little effect upon the habits of practitioners. Dentists and their employees remained at risk of infecting themselves and others.

7. Local Human Rights Commissions (HRCs) brought actions against some dentists and physicians who discriminated against patients with AIDS either by refusing to treat them or by treating them differently from other patients. In most cases the findings of the administrative court were against the practitioner and civil fines were imposed.

8. However, on appeal most cases were reversed by appellate courts on the grounds that the private offices of physicians and dentists were not "places of public accommodation" and therefore not subject to the jurisdiction of the HRC or the antidiscrimination laws. Few cases were decided in the courts on the substantive issue of whether the dentist or physician was guilty of discrimination.

9. In response to the court decisions, to prevent discrimination against those suffering from AIDS, those who are HIV-positive, or those in a high-risk population group, the federal government enacted the Americans with Disabilities Act of 1990. This act states that the private offices of health practitioners are "places of public accommodation," thus placing them within the jurisdiction of state and federal agencies charged with the responsibility of enforcing antidiscrimination laws. It ensures that physicians and dentists treat patients with infectious contagious diseases and patients suffering from other disabilities.

And so, because dentists and physicians were required to treat patients with contagious diseases (AIDS, Hepatitis B, Tuberculosis, etc), and the guidelines of the CDC did not have the effect of law, employees in high-exposure risk occupations, ie, in hospitals, dental and medical offices, etc, sought protection against accidental exposure in the workplace by having the federal agency, the Occupational Safety and Health Administration (OSHA), issue standards in infection control with which employers must comply or face heavy fines. In effect, OSHA converted the guidelines of the CDC into law, with the purpose of protecting workers. The OSHA standards include the following:

1. Written documentation:
   Exposure-control plan, job classification and description, office training, employee health status, acceptance or rejection of Hepatitis B vaccination offer, refusal of medical follow-up, exposure record, office-cleaning schedule, and exposure determination list.

2. Exposure control precautions:
   a. Gloves: Must be worn when there is any possibility of contact with blood or saliva. They must be discarded after each patient, and not washed, except that heavy-duty utility gloves used during clean-up may be reused after decontamination.
   b. Face Mask: Same conditions as with gloves. These requirements may undergo major changes as a result of fear of the transmission of TB.
   c. Eye Protective Wear: Eye shields or eyeglasses with side shields are acceptable under the same conditions as above.
   d. Face Shields: Must be worn when blood or saliva may be splashed.
   e. Gowns: Must be worn when any patient is treated. Long-sleeved gowns are required. Any type of gown may be worn that prevents blood, saliva, or splatter from reaching street clothes or skin under the gown. Fluid-proof gowns are not required. Fluid-resistant gowns are satisfactory, but there is some confusion in the definition of these terms.
   f. Handwashing: Employers must provide handwashing facilities and ensure that employees wash their hands immediately before and after removing gloves.

   There are some exceptions to these rules in the treatment of children; however, if splashing may occur, the standards in protective clothing apply. In an emergency situation protective clothing need not be worn. The employer is required to pay for protective clothing. Neither caps nor special footwear are required. Employees must remove protective clothing before leaving the work area. Records must be maintained for 30 years after an employee leaves the position, and must remain strictly confidential.

3. Sharps (including needles, scalpels, broken glass, ends of dental wires, and any contaminated object that can penetrate the skin):
   a. Recapping of needles: In general, recapping of needles is prohibited unless the needle is to be used on the same patient to enhance anesthesia. A one-handed or mechanical device is permitted.
   b. Disposal: All sharps must be placed in a puncture-resistant container that is leak-proof on all sides, red, labeled "biohazard," and marked with the universal biohazard symbol. A sharps container should be located in each operatory. The container should be disposed of as provided by local law.

4. Hepatitis vaccination:
   All employees must be offered a hepatitis vaccination, and the booster if recommended, within 10 days of employment at no cost. The employee must be educated about hepatitis and the vaccination before being offered the choice. If the employee refuses, he or she must sign an informed refusal form. The rule applies to part-time and temporary as well as full time employees. If the employee refuses to sign the form, the employer must make a record of the refusal. Recombivax HB, and Engerix-B are currently FDA-approved.

5. Housekeeping:
   The employer must keep a written schedule of cleaning and decontamination of the workplace. All equipment and work surfaces must be cleaned

and decontaminated as soon as possible after contact with blood, saliva, or any other potentially infectious material.

Plastic wraps or other coverings may be used as an alternative to decontamination procedures, but they must be replaced after the treatment of each patient.

Floor surfaces must be capable of being cleaned. Rugs are therefore not advised.

6. The Exposure-Control Plan:

Each office must develop a written exposure-control plan designed to eliminate or minimize employee exposure to blood-borne pathogens (primarily HIV and Hepatitis B). The plan must include the manner in which personnel, including the employer, are to respond when an exposure incident occurs.

An exposure incident occurs when blood, saliva, or other potentially infectious material makes contact with the eye, mouth, other mucous membrane, or non-intact skin. Accidental needle sticks are the most common form of exposure incidents that take place in the dental office.

When such a stick occurs, if the source is identified, he or she must be asked to have a blood test, and must sign a waiver if he or she refuses. The employee must be asked to give a blood sample and be tested for infectious disease, and must sign a waiver if he or she refuses. If the employee agrees only to giving a blood sample, it must be kept for 90 days.

7. OSHA-related office records:

Injury and illness records must be kept for 30 years. All other records must be kept for 3 years. If you sell your practice, you should include in the sales agreement that the purchaser must retain all your OSHA records in compliance with the law, and if you need your OSHA records for any reason, the purchaser must deliver the originals to you upon your written request. If you leave your practice without a buyer you must call the local OSHA office (or comparable state office) to determine the local rules.

The following 25 states and territories have their own OSHA-type regulations: Alaska, Arizona, California, Connecticut, Hawaii, Indiana, Iowa, Kentucky, Maryland, Michigan, Minnesota, Nevada, New Mexico, New York, North Carolina, Oregon, Puerto Rico, South Carolina, Tennessee, Utah, Vermont, Virginia, Virgin Islands, Washington, and Wyoming. In New York and Connecticut, the state plan applies only to government employees; the federal plan applies to the employees in private dental offices.

Although the passage of these laws did much to protect employees in the dental work place and ensured that dentists made their services available to disabled persons, there remained some significant omissions in preventing the spread of infectious diseases in the dental office.

1. Patients had no official standing to complain to OSHA if the dental office was not properly "OSHAized" (treating personnel were not gloved, etc).
2. OSHA had no regulations relating to patient protection equipment, eg, the sterilization of handpieces and the effectiveness of autoclaves.

3. Dentist employers were not personally required to adhere to the OSHA standards—they were required only to see to it that their employees complied with the standards. For example, an employer dentist was not required to wear gloves, a mask, etc when treating patients.
4. The penalty imposed against dentists who did not comply with OSHA's standards was limited to monetary fines and not the direct business of the licensing agencies.

To close these loopholes, Congress in October 1991 passed legislation seemingly unrelated to health care, the Postal Workers and Transportation Appropriation Act. It included a provision requiring each state to adopt laws that require health practitioners to adhere to the essentials of the infection-control guidelines of the CDC, or risk an attack upon the license to practice as well as the usual sanctions that can be imposed for professional misconduct. States were given until October 1992 to comply, or risk loss of federal public health funds. States could ask for an extension to comply, and many did. However, in a few years, all states complied.

The goals of the legislation were to make dental care accessible to all, even those with contagious infectious diseases, and to make the dental office a safer place for patients to receive care and for the dentist and the dental staff to provide it. These goals have been accomplished. The cost in dollars and time may well have been justified if only one patient, one dentist, or one dental staff member has been protected from contracting an infectious disease, particularly if that disease is AIDS. (For more information on this topic, see chapter 8.)

Americans with Disabilities Act

2.10   In 1990, President Bush signed into law the ADA. The act was designed to ensure that all barriers to services, transportation, communication, and physical facilities for the disabled would be removed. The act states that the private offices of health providers are "places of public accommodation" and therefore subject its provisions. As mentioned above, dentists are required to treat all disabled persons, those with AIDS, the HIV-positive, members of high-risk groups, etc, in exactly the same manner as all other patients—they are not permitted to discriminate against them in any manner. In addition, dentists must satisfy a host of other requirements having to do with, eg, the physical facility and communications. The rules governing the adjustment of physical facilities and the new construction of dental offices are extremely complex; dentists should contact their local building inspector or a local architect for guidance. The communications section of the law may require dentists to have all complex written instructions and consent forms printed in braille. Dentists who employ 15 or more employees must comply with the hiring regulations of the act. For details of the act, it is best to contact the offices that administer it (see chapter 8).

National Practitioners Data Bank

2.11 The purpose of National Practitioners Data Bank is for the government to collect information about physicians and dentists who are either impaired or incompetent, and to make this information available to hospitals, health facilities, and licensing agencies. When an insurance company pays a settlement or award it must be reported to the Data Bank. Though at one time a practitioner was required to report the return of a fee in response to a patient's written demand, this is no longer true. If a hospital or licensing agency takes any action against a physician or dentist that relates to the practitioner's ability to provide satisfactory care, it must be reported to the Data Bank. Hospitals are required to query the Data Bank before granting a physician or dentist privileges. A state licensing agency may query the Data Bank before issuing a license or renewing one. Neither attorneys, insurance companies, nor patients are given access to the information held by the Data Bank, though consumer groups are demanding release of the information to the public. (For more information on this topic, see chapter 8.)

Internet Access to Information About Dentists

2.12 Currently many states, including New York, have made information about punitive actions taken by the state licensing agency against dentists and physicians available on the Internet. Not all states that do the same list the malpractice records of dentists and physicians. Those that do not are feeling pressure to change.

Dental Jurisprudence

2.13 Dental jurisprudence is the application of law to dental practice. It encompasses the regulation of dental practice and those who practice it: dentists, dental hygienists, dental assistants, dental laboratory technicians, and denturists. Equally important, it includes the application of civil laws and processes that apply to allegations of malpractice brought by patients against any of these practitioners. This handbook covers the field of dental jurisprudence.

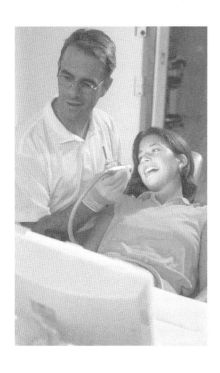

CHAPTER THREE

The Dentist-Patient Relationship: Contract Law

What Is a Contract and Why Is It Important to Dentists?

3.1   The relationship between dentist and patient has its foundation in contract law, and a suit may be brought against a dentist for breach of contract as well as for negligence or malpractice. Therefore, dentists should know the basics of the law of contracts, which this chapter is designed to provide.

A valid and enforceable contract between a dentist and a patient must include:

1. An offer
2. An acceptance
3. Consideration

The parties must be adults and of sound mind, and the contract entered into freely.

Offer and Acceptance

3.2   An *offer*, in the legal sense, is a proposal by one party to the other expressing a willingness to enter into an agreement, and made in such a way that the other party is justified in believing that his assent to, or acceptance of, that agreement is invited and, if given, will result in a binding contract between the parties. An effective offer must meet the following conditions:

1. It must describe the intent.
2. It must be certain and definite in its terms.
3. It must be communicated to the party whose acceptance is anticipated.

An *acceptance* is a voluntary act by the person to whom an offer is made, by which such person (offeree) exercises the power to create a contract conferred upon him by the offeror. An offer may be accepted only by the person to whom it is made. When a dentist says to a patient, "I will do the root canal on your front tooth," and the patient responds, "Okay, go ahead," they have the first two elements essential for a valid contract.

Consideration

3.3   For a contract to be valid, there must be *consideration*. Mutual assent by itself is not enough; there must be some bargained-for exchange that the law deems sufficient to support contractual rights and obligations. The bargained-for exchange may consist of an act, a forbearance to act, or a mere promise to act. It may be in the form of payment of a fee, goods, or services. So when a dentist informs a patient that the fee to provide a service is $500.00, and the patient agrees, the consideration is the patient's promise to pay the fee. Without such a promise, the service becomes a gift.

Forbearance—promise to forbear a claim or surrender of a claim—is always sufficient consideration where the claim is in fact valid. So when a patient demands the return of a fee, and a dentist agrees to that return provided the patient signs a "Release of All Claims Form" in which that patient agrees not to enter suit against the dentist for any services performed before the return of the fee, the forbearance by the patient is adequate consideration to support the agreement between the dentist and the patient; the dentist returns the fee; the patient agrees not to sue. The validity of a Release of All Claims Form, properly executed by the dentist and the patient, has been upheld by the courts (see chapter 17).

Contracting Parties Must Be of Sound Mind

3.4   Little needs to be said about sound mind; clearly people who suffer from mental illness or mental impairment are not able to enter into contracts enforceable against themselves, nor are people under the influence of drugs or alcohol. Thus, a treatment plan and a financial agreement entered into with a mentally retarded patient, or one who is under the influence of alcohol or drugs, is not binding on the patient, at his option, but is binding on the dentist. Conversely, if while completing the treatment agreement with the patient the dentist is under the influence of drugs, the dentist is not bound by the agreement. However, a dentist who claims to have been under the influence of drugs while practicing risks other, and severe, penalties.

Adhesion Contracts

3.5   In the provision of dental services, dentists usually control the terms of the agreement; they inform their patients what needs to be done and decide on the fee to be charged for their services. Patients are in a somewhat disadvantaged position at the outset of the relationship. However, patients are free to accept the conditions, reject them, or ask to modify them; that is, they are free to bargain. There are times when dentists may be in total control of the terms of the agreement, for example, when they are the only practitioners available in the community to provide certain services. If the terms dentists dictate in such circumstances are such that patients would not have accepted them but for their need for the services, the agreement is called an *adhesion contract*, and is unenforceable.

The following case, which came before an appellate court in New York, illustrates an adhesion contract. A patient requiring certain services agreed, in case a dispute arose, to be bound by arbitration that did not bind the dentist. The court stated:

> "Adhesion contracts" refer to a standardized contract form offered to consumers of goods and services essentially on a "take it or leave it" basis, without affording the consumer a realistic opportunity to bargain, and under such conditions that the consumer cannot obtain the desired product or services except by acquiescing to the form of the contract.

Quoting a malpractice text,[1] the court went on:

> Under the doctrine of "adhesion," contracts may be invalidated if one party, who is in an inferior bargaining position, is required to sign a contract to waive his legal rights in order to obtain [a] needed service from the party in [a] superior bargaining position.

In describing the unequal bargaining position, the court stated:

> The defendant doctor is a college, medical, and dental school graduate. The nurses employed by him are graduates of nursing schools. Counterposed to these educated people is the plaintiff, who attended school but completed an eleventh-grade education. To contrast this limited educational background against that of a professional doctor and his nursing staff could be unreasonable and unconscionable.
>
> Doctors are held in high esteem and admiration by the public. The average person is not disposed to question or doubt a doctor's treatment. Nor does the average person leave a doctor they rely upon and shop for another who does not require an arbitration agreement to be signed.

The court held the contract to be unenforceable.[2]

[1] Holder AR. Medical Malpractice Law, ed 2. New York: Wiley, 1978: 416.

[2] 422 NYS2d 335 (1979).

Must the Contract Be in Writing?

3.6   An agreement that is not valid is either void or unenforceable. A void contract is one that the courts declare not to exist. An unenforceable contract is one that exists, but cannot be enforced.

In most instances, oral contracts are valid and enforceable. However, by statute, a few types of contracts, though not void, are unenforceable if not in writing. These statutory requirements stem from the English Statute of Frauds of 1677. The following agreements fall within that statute:

1. A promise to pay the debt of another. If A says to the dentist, "if you treat B, and B does not pay your fee, I will," the agreement must be in writing to be enforceable. And so, if B does not pay the fee to the dentist, A's agreement with the dentist is not enforceable. But if instead A says "I will pay the fee for the treatment you provide to B," the oral agreement is enforceable: A must pay for the services provided to B. This may happen in dental practice when an employer refers an employee to a dentist and says to the dentist. "If my employee does not pay the fee, send me the bill." For this agreement to be valid, it must be in writing. If the employer claims he never made the statement, the dentist cannot collect the fee. If the employer said that he will pay all fees that his employee incurs, however, the oral statement is binding.
2. Contracts for the sale of land, or any interest therein (leasing agreement, etc).
3. Contracts that cannot be completed in 1 year. Theoretically, this could apply to orthodontics because few orthodontic cases can be completed in 1 year. However, the courts have treated orthodontic cases, and other cases that fall within the general health category, as a visit-to-visit contract. In most orthodontic cases there is a written agreement.
4. Agreements where the consideration exceeds a given amount of money. The amount may vary in each state. Fees for dental services often exceed this amount. However, courts have ruled that fees for dental services that require several visits may be divided by the number of visits and thus fall below the threshold amount.

Individual states may require other sorts of contracts to be written, but none appear to affect dental practice.

Though few dental-patient contracts are enforceable only if written, it is always best that they be written, so that the parties may avoid disputes as to their terms should the matter find its way into the courts. Remember, the shortest written word lasts longer than the longest memory.

Minors and Contract Law

3.7   Historically, by common law, a minor was any person under the age of 21 years. When the federal government reduced the age of voting from 21 to 18 years, states reduced the contract age to 18. Minors are no longer minors on the day of their 18th birthday.

A contract between a minor and an adult is unenforceable against the minor at the minor's option, but enforceable against the adult. Dental and other forms of health care, however, are usually excluded from this general rule. The parent or guardian of a minor has a quasi-contractual obligation to pay for the minor's "necessaries of life," such as food, clothing, shelter, and health. So if a 16-year-old patient enters into an oral agreement with a dentist to have a badly decayed third molar extracted for a fee of $75, the minor's parents or guardian cannot refuse to pay, for in making the agreement with the dentist that minor has pledged the payment of the parent or guardian.

Only the parent or legal guardian is able to enter into a binding contract on behalf of a minor. However, an emancipated minor is able to enter into a binding contract without the consent of the parent or legal guardian (see chapter 9).

Implied-in-Fact Contracts

3.8   If the promises of the parties are implied by their actions or conduct, the contract is said to be implied-in-fact. So if a patient asks a dentist to perform an oral examination, and neither patient nor dentist mentions a fee, the patient, by the act of sitting for the examination, implies a promise to pay for it. The implied-in-fact contract here is that in exchange for the service, a fee will be paid. The amount to be paid in such contracts is based on what the service is worth, its "quantum merit," which is determined by finding what other practitioners in the community charge for a like service.

Implied-in-Law Contracts

3.9   There are contracts implied-in-law, also known as quasi contracts, in which there is no mutual assent, but to avoid inequities and unjust enrichment, the law may imply a promise to pay for benefits or services rendered. For example, if a community dentist whose dental group covers the emergency room of a local hospital renders aid to an unconscious patient, the patient constructively agrees to have the service performed by the dentist, and to pay a reasonable fee for the service, by an implied-in-law contract. In deciding whether the patient is responsible for the fee, the court applies the following test: would the patient agree, if able, to have the service provided, and would a reasonable person under the same circumstances have agreed? If the answer to these questions is "yes," the patient must pay the fee, but the fee must be reasonable.

Exculpatory Clauses

3.10   One of the terms that dentists, physicians, and some health facilities may include in the provider-patient agreement is a clause in which the patient agrees not to sue the provider for any future negligence. This is called an exculpatory clause. Several courts have dealt with such clauses as in dental-care contracts, specifically in cases of patients seeking care in the clinics of several dental schools, though the decisions apply to all situations in which a patient is required to accept an exculpatory clause as a condition of receiving care.

One case of major importance found its way to the highest court of Georgia and involved Emory's dental school. The admitted facts were as follows. A patient was accepted at Emory University's dental school's clinic. She was advised that all treatment at the clinic would be performed by dental students and employees under that direction of licensed dental faculty, or directly by licensed dentists. Before accepting a patient for care, the clinic required each patient to execute an information-and-consent form, including the following exculpatory clause:

> In consideration of Emory University School of Dentistry performing dental treatment, I do hereby expressly waive and relinquish any and all claims of any nature I or my minor child or ward may have against Emory University, its officers, agents, employees, or students, their successors, assignees, administrators or executors; and further agree to hold them harmless as a result of any claims by said minor child or ward, arising out of any dental treatment rendered, regardless of its nature or extent.

Several months after beginning treatment, the patient had an impacted tooth extracted by a faculty member. The surgeon noted that her jaw was fractured. The patient alleged that the fracture was a result of negligence, and brought a suit against Emory University and the faculty member.

Emory University and the surgeon denied the allegation, pleaded the exculpatory clause contained in the information consent form as a defense, and moved for summary judgment, a judgment granted when facts are not in dispute and there is therefore no need for a trial. The trial court held that the exculpatory clause was valid and granted summary judgment to the defendants. The patient appealed. The intermediate appellate court, the Court of Appeals of Georgia, held that the exculpatory clause in the consent form was invalid as contrary to public policy. The defendants, Emory University and the faculty dentist, appealed. The Supreme Court of Georgia affirmed the judgment of the Court of Appeals.

The Court of Appeals had much to say about exculpatory clauses. Examining the impact on such clauses of constitutional and contract law, it found no prohibition by either on the right of parties to enter into contracts whose terms are neither illegal nor immoral. It also found that parties may exempt themselves by contract from liability to other parties for injuries caused by negligence. Then, however, the court stated:

> A professional person should not be permitted to retreat behind the protective shield of an exculpatory clause and insist that he or she is not then answerable for his or her own negligence. To condone a release here could mean that in the future, similar releases might be required by other dentists, physicians, and professionals.
>
> The public interest of this state would not be served if dentists . . . were permitted to relieve themselves from liability for their own negligence. We hold, therefore, that the exculpatory clause in the consent form signed by a patient as a condition of receiving treatment . . . is, for "convincing and conclusive reasons" invalid as contrary to public policy.[3]

[3] 275 SE2d 163 (1980).

The Supreme Court, in upholding the decision of the Court of Appeals, stated:

> We find that it is against the public policy of this state to allow one who procures a license to practice dentistry to relieve himself by contract of the duty to exercise reasonable care. . . . We agree with the reasoning of the court in Olson v Molzen, 558 SW2d 429, 430 (Tenn 1977), a case which held a release from medical negligence void, that "rules that govern tradesmen in the market place are of little relevancy in dealing with professional persons who hold themselves out as experts and whose practice is regulated by the state."

The court went on to say, quoting another source:

> The relationship of the parties is relevant in determining whether or not a contract is in contravention of public policy because "some relationships are such that once entered upon they involve a status requiring of one party greater responsibility than that required of the ordinary person, and therefore, a provision avoiding liability is peculiarly obnoxious." 15 Williston, Contracts 1751 (3rd ed 1972).[4]

[4]282 SE2d 903 (1981).

A New York court found a similar exculpatory clause invalid:

> It does not appear that this Court has ever previously undertaken to fully analyze the public policy ramifications of a covenant not to sue for future negligence in the context of medical or dental malpractice. Upon such analysis we conclude that the agreement in this case is in violation of public policy and should not be enforced.[5]

[5]564 NYS2d 308 (1990).

The Tennessee Supreme Court did the same:

> [T]he general rule [that] a party may contract against his or her own negligence . . . does not afford a satisfactory solution in a case involving a professional person operating in an area of public interest and pursuing a profession subject to licensure by the State. The rules that govern tradesmen in the marketplace are of little relevancy in dealing with the professional persons who hold themselves out as experts and whose practice is regulated by the state.[6]

[6]558 SW2d 429 (1977).

In California, a health center required prospective patients to complete a form containing an exculpatory clause. The court ruled the clause invalid for much the same reasons as the Georgia and New York courts.[7]

[7]60 Cal2d 92 (1963).

Exculpatory clauses, as used by health professionals, have then been repeatedly judged invalid as against public policy. Serious questions may also be raised about the morality and professional ethics of such agreements. Though some lower courts have affirmed them, the precedent law in the states of Georgia, New York, and California is that such clauses are invalid; they are therefore unlikely to be supported by any appellate court.

When Does the Dentist-Patient Contract Begin?

3.11   The contract for dental services begins when there is an agreement between a person who requests services, including a professional opinion, and a dentist. However, if a person enters a dental office after making an appointment, and the dentist, after speaking with the patient, decides not to accept the patient for care, there is no contract. As soon as the dentist either assents in any manner to provide the service or renders a professional opinion, the dentist-patient relationship, and the contract, begins (see chapter 8).

Can the Contract Begin at a Social Event?

3.11.1   At a social gathering, one of the guests says to another guest, whom he knows to be a dentist, "Yesterday (Friday) my dentist extracted a wisdom tooth. Now (this is Saturday evening) it hurts a lot and my jaw is swollen. What do you think I should do?" The dentist answers, "Rinse with warm water, take two aspirins or Tylenol, and apply a cold compress to your cheek." Here a contract between the dentist and the patient, the party-goer, has begun. The dentist is liable for any injury the patient may suffer for following this advice. The fact that the advice was gratuitous has no effect on the relationship. Dentists cannot offer "curb-side advice" without risk. Regardless of the environment, a dentist owes the same duties to a stranger as he owes to his patients of record.

Can the Contract Begin with a Telephone Call?

3.11.2   At about 9:00 p.m. one evening you receive a telephone call at home. The party at the other end of the line says that he was referred by his neighbor, one of your patients. He says he moved to New York City from Baltimore, where he recently completed some extensive dental treatment. Since his move, he has not visited a dentist and does not intend to return to Baltimore for treatment; instead he wants to become your patient. He says that he now has a dental problem that he feels needs immediate attention; he has considerable pain and swelling of his jaw. You question him about his symptoms and other matters related to his dental problem. You advise him to take aspirin or Advil, apply a cold compress, etc, and to come to your office at 8:00 a.m. the next day. On the following day he does not appear. Some months later you are served with a summons and complaint stating that as a result of this advice given over the phone the patient suffered an injury and was hospitalized; and that his subsequent dentist is now willing to testify against you.

The question is: Was a doctor-patient relationship established as a result of the telephone call? If it was, you will be held to the standard of care practiced by other dentists in the community, and experts may appear for the injured party who state that your advice departed from those standards. If it wasn't, on the grounds you never saw the patient, nor examined him, nor charged for your advice, which you gave as a courtesy to a person in distress, you owed the caller none of the duties you ordinarily owed to your regular patients of record.

A court in New York was faced with this issue. Though it involved a physician rather than a dentist, courts routinely apply case law (though not black letter law) involving physicians to dentists. An infant suffered an eye injury in a fishing accident and was taken to the emergency room of a local hospital. A physician's assistant (PA) assigned to the emergency room stated that the child might need to see a specialist. Thereafter, an emergency-room physician advised the parent to contact the defendant, an ophthalmologist who served as a courtesy-consulting physician at the hospital. Although the defendant-ophthalmologist questioned and advised the parent over the phone, he did not personally examine the child. An aunt, who was present at the hospital, testified before trial that the PA then examined the patient, gave him a prescription for eye drops and told him to take Tylenol or Advil for pain. The ophthalmologist stated that he had no direct contact with the child but rather got his information through the PA, who spoke with the ophthalmologist while the child was still present in the emergency room.

In the defendant's examination before trial, he testified that he had been on the courtesy-consulting staff since 1977 and in that capacity he answered questions of emergency room staff over the phone. He did not, however, see patients at the emergency room and he never received payment for any courtesy consultation. Although he rendered what he characterized as an informal gratuitous opinion to the PA over the phone, he did not see, examine, take a history of, or treat the patient on the date in question. He also discussed treatment management that would involve follow-up visits to his office. He told the PA that the child should avoid aspirin and aspirin-like products and suggested that he be put on a minimal activity restriction.

The parents, on behalf of the child, brought suit against the ophthalmologist, alleging that the child suffered an injury as a result of the advice given by the ophthalmologist over the phone. After answering the suit, the defendant filed a motion for summary judgment requesting dismissal of the complaint because there was no physician-patient relationship with plaintiff. The Supreme Court (the judge in the trial court) denied this motion. The defendant appealed.

The appellate court affirmed the decision of the trial judge, finding that the telephone conversation did in fact establish a doctor-patient relationship. The court, quoting a prior case,[8] stated that "a doctor-patient relationship can be established by a telephone call when such a call 'affirmatively advise[s] a prospective patient as to a course of treatment' and it is foreseeable that the patient would rely on the advice."[9]

[8]672 NYS2d 460 (1998).

[9]557 NYS2d 139 (1990).

It is clear that before giving advice about what a patient should do to allay a dental problem, the dentist should physically examine the patient and conduct tests, including necessary radiographs, to determine the cause of the problem and what should be prescribed. The most judicious way to manage a request for advice over the telephone from a person not known to you as your patient is to state that you must conduct an examination before you can give advice. If the caller cannot wait for one, advise him or her to go to the nearest hospital. Otherwise, should a suit in malpractice follow, you may well be questioned thus: "Doctor, do you give professional advice to a patient without a physical examination of the patient, and completing a health history, and is this proper?" You can readily imagine where this would lead.

Terms of the Agreement

3.12   As stated previously, to avoid disputes as to the terms of the doctor-patient agreement, it is best to put the agreement (contract) in writing and have the patient sign it. Yet in dental practice such agreements are rarely made in writing, except among orthodontists. Although a consent-to-care is a form of contract, you are cautioned not to confuse such a consent with a contract to provide care (for consent, see chapter 9).

Remember that oral agreements are enforceable. Terms that are spoken and agreed to between the parties are called *express terms*. Thus when the dentist says to the patient, "I will perform root canal therapy on your front right tooth. The charge will be $300, $100 payable when I start, and the balance when I bill you after the last visit," and the patient answers, "Go ahead," the terms are expressed; they were spoken and agreed upon. Written terms are also express terms.

However, many terms are implied simply as a result of the doctor-patient relationship, without having been spoken or written. These are called in the law of contracts *implied warranties*. In health care relationships, they are called *implied duties*.

Implied Duties Owed by the Dentist to the Patient

3.12.1   In the absence of express terms stated in a contract, the courts, in a series of cases, have identified duties owed by dentists to their patients that are based on the doctor-patient relationship. In accepting the patient for care, the dentists warrant that they will:

1. Use reasonable care in the provision of services as measured against acceptable standards set by other practitioners with similar training in a similar community
2. Be properly licensed, registered, and meet all other legal requirements to engage in the practice of dentistry
3. Obtain accurate health (medical and dental) histories of patients before making diagnoses and beginning treatment
4. Employ competent personnel and provide for their proper supervision
5. Keep up with current advances in the profession
6. Use methods acceptable to at least a respectable minority of similar practitioners in the community
7. Not use experimental procedures
8. Obtain the informed consent of patients before instituting examinations or treatment
9. Not abandon patients during the course of treatment
10. Ensure that care is available in emergency situations
11. Charge a reasonable fee for services based upon community standards
12. Not exceed the scope of practice authorized by the license, nor permit any person acting under their direction to engage in unlawful acts
13. Keep patients informed of their progress
14. Not undertake any procedure for which they are not qualified
15. Complete the care in a timely manner
16. Keep accurate records of the treatment
17. Maintain confidentiality of information
18. Inform patients of any untoward occurrences in the course of treatment
19. Make appropriate referrals and request necessary consultations
20. Take an initial blood pressure reading and monitor patients' blood pressure at appropriate intervals during treatment
21. Comply with all laws regulating the practice of dentistry
22. Make the patients' records available at trial and testify when asked by patients
23. Practice in a manner consistent with the code of ethics of the profession

A breach of any of the above will make the dentist liable to the patient for breach of contract. However, courts treat a breach of these duties as negligence or malpractice (see section 3.13).

Implied Duties Owed by the Patient

3.12.2   In accepting care patients warrant that they will:

1. Follow home-care instructions
2. Keep appointments, or notify the office if an appointment cannot be kept
3. Pay bills for services in a reasonable time
4. Cooperate with dentists in their care
5. Give honest answers to all questions related to their histories
6. Notify the office (dentist) if their health status has changed or if their physician has placed them on a new regimen of medication

Note that any of the implied duties owed by the patient may be changed and/or increased by the dentist in discussions with the patient or in writing. They then become express duties.

Breach of the Terms of the Agreement

3.13   A breach of any of the terms of the agreement, whether oral or written, express or implied, by one party relieves the other party of the duty to perform. However, the courts have added specific conditions without which a dentist is not permitted to discontinue care as a result of the patient's breach. The general rule is that care must not be discontinued when the patient's health may be compromised. For example, if you have agreed to provide orthodontic care with a fixed appliance for a child, and during the course of treatment the parent fails to make the agreed payments over an extended period of time despite notices by your office of the breach, you are not permitted to discontinue the orthodontic care at a time when the child's oral health may be compromised—to hold a child's health hostage in order to collect a fee. You have another remedy at law, to sue for the fee. However, you may remove the fixed appliance after the occlusion is stabilized.

Or if you agree to complete five veneer crowns for a patient who agrees to pay a fixed amount monthly, and the patient is delinquent despite repeated notices from your office, you may discontinue care of the patient after completing three of the crowns. Although you have breached your agreement to complete the final two crowns, you are relieved of this duty as a result of the patient's breach. But if you started the preparation of the fourth crown, you must complete it (see chapter 10).

Should a dentist breach one of these duties, and as a result the patient is injured and brings suit, the courts treat the breach as negligence rather than breach of contract. The one exception appears to be if the dentist has guaranteed a successful result (see chapter 4).

When Does the Dentist-Patient Relationship End?

3.14   The contract and all its terms end when any of the following events take place:

1. The treatment bargained for has been completed
2. The patient voluntarily seeks the services of another dentist
3. Either party breaches any of the terms of the contract
4. Both the patient and dentist agree to end it
5. Either the patient or dentist is deceased
6. The dentist terminates his practice
7. The dentist unilaterally terminates the relationship (see chapter 4)

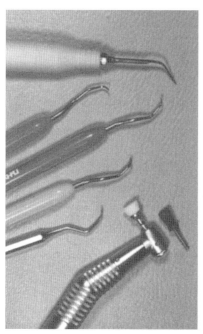

CHAPTER FOUR

Is It Negligence, Malpractice, or Breach of Contract?

Background

4.1   A single act by a dentist may lead to an allegation of negligence, malpractice, or breach of contract. This chapter will describe the differences between these, and explain how a plaintiff's attorney chooses which to allege, depending on the nature of the act; the statute of limitations; the need for and availability of experts; statements made by the dentist or the dentist's staff during, before, or after service was provided; and the amount of recovery for damages, etc.

First, an unsuccessful result alone does not make a dentist liable. Early in the legal history of medical and dental case law it was firmly established that neither a physician nor a dentist guarantees a successful result in treatment. As early as 1919 a court in New York, charging a jury in a case in which a patient alleged a tooth had been improperly removed by the dentist, declared:

> The defendant [dentist] was not a guarantor of his work, or the result that would follow; he is not an insurer as to the result. In other words, in this case, he was required to use the ordinary care of such a man having the ordinary skill in this locality; and, if he does not, the mere fact that there is a bad result is not enough, but you have got to trace it to his lack of skill, or his negligence.[1]

On appeal the appellate court affirmed the decision of the trial court and included in its opinion that the judge's charge was proper; a dentist is not a guarantor of a satisfactory result.

[1] 179 NYS2d 281 (1919).

Breach of Contract

4.2   For an action in breach of contract the plaintiff-patient must show, by a preponderance (more than 50%) of the evidence, that one of the terms of the agreement made between the dentist and the patient was breached by the dentist (see also chapter 3). The terms of agreement can be either express (written or oral) or implied. A suit for breach of contract may have some distinct advantages over one for negligence or malpractice for any one of the following reasons:

1. A suit in breach of contract may have a longer statute of limitations than one in negligence or malpractice. Should a patient do nothing following an injury, and the statute of limitations run for both negligence and malpractice, the only choice left to that patient is to sue in breach of contract. The length the respective statutes run is state regulated. In New York the statute of limitations for breach of contract is 6 years, for negligence 3 years, and for malpractice 2½ years. In New York if more than 3 years has elapsed from the time the incident took place that resulted in the injury, neither a suit in negligence nor malpractice will survive a motion to dismiss brought by the attorney for the defendant-dentist.
2. In a suit based upon breach of contract there is no need for the patient to produce an expert at trial. The jury itself is able to decide the appropriate standard of care to which the defendant-dentist is held. It is called *common knowledge*. For example, if the dentist extracted the wrong tooth of the patient, the dentist is alleged not to have complied with one of the implied duties in the dentist-patient contract; that is, to exercise care in the treatment of the patient. There is no need for an expert to testify as to the standard to be applied in a case such as this; therefore, the case for the plaintiff-patient is easier to prove.

The following is an example of a case in which an expert was not needed. During an extraction of a tooth, a dentist used excessive force, pounding on the jaw with a "chisel and mallet," as a result of which the plaintiff's jaw was broken. At the trial the plaintiff-patient did not produce an expert to inform the jury as to the standard of care, and the trial judge therefore dismissed the complaint. The appellate court reversed the decision of the trial judge and ordered a new trial:

> The question presented is whether plaintiff in the absence of expert medical testimony established a prima facie case of lack of ordinary care on the part of defendant. As a general rule, where the exercise of proper skill or care on the part of a physician, surgeon, or dentist is in issue, expert medical testimony is required by plaintiff to show that the untoward results might have been avoided by due care for under the law, the doctor does not guarantee the result. However, expert evidence is not required where the results of the treatment are of such a character as to warrant the inference of want of care from the testimony of laymen or in the light of the knowledge and experience of the jurors themselves.[2]

[2]11 NYS2d 85 (1939).

There are also some disadvantages in bringing a suit alleging breach of contract:

1. The dollar amount of the award is limited to out-of-pocket expenses (special damages); compensation for pain and suffering (general damages) cannot be included, except in rare situations.
2. Most state courts have refused to accept suits brought in breach of contract when it is related to health care. Their reasoning is that the practitioner is negligent in failing to comply with any of the contractual agreements, whether express or implied.

In one case, for example, a court, while not denying that a dentist may have breached a contract, insisted on applying the 2-year statute for malpractice rather than the 6-year statute for breach of contract: "An action against a dentist for negligence to the injury of a patient is one for malpractice within the meaning of section 384 of the Code of Civil Procedure, and must be brought within 2 years after the cause of action accrues."[3]

There is, however, an exception to this general rule, one of considerable importance to health practitioners. If a guarantee of the result of treatment is made or implied to the patient, the courts are likely to consider the failure to achieve this result a breach of contract and therefore to apply a longer statute of limitations because such a failure may not be due to negligence or malpractice. A dentist should, for this reason and others, never guarantee a result (see chapter 13).

Sometimes, in an attempt to prevent an injustice that might result from the running of the statute of limitations, the courts will bend the rules on whether the action is based on breach of contract or negligence. Here is one court on the issue: "Two or more causes of action may arise out of the same transaction with different statutes of limitations, and although one may be barred the other may be good. While the plaintiff may not be able to recover for malpractice, she may recover for a breach of contract."[4] Another court in a malpractice suit, admitting that "the limitation of the statute has run against the plaintiff's cause of action," went on to state:

> The action is one growing out of the breach of a consensual relation, and is tortious in its nature. We think it would be possible for the plaintiff still to obtain partial relief by suing strictly on the contract, against which cause of action the statute has not run. Recovery of damages could not be had for the wrong involving unskillful treatment; but plaintiff might be entitled to recover sums paid to defendants on the contract to furnish proper medical aid, and for sums paid out for nurses and medicines or other damages that flow naturally from the breach of whatever contract was made between the parties.[5]

Dentists suffer a decided practical disadvantage in being sued for breach of contract, because the typical professional liability insurance policy limits coverage specifically to negligence or malpractice (see chapter 19).

Negligence and Malpractice

4.3   There is much confusion between the terms negligence and malpractice. Unfortunately, at times they are used interchangeably; however, there is a vast technical difference between them in law. An errant dentist may be sued for

[3]161 NYS 994 (1916).

[4]135 NYS2d 696 (1954).

[5]229 NYS 60 (1928).

either, depending upon the facts leading to the injury of the patient. All acts of malpractice are the result of negligence. But not all acts of negligence are malpractice. Confusing? Consider that all dentists are health practitioners, but not all health practitioners are dentists.

Negligence is either:

1. Doing something that a reasonably prudent person would not have done—an act of commission
2. Not doing something that a reasonably prudent person would have done—an act of omission
3. Doing something that a reasonably prudent person would have done, but in doing it, failing to meet a reasonable standard of care—a breach of the standard

For negligent acts to find their way into the courts they must lead to an injury to an innocent party.

In New York, as in many other jurisdictions, there is a guide for judges in instructing a jury that summarizes the law. The following statement appears under the heading "Negligence" in *New York Pattern Jury Instructions*:

> Negligence is lack of ordinary care. It is a failure to exercise that degree of care which a reasonably prudent person would have exercised under the same circumstances. It may arise from doing an act which a reasonably prudent person would not have done under the same circumstances, or, on the other hand, from failing to do an act which a reasonably prudent person would have done under the same circumstances.[6]

[6]New York Pattern Jury Instructions, §2:10. St. Paul, MN: West, 2000.

In a court of law, the trier of facts, whether a judge or a jury without expert professional assistance, is able to determine what a reasonably prudent person would have done or not done under circumstances similar to what the defendant was faced with, or whether it was done improperly. The plaintiff, who allegedly suffered an injury as a result of what took place, is not required to present evidence as to the standard by which the defendant is to be measured. However, expert testimony may be needed to evaluate the injury to the plaintiff, whether temporary or permanent, and to determine the cost to restore the plaintiff to a reasonable state of health. Neither the judge nor the jury can decide those facts without some expert help (see chapter 13).

Negligence may be *ordinary*, at times referred to as *simple*, or *gross*, depending upon the circumstance of the act. *Black's Law Dictionary* defines ordinary negligence as: "the omissions of the care which a man of common prudence usually takes of his own concerns." It defines gross negligence as "the intentional failure to perform a manifest duty in reckless disregard of the consequences as effecting the life or property of another." The distinction is important in, for example, Good Samaritan statutes, which preclude the victim of an accident from maintaining a suit in ordinary negligence against the "Good Samaritan" but not a suit in gross negligence. Another example is professional misconduct, defined in Title VIII of the Education Law on New York, Article 130, Subarticle 3, Professional Misconduct, §6509 as "practicing the profession fraudulently, beyond its authorized scope, with gross incompetence, with *gross negligence on a particular occasion or [ordinary] negligence or incompetence on more than one occasion*." (Emphasis added.)

Malpractice is a special form of negligence. It is defined as an act of negligence committed by a member of a profession in the performance of professional services in which there has been a departure from the standard of care to which the professional is held. A more accurate term is professional negligence. In the *New York Pattern Jury Instructions*, the judge, in instructing a jury in a case in which dental malpractice is alleged, is advised to state the following:

> Malpractice is professional negligence and [dental] malpractice is the negligence of a [dentist]. Negligence is the failure to use reasonable care under the circumstances, doing something that a reasonably prudent [dentist] would not do under the circumstances, or failing to do something that a reasonably prudent [dentist] would do under the circumstances. It is a deviation or departure from accepted practice.
>
> A [dentist] who renders [dental] service to a patient is obligated to have that degree of knowledge and skill that is expected of an (average [dentist], average [dental] specialist) who (performs, provides) that (operation, treatment, [dental] service) in the [dental] community in which the [dentist] practices. The [dentist] must also comply with minimum (statewide, national) standards of care. [National standards only apply to board-certified specialists in one of the four judicial departments in the state.]
>
> The law recognizes that there are differences in the abilities of [dentists], just as there are differences in the abilities of people engaged in other activities. To practice [dentistry], a [dentist] is not required to have the extraordinary knowledge and ability that belongs to few [dentists] of exceptional ability. However, every [dentist] is required to keep reasonably informed of new developments in (his, her) field and to practice [dentistry] in accordance with approved methods and means of treatment in general use. A [dentist] must use his or her best judgement and whatever superior knowledge and skill (he, she) possesses, even if the knowledge and skill exceeds that possessed by the average [dentist] in the [dental] community where the [dentist] practices.
>
> By undertaking to perform a [dental] service, a [dentist] does not guarantee a good result. The fact that there was a bad result to the patient, by itself, does not make the [dentist] liable. The [dentist] is liable only if (he, she) was negligent. Whether the [dentist] was negligent is to be decided on the basis of the facts and conditions existing at the time of the claimed negligence.
>
> A [dentist] is not liable for an error in judgement if (he, she) does what (he, she) thinks is best after careful evaluation if it is a judgement that a reasonably prudent [dentist] could have made under the circumstances.
>
> If a [dentist] is negligent, that is, lacks the skill or knowledge required of (him, her) in providing a [dental] service or fails to use reasonable care and judgement in providing the service, and such lack of skill or care or knowledge or the failure to use reasonable care or judgement is a substantial factor in causing harm to the patient, then the [dentist] is responsible for the injury or harm caused.
>
> A [dentist]'s responsibility is the same regardless of whether (he, she) was paid.[7] [In a note, the charge states, "The charge can be used with respect to claims against other health care providers such as dentists, podiatrists, etc." Therefore, the above was modified to apply to dental malpractice cases.]

There are several major differences between malpractice and other negligence. Professional acts are usually complex and highly technical. To understand them requires special knowledge gained through long years of education

[7]New York Pattern Jury Instructions—Civil, vol 1A, ed 3. St. Paul, MN: West, 2002.

and training. The technical complexity of professional acts and services is not easily understood by laymen, ie, members of a jury; therefore, in the trial of a malpractice suit the plaintiff is required to produce an expert or experts to inform the jury and judge of the prevailing standard of care, whether the defendant-dentist departed from the standard, and if the departure was the proximate (direct) cause of the injury. Without this testimony a judge or jury would not be able to determine the standard of care to which the defendant professional is held, and whether the defendant departed from it.

The following case establishes this:

> It is not contested that plaintiffs' failure to furnish [defendant] with the discovery materials demanded was entirely attributable to law office failure. Accordingly, in seeking relief from the resulting default, plaintiffs were required to furnish an affidavit of merit demonstrating the meritoriousness of their claim. In a medical malpractice action, expert medical opinion is required to demonstrate merit as to matters not within the ordinary experience and knowledge of lay persons. The negligence alleged in the instant case, the failure to diagnose and render appropriate care and treatment for a blood clot which developed as a result of the alleged failure to properly apply and remove a cast on the infant plaintiff's leg, pertains to the level of care ordinarily expected of a physician in the community and does not encompass matters within the ordinary experience and knowledge of a lay person. Therefore, since plaintiffs failed to submit competent medical evidence, either from a treating physician or by an expert whose opinion was based on the available medical records, regarding the merits of the medical malpractice action, Special Term abused its discretion in denying the application for a final order of dismissal.
>
> Plaintiffs' assertion that expert medical opinion was not necessary to establish the merits of the instant case because plaintiffs are relying upon the doctrine of *res ipsa loquitur* to prove [defendant's] negligence is unavailing. The doctrine of *res ipsa loquitur* permits a jury possessed of the ordinary experience and knowledge of laymen to draw an inference of negligence, itself a function of the conduct of reasonable men, from the circumstantial evidence of a case when the injuries alleged by a plaintiff would not have occurred in the absence of negligence. However, in the area of medical malpractice, the jury is generally not equipped to determine the issue of negligence, in which there involves the level of care required of physicians in the community, without the aid of expert medical opinion. Specifically, "[T]he information obtained from an expert witness supplies the jury with the means by which it can evaluate the conduct of the party charged with malpractice" [quoting a prior case]. Accordingly, since, as we have previously noted, the negligence alleged here encompasses matters not within the ordinary knowledge and experience of lay persons, plaintiffs could not proceed under the doctrine of *res ipsa loquitur* without first submitting expert medical opinion regarding the level of medical care required.[8] [See chapter 13.]

[8]507 NYS2d 497 (1986).

Malpractice, thus, is tried differently than negligence; the two actions may also differ in the length of the running of the statute of limitations. Each state has independently set the time the statute begins to run, how long it runs, and under what conditions it may be *tolled,* or delayed, in beginning to run. In general, the statute of limitations for suits in negligence runs from 2 to 7 years. In some states it begins when the alleged act of negligence took place, in others when the patient discovers, or should have discovered, that the doctor's negligence caused the injury. In New York the statute of limitations for negligence is 3 years and for malpractice $2^1/_2$ years after occurrence. (See chapter 5 for a full discussion of statutes of limitation.)

Some courts have ruled that when a dentist extracts a wrong tooth, the act constitutes negligence rather than malpractice, and the jury need not be informed as to the standard of care to which the dentist is held; it is within the common knowledge of lay persons. In a recent case decided in New York, a physician was sued for not informing the patient about how and when a pre-scribed medication should be taken. The court decided that the act was not malpractice but negligence. In that case the judge stated:

> An act of omission or commission may be negligent conduct and if com-mitted by a physician is designated as a medical malpractice action.
>
> Since these issues may readily be assessed based upon common every-day experience of the trier of facts, without the need for expert testimony, the action sounded [fell within the class of legal action] in ordinary negli-gence.[9]

[9]New York
Law Journal.
1 October
1991, p 1,
col 7.

Errors in Judgment

4.4   Not all errors in treatment are malpractice. The courts have set out specific conditions that must be met before the practitioner may be relieved from lia-bility despite committing error that was the proximate cause of the injury to the patient. The following case illustrates these conditions:

> Plaintiff, an unemployed alcoholic construction worker, was injured as the result of "a little argument with some guy" who "belted" him to the extent that he was brought on January 5, 1977 to hospital with multiple fractures of both sides of the jaw, compounded to the extent that a piece of jaw had cut through a nerve and protruded through the skin, and another piece of bone had become lodged under the skull. His condition as to sobriety was such that it was necessary to apply restraints before he could be examined, and it was necessary, before X rays could be made, to devise a bandage sling to support the injured jaw. Defendant-appellant, a certified oral sur-geon, examined and treated plaintiff-respondent. The patient had no natur-al upper teeth, and had theretofore broken an upper plate, never replaced. There being no upper anchorage for wires to keep the jaw bones in position during healing, defendant devised a supportive structure consisting of wires running under the skin across the cheek bones and through the nose. A similar structure, anchored to the seven lower teeth, held the lower jaw in place. Antibiotics were administered on each visit except at one specified below.[10]

[10]430 NYS2d
78 (1980).

In a footnote the court noted that the defendant's records "did not reflect rou-tine administration of antibiotics but he testified to this, and it was verified by plaintiff himself during his testimony that antibiotic pills were given to him."

The court reported the following sequence of events:

> On January 23, 1977, plaintiff was advised, after treatment, to return to defendant's office in 48 hours; he did not return for 8 days and no commu-nication could be had with him in the interval because the address and phone number he had left were false. After irrigation and self-care instruc-tion, he was again told to return in 48 hours; he returned in 4 days, and was

found to have developed an infection. This condition was treated by incision and insertion of a drain. The next day, he was again irrigated, medicated, and dressed, and two days thereafter a molar, originally left in the fracture line so as not to impede aligned healing, was extracted. On February 8, all signs of infection having gone, indicated by discharge of blood only, the abscess was permitted to heal without further draining. Three days later, some of the wire structure was removed and, on February 17, the swelling at the site being reduced in size, no antibiotic was administered in order that plaintiff's situation might be evaluated, and to avoid building up an immunity to the antibiotic in the infective microorganisms. Plaintiff was told to return a week later, at which time the evaluation was to be made; instead, he went to the hospital's emergency room, complaining of pain. Personnel there telephoned defendant's office, and transmitted to plaintiff defendant's instruction to come to the office on the following day; he did not come then, but he did appear on March 19.

When plaintiff did come to the office, defendant indicated that the time had come to remove the rest of the wire structure, but, since the original hospital would not receive him for the necessary surgery because of an unpaid bill for prior service, it was suggested that he sign himself into the alcoholic facility at a State Hospital. He did so, the wires were removed, and the professional relationship terminated; plaintiff did not thereafter appear at defendant's office.

The patient charged the defendant with malpractice for his suspension of antibiotics on February 17. The court in relieving the defendant from liability stated:

> As to the cutoff intended to be only temporary of the antibiotic, plaintiff's expert conceded its propriety if defendant had reason to believe the infection was under control. At its worst, it would have been an error in professional judgment, and not malpractice. "The rule requiring him to use his best judgment does not hold him liable for a mere error of judgment, provided he does what he thinks is best after careful examination" [the court quoted a prior case].[11]

[11]155 NY 201 (1898).

Summary

4.5   In general, if the act that caused the injury to a patient is considered administrative in nature, and a jury of lay people is able to judge, without the assistance of experts, the standard of reasonable care, the action will sound in negligence. The general negligence statute of the jurisdiction will apply, and the plaintiff will not be required to provide expert testimony. If the act falls within a professional field where technical information is required to determine the standard of care, the action will sound in malpractice, or professional negligence, the plaintiff will be required to provide expert testimony, and the statute for suits in malpractice will apply. And so, what matters is not so much whether the defendant is a member of a profession, but rather what the defendant did that initiated the suit. If the act performed by a dentist falls within the class of negligence rather than the subclass of malpractice, the dentist is exposed to additional legal risks:

1. In some jurisdictions the statute of limitations for negligence may exceed that for malpractice.

2. The burden placed upon the patient-plaintiff in the trial of the case is considerably reduced when negligence rather than malpractice is alleged because no expert is needed.

As between negligence/malpractice and breach of contract, the advantages to the plaintiff-patient of the former are:

1. The general damages are included in the award (and general damages may far exceed special damages).
2. In negligence and malpractice actions, if the plaintiff is married, the spouse can claim loss of services and be awarded a significant amount of money.

The disadvantages to the plaintiff-patient to allege negligence or malpractice over breach of contract are:

1. The statute of limitations may be shorter than for breach of contract.
2. Suits in malpractice are more difficult to prove—experts are needed by the plaintiff-patient to establish a standard of care and that there was a departure from the standard.

The advantages to the plaintiff-patient in alleging negligence rather than malpractice are:

1. No expert is needed to establish the standard of care.
2. The statute of limitations may be longer.

The disadvantage to the plaintiff-patient in alleging negligence rather than malpractice is only that the judge may declare the action one of malpractice and not negligence, and the patient may not be prepared to produce an expert.

CHAPTER FIVE

Statute of Limitations and Statute of Repose: How Long the Patient Has to Sue

Statute of Limitations

5.1   Dentists may be sued for negligence, malpractice, and breach of contract. Each state has its own statutes of limitations for these actions that determine how long dentists may be sued and under what conditions that period may be *tolled* (delayed in its start). Such statutes are designed to prevent the threat of a suit from lasting forever, and to allow for the fact that memories fade over time and witnesses become unavailable through death or relocation. If a statute of limitations has run, the right continues, but the remedy is lost. The patient may still enter suit against the dentist, who then has the burden, through his attorney, of answering the initial filing of the claim with an affirmative defense raising the expiration of the running of the statute. The court will then rule on whether the suit will continue.

When the Statute of Limitations in Malpractice Suits Begins to Run

5.1.1   Each state has a rule that determines the date on which the statute of limitation begins to run. It may be when the act of negligence alleged to have caused the injury to the patient took place, or it may be when the patient discovered, or should have discovered, that that act of negligence took place. The first is called the *occurrence rule,* the second the *discovery rule.* Fourteen states are discovery states (Table I). Clearly, the occurrence rule favors the defendant-dentist, because the patient may not be aware of an injury alleged to have been

[1]Louisell DW, Williams H. Medical Malpractice. New York: Matthew Bender, 1997.

Table 1 Rules for malpractice statute of limitations by state or territory[1]

State or territory	Length of statute (y)	Rule determining when statute begins to run*
Alabama	2	O, X
Alaska	2	O
Arizona	2	O
Arkansas	2	O
California	3	O, X
Colorado	2	D
Connecticut	2	O, X
Delaware	2	O
District of Columbia	3	D
Florida	2	O, X
Georgia	2	O
Hawaii	2	O, X
Idaho	2	O
Illinois	2	O, X
Indiana	2	O, X
Iowa	2	D
Kansas	2	O, X
Kentucky	1	D
Louisiana	1	O, X
Maine	3	O
Maryland	5	D
Massachusetts	3	D
Michigan	2	D
Minnesota	2	O
Mississippi	2	D
Missouri	2	O, X
Montana	3	O, X
Nebraska	2	O, X
Nevada	4	O, X
New Hampshire	3	O, X
New Jersey	2	D
New Mexico	3	O
New York	$2\frac{1}{2}$	O, X
North Carolina	3	O, X
North Dakota	2	D
Ohio	1	O, X
Oklahoma	2	D
Oregon	2	O
Pennsylvania	2	O, X
Puerto Rico	1	D
Rhode Island	3	O, X
South Carolina	3	O, X
South Dakota	2	O, X
Tennessee	1	D
Texas	2	O, X
Utah	2	D
Vermont	3	O, X
Virgin Islands	2	O
Virginia	2	O
Washington	3	O, X
West Virginia	2	O, X
Wisconsin	3	O, X
Wyoming	2	O, X

*O, Occurrence; X, tolled; D, discovery.

caused by a dentist until many years after the incident that caused the injury took place.

In the some occurrence states, the running of the statute of limitations may be tolled for one or more of the following reasons:

1. *Foreign Object.* Should the negligence result in leaving a foreign object in the body, the statute is tolled until the patient discovers, or should have discovered, that object. The exception applies only to objects not intended to be left in the body: to broken reamer tips, for example, but not prosthetics.
2. *Continuous Treatment.* The statute begins to run at the end of the course of treatment in which the negligent act took place. For example, if a reamer tip breaks in the root canal on July 1st, but the root canal treatment is not completed until September 1st, the statute begins to run on September 1st.
3. *Fraudulent Concealment.* Should the practitioner have been guilty of fraudulent concealment, the statute begins to run when the patient discovers the fraud. Therefore, the running of the statute is governed by the statute that applies to fraud rather than malpractice. For example, if a dentist knows but fails to inform the patient of a broken reamer tip left in a canal, the statute begins to run when the patient discovers it.
4. *Infancy.* The statute tolls for the infancy of the patient and then, as in New York, runs for 10 years from the date of the occurrence or for three years after the minor reaches majority, whichever is longer.

For illustrations of these exceptions, see sections 5.1.1.1 to 5.1.1.4.

Foreign Object

5.1.1.1   In a New York case the facts were as follows. During the course of endodontic therapy, a file broke inside a root canal and remained there, despite the dentist's attempts to remove it. The dentist did not tell the patient about the file; it was discovered long afterwards by another dentist, who advised the patient of the need to remove it surgically. The patient entered suit against the errant dentist after the 2½-year statute of limitations had run. The dentist filed a motion to have the suit dismissed because the statute had run. The trial judge ruled in favor of the patient. The dentist appealed.

The appellate court upheld the decision of the trial judge: "The broken dental file which was left inside of the plaintiff's tooth is a 'foreign object' within the meaning of CPLR 214-a, which delayed the running of the Statute of Limitations until the date the foreign object was or reasonably should have been discovered."[2] New Jersey is a discovery state. The statute of limitations for malpractice actions runs for 2 years, which do not begin to run until the patient discovers, or should have discovered, the negligent act that caused the injury. In states which, like New York and New Jersey, do not have a statute of repose (defined in 5.2 below), dentists are at risk in such cases as these for an indeterminate length of time—another reason they should retain the records of their patients for as long as they are able (see chapter 12).

[2]702 NYS2d 85 (2000).

Continuous Treatment

5.1.1.2   *Continuous treatment* has proved difficult for both courts and practitioners to define. One issue is whether the recall of a patient for a periodic examination qualifies as continuous treatment. In a New York case on this issue, the patient, a physician, sought treatment by the defendant physician for ringing in his ears. The patient was admitted to a hospital where inconclusive tests were performed and was discharged. There was no further contact between the parties until 3½ years later, when the defendant doctor contacted the patient and suggested that another cat scan be taken and a new noninvasive audiometric test, unavailable during the initial course of tests, be performed. The new test revealed the cause of the patient's problem, and the defendant performed surgery to correct it. The patient claimed that the surgery left him permanently injured and entered suit against the surgeon, the physician whom he had seen originally, for fraudulent misrepresentation and negligence.

Given that the suit was filed more than 2½ years after the end of the initial series of visits, was it barred by the running of the statute of limitations, or did it fall within the continuous treatment tolling of the statute? The Court of Appeals, the highest court in the state, quoted the statute: "An action for medical, dental, or podiatric malpractice must be commenced within two years and six months of the act, omission or failure complained of or last treatment where there is continuous treatment for the same illness, injury or condition which gave rise to the said act, omission or failure." The court ruled against the patient: "allowing continuous treatment to be invoked solely on a doctor-initiated communication might, we fear, encourage" doctors not to recall their patients.[3]

[3]538 NYS2d 229 (1989).

Though recalls to evaluate a specific treatment may fall within the continuous treatment tolling of the statute, periodic recalls following completion of care do not: sending out recall notices presents no apparent risk.

In a case decided in Idaho, the facts were as follows. On December 15, 1978, the defendant dentist extracted a wisdom tooth for the plaintiff. On December 20, 1978, the defendant removed the stitches. There was no further contact between plaintiff and defendant. The plaintiff, complaining that the dentist had failed to warn him of the risks, claimed that the statute of limitations for this did not begin to run until the time the stitches were removed. Idaho has no law tolling the statute of limitations for continuous treatment.

The Supreme Court held:

> *(1)* patient's cause of action for the alleged negligence accrued as of date of the extraction, the time when the negligent act, if any, was fully accomplished, not as of subsequent date in which patient returned to have stitches removed; *(2)* alleged failure to warn patient of risks inherent in the procedure would of necessity have had to have occurred prior to date of extraction and, therefore, limitations period would also have run on that claim.[4]

[4]106 Idaho 561 (1987).

[5]538 NYS2d 229 (1989).

In New York a court ruled that by routinely recalling patients, the practitioner does not toll the statute of limitations.[5]

Fraudulent Concealment

5.1.1.3   Fraudulent concealment is the dentist's withholding of information from the patient about negligence that resulted in an injury to the patient. Dentists should protect themselves by informing patients about any untoward event, entering it in the patient's treatment record, and, if possible, having the patient initial, or better still, sign the entry. The statute of limitations will then run from the date on which the entry on the record was made, in both occurrence and discovery states (see chapter 17).

States with fraudulent concealment tolling of the statute of limitations are California, Colorado, Connecticut, Delaware, Florida, Georgia, Hawaii, Idaho, Illinois, Indiana, Kentucky, Louisiana, Maryland, Massachusetts. Michigan, Minnesota, Mississippi, Missouri, Montana, Nebraska, New Jersey, New Mexico, New York (for fraud in one of its four departments), North Dakota, Ohio, Oregon, Pennsylvania, Rhode Island, Tennessee, Texas, Utah, Vermont, Virginia, Washington, West Virginia, and Wisconsin. Others may recognize fraudulent concealment in case law. A federal court ruled that fraudulent concealment will toll the statute.[6] Whether or not fraudulent concealment is a matter of law in the state in which you practice, the patient-dentist contract includes the implied duty of keeping patients informed about their health status (see chapter 3).

[6]481 F2d 257 (1973).

Infancy

5.1.1.4   The statute is tolled during infancy and generally does not begin to run until the minor reaches majority. However, during the malpractice crises of the 1970s and again in the 1980s, states enacted tort-reform legislation in an attempt to control the growing number of malpractice suits. Some limited the number of years the statute may toll regardless of the age of the child at the time the injury took place. Other factors that toll the statute, of relatively little importance to dentist, include the imprisonment of the plaintiff, periods of mental incompetency, and the absence of the plaintiff from the jurisdiction of the court.

Statute of Repose

5.2   The statute of repose is a close relative of the statue of limitations: It sets an outer limit to the time in which the injured party can enter suit, regardless of circumstances. Twenty-one jurisdictions superimpose the statute of repose on the statute of limitations (Table 2).

Some Examples

5.3   To define the statute of repose is relatively simple, but to fully understand how it operates can best be explained using examples. Say that, in a certain state, the statute of limitations for malpractice is 3 years from the time the patient discovers, or should have discovered, the injury due to the negligence of the dentist, and the statute of repose is 6 years. A dentist, in removing an impacted third molar, fractures the tooth, leaves the root tips in the bone, and does not inform the patient of this. If the patient is discovers it and enters suit within 3 years, the suit will proceed. If the patient discovers it and enters suit with-

[7]Louisell DW, Williams H. Medical Malpractice. New York: Matthew Bender, 1997.

Table 2 Length of statute of repose by state[7]

State	Length of statute of repose (y)
Alabama	4
California	4
Connecticut	3
Florida	7
Hawaii	6
Illinois	4
Iowa	6
Kansas	10
Kentucky	5
Louisiana	3
Missouri	10
Montana	5
Nebraska	10
North Dakota	6
Ohio	4
Oregon	5
South Carolina	6
Tennessee	3
Vermont	7
Washington	8
Wisconsin	5

in 4 years, the courts will let the suit go forward because this is a discovery state. But if the patient does not discover it until the 7th year, the suit will be barred by the statute of repose.

Should dentists practicing in a discovery state with no statute of repose commit negligent acts that result in injury and not inform their patients, such dentist can never rest without fear of a suit. Should dentists practicing in an occurrence state with no statute of repose commit such acts, they also may never rest without fear, because of exceptions for continuous treatment, fraudulent concealment, or foreign object.

Again, the only safe procedure is to notify the patient at the time the adverse occurrence takes place and document on the record that the patient was informed. The most common circumstances under which this is necessary are broken instrument tips lodged in root canals, fractured root tips left in bone, and root canals that have been unintentionally overfilled or underfilled.

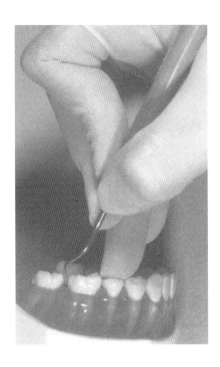

CHAPTER SIX

Experts and the Standards of Care

Avoiding Confusion Regarding "Standards"

6.1   The use of the word *standards* in court proceedings confuses many practicing dentists who identify the standards set by the courts with the standards set by professional organizations for their members. In fact the courts do not accept the standards of professional organizations as the standards to which practitioners are to be held in malpractice cases. Some professional organizations use the phrase "parameters of practice" to prevent the courts from using them as legal standards. However, they have little to fear: The hearsay evidence rule prevents their "parameters" or "standards" from being entered directly into evidence (see chapter 13).

Need for Experts

6.2   When a dentist is tried for malpractice, the standard to which she is held is decided by whoever tries the facts—a judge alone or a jury. In a malpractice suit against a dentist, no member of the jury will be a dentist. The attorneys selecting jurors will disqualify anyone remotely connected to the dental profession. Further, in most states health practitioners are excluded from jury lists so that they may continue service to the community and treatment to their patients uninterrupted. Therefore all members of any jury will be equally uninformed before trial about the standard of care to be applied to a defendant-dentist. To compensate for this, the court admits the testimony of experts to educate the jury. Experts will testify to the following:

1. The standard to which the defendant-dentist is held
2. Whether the dentist, in the provision of the service that caused the injury, departed from the standard
3. The extent of the injury that was caused by the departure, whether temporary or permanent
4. Whether the departure was the proximate (direct) cause of the injury
5. The treatment needed to restore the patient to optimum health given the severity of the injury
6. The cost of this restorative treatment

In all cases of alleged malpractice, in all jurisdictions, the plaintiff-patient is required to produce expert testimony initially to inform the jury of 1 and 2 above, without which the case may be dismissed by the judge on the motion of the defense attorney. This may take place before the defense puts on its case. Although it is not required that the defense produce an expert, it invariably does. The defense expert may testify either that the plaintiff's expert's supposed standard of care did not apply in this case, or that the defendant adhered to it. Malpractice trials have often been characterized as battles of the experts.

Cases in Which Experts Are Not Required

6.3   Plaintiffs are required to produce experts in malpractice cases, but not in negligence cases, where a jury of laymen, without assistance, can determine the standard of care and whether the dentist departed from it: No expert is required to prove that a dentist who extracted a wrong tooth was negligent. The difference between negligence and malpractice is discussed more generally in chapter 4; the following case makes it clear as it relates to expert testimony:

> The question presented is whether plaintiff in the absence of expert medical testimony established a prima facie case of lack of ordinary care on the part of defendant.
> As a general rule, where the exercise of proper skill or care on the part of a physician, surgeon, or dentist is in issue, expert medical testimony is required by plaintiff to show that the untoward results might have been avoided by due care for under the law, the doctor does not guarantee the result. However, expert evidence is not required where the results of the treatment are of such a character as to warrant the inference of want of care from the testimony of laymen or in the light of the knowledge and experience of the jurors themselves.[1]

[1] 11 NYS2d 85 (1939).

A host of other cases in other jurisdictions draw the same conclusion. Where a jury of lay people can decide the standard of care to be applied to a case where negligence is evident, and where the alleged act was a departure from the standard, the plaintiff-patient is not required to produce the testimony of an expert.

Cases in Which Experts Are Required

6.4   A long-established rule in case law is that in a trial in which the patient of a physician or dentist claims to have sustained an injury as a result of malpractice, the plaintiff-patient must, in the presentation of his case, produce an expert. Otherwise, the case will be dismissed, sometimes before the defense is presented. The defendant is not required to produce an expert but almost always does. The standard of care to which a physician or dentist is held in the trial of a suit in malpractice is directly related to whom the trial judge will permit to present testimony. In a case decided in Massachusetts the appellate court began by stating, "although a trial judge has broad discretion in determining the qualifications of a witness to testify as an expert, his decision will not be upheld if it is erroneous as a matter of law."[2]

[2]401 Mass 65 (1987).

Case Law and the Standard of Care

6.5   In a landmark case decided in 1898, concerning treatment of a man whose kneecap was broken by a kick from a horse, a court in New York set out in detail the standard of care to which a physician was held. Over the years the case has been cited and quoted in many states and represents the basic standards to be applied in malpractice cases that involve health practitioners:

> The law relating to malpractice is simple and well settled, although not always easy of application. A physician and surgeon, by taking charge of a case, impliedly represents that he possesses, and the law places upon him the duty of possessing, that reasonable degree of learning and skill that is ordinarily possessed by physicians and surgeons in the locality where he practices, and which is ordinarily regarded by those conversant with the employment as necessary to qualify him to engage in the business of practicing medicine and surgery. Upon consenting to treat a patient, it becomes his duty to use reasonable care and diligence in the exercise of his skill and the application of his learning to accomplish the purpose for which he was employed. He is under the further obligation to use his best judgment in exercising his skill and applying his knowledge. The law holds him liable for an injury to his patient resulting from want of the requisite knowledge and skill, or the omission to exercise reasonable care, or the failure to use his best judgment. The rule in relation to learning and skill does not require the surgeon to possess that extraordinary learning and skill which belong only to a few men of rare endowments, but such as is possessed by the average member of the medical profession in good standing. Still, he is bound to keep abreast of the times, and a departure from approved methods in general use, if it injures the patient, will render him liable, however good his intentions may have been. The rule of reasonable care and diligence does not require the exercise of the highest possible degree of care, and, to render a physician and surgeon liable, it is not enough that there has been a less degree of care than some other medical man might have shown, or less than even he himself might have bestowed, but there must be a want of ordinary and reasonable care, leading to a bad result. This includes not only the diagnosis and treatment, but also the giving of proper instructions to his patient in relation to conduct, exercise, and the use of an injured limb. The rule requiring him to use his best judgment does not hold him liable for a mere error of judgment, provided he does what he thinks is best after

[3]155 NY 201 (1898).

careful examination. His engagement with his patient does not guaranty a good result, but he promises by implication to use the skill and learning of the average physician, to exercise reasonable care, and to exert his best judgment in the effort to bring about a good result.[3]

To summarize, the court stated that a doctor must:

1. Possess a reasonable degree of learning and skill that is ordinarily possessed by physicians in the locality where she practices
2. Use reasonable care and diligence in the exercise of his skill
3. Keep up with the latest advances in the profession
4. Use her best judgment in exercising skill and applying knowledge
5. Exercise the skill and learning possessed by the average member of the medical profession in good standing, not necessarily of the best practitioner
6. Keep abreast of the times
7. Use approved methods in general use
8. Give proper instructions to his patient

The court added that a doctor is not liable for a "mere error of judgment, provided he does what he thinks is best after careful examination," and does not "guaranty a good result."

The judge instructs the jury as to the law to be applied to the facts, and the jury decides the facts. Texts published for all states contain recommended jury instructions that represent the current precedent law of the state in which the issue is to be decided. Compare the recommended jury instructions for malpractice in the 2002 edition of the New York text (see chapter 4, section 3) with the case decided in the same state more than 100 years earlier. According to these most recent instructions, if a patient should sustain an injury while undergoing medical care and that injury results from the doctor's lack of knowledge or ability, or from his failure to exercise reasonable care, or to use his best judgment, then he is responsible for the injuries that are the result of his acts.[4]

[4]New York Pattern Jury Intructions— Civil, vol 1A, ed 3. St. Paul, MN: West, 2002.

The only addition to the 1898 standards is that the standards apply whether the service provided is paid for or given gratuitously. In the 1990s, however, the general standards of 1898 underwent two changes in New York and many other states. The old standards require the practitioner to do what other physicians do (the *community practitioner standard*) in the local community in which the defendant practices (the *locality rule*). The *community practitioner standard* has in some places given way to the *reasonably prudent practitioner standard* and, more importantly, the *locality rule* has in some places been weakened or dropped.

Community Standard

6.6   In some states the standard to which a defendant practitioner is held is still determined by what other practitioners in the community would have done under the circumstances. Suppose that a general dentist is sued for malpractice because in performing root canal therapy on an upper central incisor he failed to use rubber dam and, as a result, the patient aspirated the tip of a broken file and suffered an injury. If it can be shown that other dentists in the community did not use a rubber dam to perform the same service, the dentist would be absolved of any malpractice, despite the fact that such a dam would have prevented the injury. One of the many states that apply the community practitioners rule is Minnesota. In a case brought against a dentist for having cut the mucous membrane at the base of the patient's tongue during the preparation of a tooth to which a fixed bridge was to be attached, the court stated, "The question as to whether the defendant was negligent in treating the plaintiff is whether he used that degree of care and skill used by dentists in the same and similar localities."[5] Other states, including New York and California, have continued to apply the community practitioners standard.

[5] 189 Minn 68 (1933).

Reasonable Prudent Practitioner Standard

6.7   Some courts have abandoned the community practitioner standard, claiming that it allows doctors to set a low standard of care, and instead hold a practitioner to what a reasonably prudent practitioner would have done under a certain set of circumstances. A landmark decision was reached in a case in 1974 in which a physician did not perform a test for glaucoma on a patient in her twenties who later contracted the disease. It was shown that ophthalmologists in the community did not perform the test on patients under the age of 40. The court stated the issue thus: "whether the defendants' compliance with the standard of the profession of ophthalmology, which does not require the giving of a routine pressure test to persons under 40 years of age, should insulate them from liability under the facts in this case where the plaintiff has lost a substantial amount of her vision due to the failure of the defendants to timely give the pressure test to the plaintiff." The court continued,

> The incidence of glaucoma in one out of 25,000 persons under the age of 40 may appear quite minimal. However, that one person, the plaintiff in this instance, is entitled to the same protection, as afforded persons over 40, essential for timely detection of the evidence of glaucoma where it can be arrested to avoid the grave and devastating result of this disease. The test is a simple pressure test, relatively inexpensive. There is no judgment factor involved, and there is no doubt that by giving the test the evidence of glaucoma can be detected. The giving of the test is harmless if the physical condition of the eye permits. The testimony indicates that although the condition of the plaintiff's eyes might have at times prevented the defendants from administering the pressure test, there is an absence of evidence in the record that the test could not have been timely given.[6]

[6] 82 Wash2d 514 (1974).

The court referred for general principles to Oliver Wendell Holmes: "What usually is done may be evidence of what ought to be done, but what ought to be done is fixed by a standard of reasonable prudence, whether it usually is complied with or not"[7]; and Learned Hand:

[7] 189 US 468 (1903).

> In most cases reasonable prudence is in fact common prudence; but strictly it is never its measure; a whole calling may have unduly lagged in the adoption of new and available devices. It never may set its own tests, however persuasive be its usages. *Courts must in the end say what is required; there are precautions so imperative that even their universal disregard will not excuse their omission.*[8] (Emphasis added.)

[8] 60 F2d 737 (1932).

The same reasoning may apply to our hypothetical case of the broken file tip: the placement of a rubber dam before treatment is simple. It takes a few minutes, if not seconds; it's painless, and it may prevent a serious injury. The fact that no other general practitioner uses a rubber dam under the same set of circumstances may not shield the errant practitioner from liability.

Locality Rule

6.8   The locality rule determines the geographic area in which the courts will look in setting the standard to which a health practitioner is held. The general and traditional rule states that a practitioner is held to the standards of care *in the community in which the practice is conducted*. Thus a dentist who practices in a rural community is not held to the same standard of care as one who practices in an urban community, notwithstanding they both practice in the same state because, as one New York court put it, of "such variables as geography, availability of medical facilities, consultants, specialists, equipment, personnel and the like."[9] Courts have also noted that educational resources, or transportation to them, are not equally available to all areas. As late as 1978, a court in New York applied the strict locality rule. In deciding a case against a dentist the court stated, "the jury, from the evidence, could properly determine that the testimony of Dr [W.] was sufficient to prove that Dr [M.] did not properly prepare and treat Mrs [T.]'s dental condition in accordance with the standard practice of dentists in the area where defendant practiced dentistry and was, therefore, liable for his malpractice."[10]

The continued application of the strict locality rule led to many problems, not the least of which was the recognition by the courts of the "conspiracy of silence" that often faces a patient looking for a dentist in a small town willing to testify against a neighbor dentist accused of malpractice. As a result, courts began to extend "local community" to "similar community." Moreover, improvements in travel and communication have given practitioners from around the country easy access to new modes of treatment in areas other than their own; some courts therefore further extend the "similar community" to the entire state, others, under certain circumstances, to the whole nation.

In a case decided in the state of Washington in 1967, the court discussed whether to abandon the locality rule as it applied to dentists as well as physicians and hospitals. The facts, as found by the court, were that the patient was injured in an automobile accident and taken to a local hospital. On admission, the physician discovered the patient had a broken jaw. He summoned a dentist on the staff who reduced the fracture under a general anesthetic in the operating room of the hospital. A nurse employee of the hospital administered the anesthetic. The dentist testified that he had no knowledge of the use or administration of a general anesthetic and had left the responsibility and control of the anesthetic to the nurse. No physician was present during the procedure; the admitting physician left the hospital before surgery commenced. The dentist testified that on 11 prior occasions, when he had reduced a fractured jaw under a general anesthetic in the hospital, a medical doctor had been present; that on only one prior occasion a medical doctor had not been present.

[9] 552 NYS2d 978 (1990).

[10] 401 NYS2d 914 (1978).

Shortly after noon, and while in the recovery room, the patient suffered convulsive seizures. The physician could not be located; it was his "afternoon off." No medical doctor was available in the hospital at the time. Later that day another physician was located to treat the patient and found that the patient was suffering "some type of brain injury." The nurse anesthetist testified that she had been a narcotics user from 1958 or 1959 until the month before the surgery, when she had replaced the narcotics with alcohol. Two months after the surgery she was committed to Western State Hospital, where she was a patient for seven months. At the trial, she had a bare minimum of independent recollection and relied almost entirely on the anesthesia chart to describe the surgery. The nurse was hired and paid by the hospital; the hospital billed the patient for her services. Testimony was admitted that the patient suffered severe and permanent brain damage from cerebral anoxia due to inadequate ventilation during the anesthesia or post-operative period.

The trial court rendered judgment in favor of the defendants and the patient appealed. One of the several issues to be decided by the appellate court was the correctness of the instructions of the trial court concerning the standard of care applicable to physicians, dentists, and hospitals. The court's lengthy opinion, which thoroughly reviews the history of the locality rule, the reasons for its abandonment, and other matters relevant to the standard of care, holds important lessons for practicing dentists:

> The standard, I remind you, was set by the learning, skill, care and diligence ordinarily possessed and practiced by others in the same profession in good standing, engaged in like practice, *in the same locality or in similar localities, and under similar circumstances and at the same time.*
>
> The same thought is threaded through each of the standard-of-care instructions as they apply to [physicians], dentists, and hospitals.
>
> We find some conflicting language in Washington cases concerning the scope or area qualifications of the standard of care applicable to medical doctors. Cases in the first group refer to the standard "in the same community" or "in the locality where he practices." Cases in the second group refer to the standard of care "in the same or similar communities."
>
> Each line of decisions appears to have overlooked the other; although, as early as 1913 this court said in a malpractice case: The instruction is faulty in that it makes the standard of treatment that of the locality alone in which the appellant was practicing; whereas, the true standard is that of all similar localities [citing a 1913 case].
>
> The original reason for the "locality rule" is apparent. When there was little intercommunity travel, courts required experts who testified to the standard of care that should have been used to have a personal knowledge of the practice of physicians in that particular community where the patient was treated. It was the accepted theory that a doctor in a small community did not have the same opportunities and resources as did a doctor practicing in a large city to keep abreast of advances in his profession; hence, he should not be held to the same standard of care and skill as that employed by doctors in other communities or in larger cities. Parenthetically, we note that the law of this jurisdiction has never recognized a difference in the professional competency of a lawyer in a small community from that of the professional competency required of a lawyer in a large city. (Emphasis added.)

The court went on:

> The "locality rule" had two practical difficulties: first, the scarcity of professional men in the community who were qualified or willing to testify about the local standard of care; and second, the possibility of a small group, who, by their laxness or carelessness, could establish a local standard of care that was below that which the law requires. The fact that several careless practitioners might settle in the same place cannot affect the standard of diligence and skill which local patients have a right to expect. Negligence cannot be excused on the ground that others in the same locality practice the same kind of negligence. No degree of antiquity can give sanction to usage bad in itself.
>
> Broadening the rule to include "similar localities" or "similar communities" alleviated, to a certain extent, the first practical difficulty of the "locality rule"—additional witnesses might be available....
>
> Now there is no lack of opportunity for a physician or surgeon to keep abreast of the advances made in his profession and to be familiar with the latest methods and practices adopted. The comprehensive coverage of the *Journal of the American Medical Association*, the availability of numerous other journals, the ubiquitous "detail men" of the drug companies, closed circuit television presentations of medical subjects, special radio networks for physicians, tape recorded digests of medical literature, and hundreds of widely available postgraduate courses all serve to keep physicians informed and increasingly to establish nationwide standards. Medicine realizes this, so it is inevitable that the law will do likewise. Louisell and Williams, *The Parenchyma of Law* (Professional Medical Publication, Rochester, N.Y.1960) p. 183.
>
> We have found no better statement of existing conditions. The "locality rule" has no present-day vitality except that it may be considered as one of the elements to determine the degree of care and skill which is to be expected of the average practitioner of the class to which he belongs. The degree of care which must be observed is, of course, that of an average, competent practitioner acting in the same or similar circumstances. In other words, local practice within geographic proximity is one, but not the only factor to be considered. No longer is it proper to limit the definition of the standard of care which a medical doctor or dentist must meet solely to the practice or custom of a particular locality, a similar locality, or a geographic area.
>
> The "locality rule" has never been suggested in any English case. (Nathan, Medical Negligence, Butterworth & Co, Led 1957, p 21). In England, the same standard is applicable throughout the country. The extent of our country is such, however, that we hesitate to fix a definite geographic limit upon the standard of care—be it statewide or expanded to the Pacific Northwest, as suggested by plaintiff's requested instruction.[11]

[11]431 P2d 973 (1967).

New York, unlike Washington, chose to extend the same standard of care state-wide. In 1990 an appeal court in New York was to decide a case in which a patient brought an action against five general practitioners and an endodontist who was not board certified, all of whom practiced in an upstate county in New York. The patient alleged that the dentists failed properly to diagnose and treat her trigeminal neuralgia: tic douloureux. The judge in the trial court refused to permit the plaintiffs' expert, a board certified oral and maxillofacial surgeon whose practice was limited to the New York City area, to testify concerning the standard of care of the defendants. Because the plaintiffs offered no other medical support for their allegations, the trial judge dismissed the complaint at the close of the plaintiffs' proof. The trial court applied the strict locality rule, stating that a dentist practicing in New York City could not be familiar with the standards of dentists practicing in a smaller community and that an oral and maxillofacial surgeon could not be familiar with the standards to be applied to general dentists, or to one limiting practice to another specialty. The plaintiff appealed the decision of the trial court.

The appellate court, in its decision, had much to say about the locality rule and the testimony of a specialist when the defendant is a generalist.

> The locality rule, premised as it is on such variables as geography, availability of medical facilities, consultants, specialists, equipment, personnel and the like, does not, however, prohibit him [the oral and maxillofacial surgeon] from testifying to what we perceive plaintiffs proposed to show; namely, that there is a minimum standard of care that dentists licensed to practice in this State are expected to exercise in diagnosing and treating tic douloureux, that this standard is uniform throughout the State, and presumably that the treatment furnished in this instance fell below this threshold. Whatever may actually be the standard of care practiced by general dentists in any particular locality in this State, if it is less demanding than the minimum level of skill and expertise which general dental practitioners are required to achieve to attain and maintain licensure in the State, it is unacceptable. If that were not true, spectacular ineptitude could be condoned under the guise of the locality rule. Simply put, certain rudimentary criteria must be met before one can practice dentistry in New York.
>
> Nor are we persuaded that [the witness] is foreclosed from testifying because he is a specialist. All that need be demonstrated is that he has knowledge of the standard of care about which he is testifying. That he has such knowledge is readily apparent from his credentials. He graduated from New York University College of Dentistry, one of four accredited dental schools in this State, and obtained a license to practice all phases of general dentistry in New York. He continued his dental education and became a specialist certified by the American Board of Oral and Maxillofacial Surgeons. For one of his three years of specialized training, he practiced general dentistry in Boston, Massachusetts, during evenings and weekends.
>
> [He] is a member of a multitude of dental associations including the Queens County Dental Association, the Dental Society of the State of New York, the American Dental Association, the New York State Society of Oral and Maxillofacial Surgeons, and the American Association of Oral and Maxillofacial Surgeons. As representative for the New York State Society of Oral and Maxillofacial Surgeons, [he] serves on the New York State Dental Advisory Committee. In this capacity he helps define policies bearing on all aspects of the practice of dentistry as it relates to Federally funded dental care, such as Medicaid, within the State. He also co-chairs the New York State Society of Oral and Maxillofacial Surgeon's Committee on health plans and legislation. Additionally, he helped found the American College of Oral and Maxillofacial Surgery. Finally, [he] serves as the senior attending oral surgeon for Astoria General Hospital and for five hospitals in New York City comprising the Catholic Medical Center.
>
> Admittedly, [he] currently limits his practice to his specialty. His expertise, however, does not imply that he is unacquainted with the minimal standards of general dentistry. In fact, [he] routinely reviews the work of general practitioners, for a substantial number of patients who have complications arising from general dentistry are referred to him. Moreover, in this State all dentists must first be licensed as generalists before practicing

any form of specialized dentistry. To obtain this license, a dentist must graduate from an accredited dental school (the accreditation standards for all four dental schools in New York are the same), and pass a written and a practical examination covering all phases of general dentistry. In sum, Supreme Court [the trial court] was mistaken when it refused to afford [Oral and Maxillofacial Surgeon] the opportunity to testify, for plaintiffs satisfactorily established that the doctor was skilled in the field of dentistry and familiar with the accepted minimum standards of dental care for a general practitioner in New York.

Criticism of an expert's experience goes not to the admissibility of his testimony, but simply affects the weight the fact finder [jury or judge] ascribes to that testimony.[12]

[12]552 NYS2d 978 (1990).

With this decision New York abandoned the strict locality rule for a state-wide standard of care. In so doing the court permitted a specialist to testify as to the standard of care to be followed by a generalist.

A case previously decided in Massachusetts came to the same conclusion. A patient brought an action against a pedodontist who had placed for her an orthodontic appliance. The patient claimed that "as a result of the defendant's malpractice she developed root resorption in several of her teeth, necessitating years of expensive corrective procedures and the likely loss of the affected teeth." During the trial, the plaintiff called an orthodontist to testify as an expert. The trial judge accepted him as such. However, the judge precluded him from testifying to the appropriate standard of care for the plaintiff's course of treatment because he was not a pedodontist. Without expert testimony on this issue in evidence, the judge felt compelled to order a directed verdict for the defendant. The plaintiff-patient appealed. The appellate court, in remanding the case for retrial, stated:

A medical expert need not be a specialist in the area concerned nor be practicing in the same field as the defendant. "It is well established that the professional specialty of a medical practitioner offered as a witness need not be precisely and narrowly related to the medical issues of the case. Thus, it has been held that a judge, in his discretion, properly admitted the opinions of a general practitioner in a case which related to specialized medical issues."

The court continued:

The crucial issue is whether the witness has sufficient "education, training, experience and familiarity" with the subject matter of the testimony. [The] expert['s] testimony was particularly appropriate here, since his expertise was in the very field at issue. The defendant's allegedly negligent treatment was orthodontic in nature. In such circumstances, it was error to exclude [his] opinion regarding the appropriate standard of care on the ground that he has a different specialty from that of the defendant. His training and experience as an orthodontist, rather than a pedodontist, goes to the weight accorded his testimony but not to its admissibility.[13]

[13]401 Mass 65 (1987).

What the court said was that for a specialist to testify as to the standard of care to be exercised by a generalist, or a specialist in another specialty field, he must be familiar with the standards of care related to the service at issue. Neither court ruled that generalists should be held to the same standard of care as specialists.

National Standard of Care: Is There One?

6.9   New York, after its rulings about using the standard of care in a similar community and, in one case, in the state, made an even bolder move in deciding a case in 1988. The facts were that a board certified radiologist, practicing in a small village in upstate New York, was alleged to have been guilty of malpractice during the performance of a sigmoidoscopy and a barium enema, as a result of the which the patient died. One of the experts for the plaintiff (who was the patient's husband and executor) was a board certified radiologist practicing in California. He testified that the defendant departed from acceptable standards. The defendants objected to this testimony on the ground that the radiologist practicing in California was incompetent to express such an opinion because, admittedly, he was unfamiliar with the general accepted medical practice in the community where this action arose or with the practice in upstate New York as it existed in 1981, the date of the alleged malpractice. The objections were overruled by the trial judge, and the defendant contended this violated a long-standing locality rule articulated by the New York Court of Appeals stating that the doctor is required to possess "that degree of learning and skill . . . ordinarily possessed by physicians and surgeons in the locality where he practices."

The appellate division, in deciding against the defendant's contention, stated:

> We cannot accept defendants' strict application of the "locality rule" in view of leading current authority. Although the rule is still extant, the standards upon which it is based are no longer the same as articulated in [P.] v. [H.] (supra). In [T.] v. Community Hosp. at Glen Cove (supra), the Court of Appeals in discussing the locality rule observed that "conform[ing] to accepted community standards of practice usually insulates [the doctors] from tort liability."[14]

[14]528 NYS2d 925 (1988).

However, the court then applied the locality rule as a minimum standard, inserting the further requirement that doctors use their "best judgment and whatever superior knowledge, skill, and intelligence [they have]." Thus, a specialist may be held liable where a general practitioner may not. The resulting two-tiered standard preserves the benefits of the locality rule while compelling doctors to use available methods that may exceed local standards. The court went on to state,

> Accordingly, [the radiologist from California's] testimony was properly admitted into evidence and, although the standards he would impose upon the treatment and care rendered by [the defendants] were rebutted by the testimony of defendants' local radiologist as not representative of the local norms, his testimony described the "superior knowledge, skill and intelligence" that [the defendant] should possess as a board-certified specialist under the rule established in [the 1898 case]. Since these standards are national standards and [defendant's] practice included the practice of radiology in Georgia, New York City, and Rochester, as well as Tioga County, it was for the jury to conclude whether he knew of these standards and should have complied with them.

It is well to note two sentences of the decision: "a specialist may be held liable where a general practitioner may not," and there results a "two-tiered" standard; one for generalists and a higher one for board certified specialists." The holding applied to one of the four divisions of the state. The others have not as yet ruled on the issue, but it is probable that the New York Court of Appeals, the highest court in the state, will provide a similar decision, which will then apply to the entire state.

In a decision reached by the South Dakota Supreme Court, in the same year as the cases in New York, the court adopted a national standard of care for board certified medical specialists. The court noted that the defendant physician was certified by the American Board of Surgery and was a Fellow of the American College of Surgery. The expert for the plaintiff, though not familiar with local standards, testified as to those of the specialty board, and went on to state that the defendant did not meet those standards in the care of the patient. The trial court allowed the testimony, and instructed the jury on a national standard. The jury found for the plaintiff. The defendant appealed. The Supreme Court affirmed the decision of the trial court, stating that "a medical specialist who holds himself out as such should be measured against the national standards of his profession."[15] In a footnote the court cited many state decisions in which a national standard for specialists was adopted. Among the states are Alabama, Alaska, Arizona, Colorado, Connecticut, Georgia, Iowa, Kansas, Louisiana, Maine, Massachusetts, Michigan, Minnesota, Missouri, Nevada, New Jersey, New Mexico, Ohio, Pennsylvania, South Carolina, and Wisconsin. The trend toward a national standard of care is evident.

[15]418 NW2d 299 (S.D. 1988).

Inference Testimony

6.10

When the plaintiff's expert takes the stand and is questioned by the plaintiff's attorney, the expert is expected to describe the defendant's act as a "deviation or departure from the requisite standard of care." If these words aren't spoken, can they be inferred? A court in New York was faced with deciding if the "inference of departure" from the standard would satisfy the requirement. The case was of additional interest because the defendant was called as an expert witness against himself. The trial court granted the defendant's motion for judgment as a matter of law based upon the fact that there was no testimony that the defendant departed from the requisite standard of care. The appellate court overturned this decision.

The facts were as follows. The plaintiff claimed that the defendant, an oral surgeon, "improperly implanted two of the three titanium fixtures into the inferior alveolar nerve canal of the right mandibular bone, one of which extended into the alveolar nerve, and one of which obliterated the alveolar nerve." Two expert witnesses testified for the plaintiff that "a primary concern in planning a case for dental implants was that care should be taken to avoid intrusion of the titanium fixtures into the inferior alveolar nerve canal of the mandibular bone . . . in order to prevent damage to the nerves therein." However, "none of the plaintiffs' experts . . . stated in specific words or phrases that the defendant-oral surgeon's act . . . constituted a departure from the requisite standard of oral surgery." The plaintiff also called the defendant to testify; he stated that "it is vital to the success of dental implant surgery that an oral surgeon avoid going below the bone ridge and intruding into the inferior alveolar canal of the mandibular bone or impinging on the inferior alveolar nerve." He testified also that he had warned the plaintiff of the risk of such intrusion.

The court ruled:

> The testimony of these experts that it was imperative to avoid violation by the titanium implants of the inferior alveolar canal should be accorded great probative force in determining whether the defendant-oral surgeon's conduct was a departure from the requisite standard of oral surgery. A determination that the defendant-oral surgeon's conduct was a departure from the requisite standard of oral surgery is not contrary to reason, common conclusion, or natural and physical cause. So long as the inference of departure from the requisite standard of care is fairly supported by the evidence and consistent with a party's argument or theory of the case, it may be drawn. . . .
>
> Posited against the background of plaintiffs' experts' testimony, it is pivotal to our determination that during the plaintiffs' case-in-chief the defendant-oral surgeon, testifying as an expert, admitted that he was to avoid placing a titanium fixture into the inferior alveolar nerve canal of the mandibular bone.
>
> It is well settled that a plaintiff in a medical/dental malpractice action may call as a witness the [physician], dentist, or other health-care provider against whom the action is brought in order to elicit testimony both as to fact and opinion.
>
> Since all the experts agreed that intrusion into the inferior alveolar canal of the mandibular bone must be avoided, the occurrence of that act compels the inference that the intrusion was a departure from the requisite standard of dental practice. . . .
>
> By enacting CPLR 4515 in 1962, the New York State Legislature abolished the common-law rule requiring that a hypothetical question be posed to an expert in order to elicit an expert opinion. The statute permitted an expert witness to state what he or she knows in natural or conventional language and thought. . . . The Legislature, thus, trumpeted its intention to relax the rigidity of the common law. By analogy, in considering the substance of the legislative commentaries, the courts have made clear their intention to focus on the probative force of opinion evidence, rather than a particular combination of words and phrases used to express the opinion. This guards against the defeat of expert opinion "by semantics if it is reasonably apparent that the [witness] intends to signify a probability supported by some rational basis" [The court quoted several prior cases.]
>
> A court's duty, therefore, is not to reject opinion evidence because non-lawyer witnesses answer questions that are not hypothetical or fail to use the words and phrases preferred by lawyers and judges, but rather to determine whether the whole record exhibits substantial evidence that there was a departure from the requisite standard of care. . . .
>
> In the circumstances of this case, there was no need for experts to state a special or particular combination of words and phrases that the conduct of the defendant-oral surgeon constituted a deviation or departure from the requisite standard of care. . . . Such a combination of particular words is ineluctably unnecessary in view of the defendant-oral surgeon's express admission that he was not to permit titanium fixtures to intrude into the inferior alveolar canal of the mandibular bone. . . .
>
> Inasmuch as the plaintiffs' experts opined that the conduct of the defendant-oral surgeon was to be avoided and was a proximate cause of the plaintiff's injuries, together with the defendant-oral surgeon's judicial admis-

sion that he was not supposed to intrude into the inferior alveolar canal of the mandibular bone, an inference could be drawn that this complained-of conduct was a deviation or departure from the requisite standard of care to be followed with respect to dental implantations. Under these circumstances, the weight and probative effect of the defendant-oral surgeon's judicial admission should have been determined by the jury, not the court. Since the question of the defendant–oral surgeon's liability was not submitted to the jury, the matter must be remitted for a new trial.[16]

[16] 725 NYS2d 350 (2001).

The court noted that the matter was one of first impression—one that had not been decided before. The case appears to have reversed a decision 8 years earlier in which the same defendant was alleged to have been guilty of malpractice and failure to obtain the informed consent of the patient.[17]

[17] 580 NYS2d 458 (1992).

Summary

6.11 The standard of care will depend solely upon who the trial judge will permit to qualify as an expert, and the trial judge is given wide discretion by the appellate courts. The result is that it is difficult to predict with any degree of certainty, despite appellate court rulings, who is qualified to appear as an expert.

The trend in the courts is to move away from the traditional locality rule, in which practitioners were held to the standard of care present in the community in which the patient received treatment. Courts generally became disenchanted with the rule for several reasons. The "conspiracy of silence" engaged in by community practitioners placed plaintiffs at an insurmountable disadvantage, and courts therefore recognized a "similar community" standard. Courts have adopted a national standard of care for board certified specialists, but generalists in both medicine and dentistry are still commonly held to a "similar community" standard, though in some states this has been extended to a state-wide standard.

The general rule adopted by all states is that if an expert is familiar with the standards of care of the defendant, her testimony will be admitted by the trial judge, regardless of whether she is a specialist testifying against a generalist or a generalist testifying against a specialist. In addition, it appears from several court decisions that because all dentists must pass a state's general dental licensing examination and the educational program of all dental schools is in general dentistry, a specialist should be familiar with the standard of care of generalists and therefore may testify about it. Some courts have ruled that if the service provided by a generalist falls into the scope of practice of a specialist, the generalist will be held to the standard of care of the specialist.

Given all of the above, the prudent dentist will limit his scope of practice to the level of his ability, training, and experience. If he undertakes to provide a service commonly provided by a specialist, he should meet the standards set by specialists; most likely his care will be judged by specialists. The same may be true in a situation in which a patient refuses care by a specialist, and the dentist undertakes to provide the care he recommended the specialist provide: He will be held to the standard of care of the specialist who will be permitted to testify as an expert.

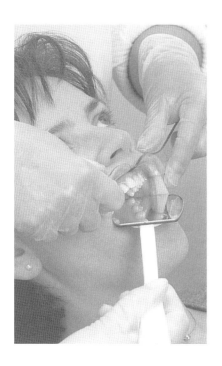

CHAPTER SEVEN

Vicarious Liability
and *Respondeat Superior*

Definitions and Applications

7.1 *Vicarious liability* is a theory under which courts will hold an innocent party liable for someone else's negligence. The innocent party stands in the shoes of a guilty party who committed an act that injured a third party. *Respondeat superior* literally means "let the master answer." It is the form of vicarious liability that applies to all master-servant relationships, including an employer's to an employee. All jurisdictions recognize the legal concepts of vicarious liability and *respondeat superior*.

Vicarious liability is based upon the fact that the innocent party who is held responsible for another's act:

1. Derives a benefit from the acts of another
2. Is in control of the other's activities
3. Selected the other to act

Thus, the conditions needed for the transfer of liability are benefit, control, and selection.

The historical basis for the transfer of liability is found in English common law (see chapter 1), which holds that:

1. A party injured through the negligence of another and innocent of the events that caused the injury should be compensated.

2. The party that committed the negligent act should be made to compensate the injured party.

In modern society, without stating it, the courts look for compensation from the person or entity with the "deepest pockets," in most situations an employer. It may appear that the guilty party is relieved by vicarious liability of the common law responsibility for compensation; however, an employer in such cases may seek indemnification from a guilty employee. In health professional practice this rarely happens—hospitals whose insurance carriers have paid damages to a patient injured through the negligence of a nurse rarely seek indemnification from the nurse—but the fact that it may happen in theory satisfies the common law.

Applications to Dental Practice

7.2   In applying the principles of vicarious liability and *respondeat superior* to a case, the courts look for the following:

1. *Who benefited?* The acts of an employee in a dentist's office are performed for the benefit of the employer-dentist; therefore, the employer should bear any losses resulting from such acts. In the typical dental practice, the dentist-owner may be liable for the negligent acts of assistants, hygienists, receptionists, office managers, laboratory technicians, other employee dentists, dentist partners, etc.
2. *Was there control?* The employer-dentist has the right and duty to control and supervise the employee, to dictate what is to be done and how.
3. *Who made the selection?* The employer-dentist selected (hired) the employee and placed the employee in a position in which a negligent act might be committed. The dental patient did not hire or select the employee to provide the specific service and had no control over how the employee's service was to be provided.

The defining words, again, are *benefit, control,* and *selection.* Find those, and you find liability. Dentists should be aware that the more complex the arrangements of practice, the more exposure there is to legal entanglements.

Employees

7.2.1   The relationship between a dentist and his employee is the simplest involving vicarious liability and *respondeat superior.* Take, for example, a dental assistant who, while assisting a dentist in retracting the tongue during the preparation of a tooth to receive a crown, is distracted. He releases the tongue and it moves into the area in which the high speed drill is in contact with the tooth. The tongue is lacerated. When the patient reacts to the pain, he moves, and as a result the patient's lip also is lacerated and requires suturing. The lip becomes permanently scarred. The assistant was negligent, but by application of the theories of *respondeat superior* and vicarious liability, the dentist is sued and must pay the award. The patient may sue the assistant; but the dentist will have the "deepest pockets." The dentist, or the dentist's insurer, may then bring an action against the assistant for the indemnification of losses, and although this almost never happens, the fact that it is possible satisfies the common law principle that the one who commits the act causing the injury must pay the injured party.

An injured patient may sometimes choose to sue both an employee and a dentist, because:

1. The employee may be treated as a hostile witness on the stand—an advantage to the plaintiff's attorney during the examination of the employee.
2. The employee is certain to show up for the trial.
3. No lawyer is certain what a jury might find or how a judge might rule.

This is a matter of trial tactics.

Let us suppose that a dentist instructs his hygienist never to provide a specific service to any of his patients, although the service in question is permitted by law. The hygienist, without knowledge of the dentist, does provide the service to a patient, and as a result the patient suffers an injury due to the hygienist's negligence. The dentist will not be able to defend himself from liability with the claim that the hygienist defied his instructions. *Respondeat superior* still applies: The dentist selected the hygienist, is in control of what he does, placed him in a position where it was possible for him to commit an act of negligence, and derived a benefit in income from the services he provides. The principles have been met.

Suppose instead that the dentist instructs the hygienist never to perform a service not permitted under the state's law listing the permitted duties of hygienists. The hygienist admits knowing the law regulating the practice of dental hygiene in the state. In addition, the dentist provides him with a copy of the law and insists that he become familiar with all its provisions. Some time following these events, the hygienist, without the knowledge of the dentist, injures a patient through negligence during the commission of an unlawful act. The dentist's defense appears to be stronger than in the situation described above in that the act was unlawful, the hygienist knew it, and despite all that, he did it. Worst of all, he did it negligently. However, the result would be the same as to who compensates the patient: the dentist-employer. The rules of *respondeat superior* still apply.

If the employee of a dentist is a dentist, there may be some modifications in the transfer of liability. It may be that, by either written or oral agreement, under certain circumstances the employee-dentist may be given the right to exercise independent judgment, or in the contract of employment there might exist a "hold harmless clause" in which the employer is held harmless for any negligence committed by the employee. But in the absence of such agreements, the basic principles remain the same; and even in the face of such agreements, the plaintiff's attorney is likely to name both dentists as defendants in the suit and to let the judge or jury decide who must pay damages to the patient.

If you, as a dentist, do not like the transfer of liability to you as an innocent party, think of the following: Suppose your automobile, with you in it, is struck by a Macy's truck that went through a red light while on its way to deliver furniture. Who would you sue? Macy's, of course, for all the reasons related to vicarious liability and *respondeat superior*, not forgetting the "deep pockets."

Associates

7.2.2   Associations in practice may take many forms, of which some decrease, while others increase, legal risks. One form that increases legal risk is the employer-employee relationship discussed above. Another is the partnership, because all partners, including the innocent ones, are individually liable for the negligent acts of each. Each partner may be jointly (as a group) and severally (individually) liable. The choice of whom to sue is the plaintiff's, often on the advice of an attorney. It is not unusual for all partners, the guilty and innocent, to be joined in the suit. The principle of vicarious liability is supported by the legal theory that all partners are united in interest; each benefits from the acts of the others. Control is somewhat limited, but selection was voluntary. Even where there is not a partnership agreement between dentists, in several cases courts have stated that if the patient considers the practice to be a partnership, and it looks like a partnership, the courts will consider it to be a partnership and apply the principle of vicarious liability. Contributing to the appearance of a partnership are such circumstances as a shared waiting room, other jointly used rooms in the office, and shared receptionists, hygienists, assistants, etc. To avoid serious complications, it is best for all dentists in such an arrangement to be covered by the same professional liability insurance company.

A third form of associateship practice, involving less legal risk, is the professional corporation, known in some states as a *professional corporation*, or PC, in others as a *professional association*, or PA. The letters follow the names and degrees of the practitioners on stationery, business cards, etc. In this arrangement, dentists are shareholders in a corporation, and innocent shareholders are not liable for the negligent acts of other shareholders. There is no transfer of liability; only the guilty practitioner and the corporation are liable. However, it is best for all dentist-shareholders and the corporation to be insured by the same professional liability insurance company (see chapter 19). A 1981 case was decided in New York on this issue:

> The real question in this case is whether plaintiffs have a viable claim that [S.] is vicariously liable for the acts of [Pe.] and [Pa.]. Plaintiffs' complaint alleged a partnership and in their answer [Pe.], [Pa.], and [S.] admitted that they were partners. It subsequently developed that [Pe.], [Pa.], and [S.] were actually coshareholders, officers, and employees of a professional service corporation (a PC). In their brief on appeal, plaintiffs concede that that was the true form of the professional entity employed by those defendants, and that they were not partners. That concession thereby vitiated the effect of the improvident admission of a partnership in the joint answer of [Pe.], [Pa.], and [S.]. We hold, as explained in [case cited] that while partners are, by statute, vicariously liable for the tortious acts and omissions of their copartners committed within the scope of the partnership business (Partnership Law, §§ 24, 26), neither the common law nor section 1505 of the Business Corporation Law imposes vicarious liability upon a shareholder, officer, or employee of a professional service corporation for the tortious acts of his coshareholders, officers, or employees.[1]

[1]443 NYS2d 403 (1981).

Another form of associateship practice that reduces legal risk has recently emerged: the *limited liability company*, or LLC. This is fast replacing the corporation in business and industry. Where signs and announcements once read "ABC Inc," many now read "ABC, LLC." Newly enacted laws in all states permit some form of the new legal entity. Professionals such as attorneys, physicians, dentists, and others are permitted to form professional LLCs known as LLPs or PLLs. The advantages of LLCs or LLPs over the corporation are that, while they afford the same liability protection as the corporation, they are simpler and cheaper to form and maintain. Currently, two states permit a single practitioner to form a PLL: New York and Texas. Others are sure to follow.

The *independent contractor* (IC) also has legal advantages. The Internal Revenue Service, the unemployment agency of the state, and worker's compensation boards have a financial interest in whether the relationship between the parties is one of employer-employee or principal and independent contractor. If the relationship is one of employer-employee, the employer must withhold tax and make contributions to the Social Security Administration, the Workers Compensation Fund, and the Unemployment Fund—a lot of work and expense for the owner of the practice. If the relationship is one of independent contractors, no such payments must be made, and the contractors collect the full amount of their earnings, with no deductions. A case in which such issues were considered was decided in New York:

> During the period between January 1983 and December 1985, the corporation provided the premises, all centralized services, and a full support staff, which it shared with three different dentists to whom it leased space. The lessee dentists received 35% of the gross billings less laboratory fees and were paid a weekly draw based on the prior 6-month billing period. Actual earnings were adjusted every 6 months.
>
> The corporation retained 65% of each dentist's gross billings to cover centralized services and overhead such as rent, utilities, maintenance, and a complete support staff composed of a hygienist, receptionist, office manager, and a sterilization person. While the corporation provided most of the tools and equipment, the other dentists paid for any specialized equipment and for their own chairside assistants. The corporation's receptionist made all appointments and patients were assigned to the corporation and the other dentists on an alternating basis. All patients were charged uniform fees, which the corporation established after consultation with the other dentists. All patient billing and collection was done centrally by the corporation's office manager.
>
> Based on these facts, the Unemployment Insurance Appeal Board reversed the decision of an Administrative Law Judge and sustained the initial determination assessing the corporation $1,297.28 as additional contributions due for the period January 1, 1983 through December 31, 1985 based on remuneration paid to dentists employed by the corporation. The Board rejected the corporation's contention that the dentists it engaged were independent contractors.
>
> The determinative issue of whether one is an employee rather than an independent contractor is a mixed question of fact and law for the Board to resolve. Many factors are considered, but the primary one is the degree of control exercised by the employer. Here, the corporation provided the premises, all centralized services, and a full support staff. This evidence is more than adequate to support the Board's determination of an employer-employee relationship.[2]

[2]551 NYS2d 409 (1990).

The courts examine the arrangement between the parties before determining the financial liability of the principal. Courts consider how independent the independent contractor is from control by the principal, whose the patients are, who provides the supplies and equipment, who supplies the auxiliary help: assistants, secretaries, receptionists, etc, who sets the hours. There are 20 such questions upon which the Internal Revenue Service will judge whether the dentist is an employee or an independent contractor. Courts may, and often do, use the same questions in deciding whether to treat the IC as an employee and hold the employer-dentist financially liable to the various government agencies.

Given the fact the an IC is rare in multidental associateships, the question of vicarious liability and *respondeat superior* is usually moot. It does not matter that both the owner of the practice and the supposed IC refer to their association as principal-IC. If the relationship does not meet the tests, the owner will be held liable for the negligent acts of the supposed IC. One case that may meet the tests is that of an oral and maxillofacial surgeon who provides services in several different dental offices. If the surgeon commits the negligent act, an experienced attorney will sue the owner of the practice and the IC jointly, and let the judge and jury decide who is to pay the damages. A "hold-harmless" clause in the agreement between the owner and the IC will avert trouble, as will the owner's and the IC's holding insurance from the same company (see chapter 19).

Referrals and Substitute Practitioners

7.2.3

It is rare in today's dental practice for a dentist to provide all professional services available to patients. The typical dentist makes many referrals to specialists in order to provide patients with the latest advances in the profession and the best standard of care. In addition, it is unusual for a dentist to be always available to patients; during periods of absence, a dentist is required to provide substitute service for patients requiring care. Is the referring or absent dentist liable for the negligent acts of the specialist or substitute? The answer in the case of the referral is *no,* except under any of the following circumstances:

1. If the referring dentist knew, or should have known, that the specialist or substitute had a history of impairment or incompetence
2. If the referring dentist benefited in any material way from the referral
3. If the referring dentist participated in any way in the treatment provided by the specialist or substitute, eg, if the referring dentist assisted during the procedure or took an active role in directing what should be done

The first situation is simple to understand: A referral to a specialist or a substitute practitioner who is known to have a problem with alcohol or drugs, has been found culpable in several malpractice suits, or has been investigated and found guilty by the licensing agency places the referring dentist at risk.

The second situation, however, is more complicated. The form of the benefit the referring dentist receives may decide that dentist's liability, either jointly or severally. Clearly, a cash payment from the specialist or substitute to the referring dentist establishes liability. This form of fee-splitting is prohibited by black letter law (BLL) in many states. The New York State Education Law, Section 6509a, defines as professional misconduct:

> That any person subject to the above enumerated articles [includes dentistry], has directly or indirectly requested, received, or participated in the division, transference, assignment, rebate, splitting, or refunding of a fee for, or has directly requested, received, or profited by means of a credit or other valuable consideration as a commission, discount, or gratuity in connection with the furnishing of professional care, or service, including X-ray examination and treatment.

However, it is customary for specialists to send a Christmas or holiday gift to referring dentists. The size of the gift may affect liability. The most common form of a "gift" that opens the door to liability is a much-lower-than-average office rent charged a referring dentist by a specialist who owns the building. If all referrals from the dentist-tenant are made to the specialist landlord, the door to liability is wide open.

As to the liability of an absent dentist for the malpractice of a dentist substituting for him, a court had the following to say:

> Although the movement of the law has been in the direction of broadening the base of derived liability to others from the professional acts of physicians, this has been largely achieved by looking differently than we formerly did at the highly individualized independence of judgment of a physician in the area of professional diagnosis and treatment.
>
> But this limitation of liability has been broken through in situations of control to which the physician has submitted himself. Although the rule of liability is broadening out in this area, we think it ought not be extended to rest on a situation where there is neither a legal nor an actual control of the treating physician by the other physician and the relationship between them upon which responsibility is sought to be imputed turns upon a shared office and an agreement to service each other's patients for a shared fee.
>
> This is something less than, and quite different from, a relationship of master and servant or agency upon which vicarious liability has thus far rested. *The implications of such an enlarged liability would tend to discourage a physician [dentist] from arranging to have another care for his patients on his illness or absence and thus curtail the availability of medical service.*
>
> On the whole this extension of liability should not be made on the record now before us. If splitting of fees in the absence of active participation in the service or of a written partnership agreement was professionally irregular (Education Law, § 6514) [sig § 6509-a] that should be dealt with rather by appropriate disciplinary action than by an extension of vicarious liability.[3] (Emphasis added.)

[3]243 NYS2d 940 (1963).

Keep in mind, however, that in all situations of associated dentists there is the possibility of joint and several liability. What may determine who is sued is the extent of the damages anticipated by the patient's attorney. If the attorney feels that the award may exceed the level of insurance of one of the possible defendants, she is likely to include both in the suit, or if she is not certain who the court will hold responsible, she will sue both and let the court decide who must pay.

Summary

7.3   It is clear that liability for an act of negligence is not always limited to the one committing the act. Others may place an innocent dentist at risk of losing a suit in malpractice. The legal doctrine of vicarious liability transfers liability to an innocent party. Transfer of liability may take place in an employer-employee situation (*respondeat superior*), in partnership arrangements, in referrals, and in the provision of substitute practitioners. To minimize the risk, dentists should select with care those who might expose them to vicarious liability. As an alternative to partnership practice, prudent practitioners should consider forming a professional corporation, or better still, a professional limited liability company (see chapter 17).

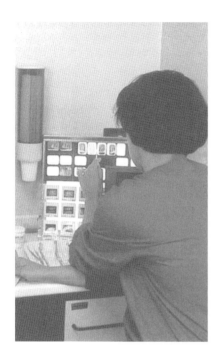

CHAPTER EIGHT

Does the Dentist Have to Treat?

Freedom to Refuse to Treat

8.1   The landmark case on whether a doctor must treat everyone who demands to be treated was decided as early as 1901. The facts were as follows:

> At and for years before decedent's death appellee was a practicing physician at Mace, in Montgomery county, duly licensed under the laws of the state. He held himself out to the public as a general practitioner of medicine. He had been decedent's family physician. Decedent became dangerously ill, and sent for appellee. The messenger informed appellee of decedent's violent sickness, tendered him his fee for his services, and stated to him that no other physician was procurable in time, and that decedent relied on him for attention. No other physician was procurable in time to be of any use, and decedent did rely on appellee for medical assistance. Without any reason whatever, appellee refused to render aid to decedent. No other patients were requiring appellee's immediate service, and he could have gone to the relief of decedent if he had been willing to do so. Death ensued, without decedent's fault, and wholly from appellee's wrongful act.

In deciding, the court stated,

> The [licensing] act is a preventive, not a compulsive, measure. In obtaining the state's license (permission) to practice medicine, the state does not require, and the licensee does not engage, that he will practice at all or on other terms than he may choose to accept. Counsel's analogies, drawn from the obligations to the public on the part of innkeepers, common carriers, and the like, are beside the mark.

[1] 59 NE 1058 (1901).

Judgment was in favor of the physician.[1]

From this case a lasting precedent, with some future modifications, was established that a health practitioner was free, even in emergency situations, to refuse to treat anyone except a patient of record. With the spread of civil rights legislation many states and smaller jurisdictions passed legislation that declared discrimination on the basis of color, creed, religion, national origin, or disabilities a violation of the law. The targets of these proscriptions were "places of public accommodations," eg, public transportation, restaurants that invited the public, hotels, public hospitals, businesses that invited the public, etc. Private institutions were not the targets of the antidiscrimination laws; they were not places of "public accommodation" and therefore were permitted to discriminate.

In 1951, in Ohio, an African American presented herself to a dentist's private office and asked to have a tooth extracted. The dentist refused to treat her because of her race. The woman brought an action against the dentist alleging he violated the antidiscrimination law of the state.

The court began by quoting the applicable statute:

> "Whoever, being the proprietor or his employee, keeper or manager of an inn, restaurant, eating house, barber shop, public conveyance by air, land, or water, theater, store or other place for the sale of merchandise, or any other place of public accommodation or amusement, denies to a citizen, except for reasons applicable alike to all citizens and regardless of color or race, the full enjoyment of the accommodations, advantages, facilities, or privileges thereof, [the dentist] shall be fined."

The narrow issue before the court was whether the law applied to the private office of the dentist. In reaching its decision the court stated:

> The narrow question presented is the meaning of "any other place of public accommodation" as employed in the statute. . . . The places particularly designated in the section of the Code under consideration may be classified: (1) restaurant, eating house, (2) barber shop, (3) public conveyance by air, land, or water, (4) theater, (5) store or other place for sale of merchandise. No one of these descriptive words nor the classes into which they fall include a dentist's office nor are they so like any of the places described as to come within any one of the specific classifications of the statute. We are of opinion that the trial judge did not err in holding that "any other place of public accommodation" did not include the office of the defendant.

The court continued:

> Although the application of the rule which we have discussed seems to be appropriate in interpreting the meaning of Section G.C. § 12940 and the particular words "any other place of public accommodation," it is possible that giving the broadest possible interpretation to place of public accommodation it would not include the office of a dentist. A dentist may be classified as one of the learned professions like unto a physician or surgeon. An office of a physician or surgeon does not connote that it is a place of public accommodation.[2]

[2]119 NE2d 657 (1951).

The First Limit: Protection of People of Color from Discrimination

8.2 To prevent health practitioners from discriminating in their private offices against people of color, a practice considered unjust by all health professional organizations, state laws were passed declaring that refusing treatment because of race, creed, color, national origin, etc, was professional misconduct subject to penalties. For example, in New York, Section 6509 of the Education Law lists as Professional Misconduct, "6. Refusing to provide professional service to a person because of such person's race, creed, color, or national origin."

These special rules did not, however, address whether the private office of a health practitioner was a "place of public accommodation," a question that would arise during a later conflict that would further limit the right of health practitioners to refuse patients.

The Second Limit: Protection of People with AIDS and Other Infectious Diseases

8.3 The spread of AIDS gave impetus to a major movement among legislative bodies and administrative agencies to prevent health practitioners, particularly physicians and dentists, from discriminating against persons afflicted with AIDS or other infectious diseases. Balancing this concern, however, was the fear that if practitioners were made to treat these people, their disease would spread to non-infected patients.

Human Rights Agencies

8.3.1 In the early 1990s many cases were brought by local human rights commissions accusing dentists of violating local civil rights laws. Such dentists were led to refuse treatment to AIDS victims by their fear that in the course of treatment the disease could be transmitted to other patients, themselves, and their office staff. Although the American Medical Association and the American Dental Association declared refusal to care for these patients unethical, such refusal remained widespread. In New York, the Commissioner of Health threatened to (but never actually did) revoke the license of any physician or dentist who refused treatment to AIDS patients.

State and local antidiscrimination agencies targeted dentists, sometimes entrapping them; many of these cases found their way into the media. They were decided at hearings by an administrative law judge, usually a member of the agency, who invariably found the dentist guilty. The slightest modification in the treatment of the AIDS or HIV-positive patient, such as gloving, referrals if the dentist did not treat the condition presented by the patient, separate office hours, or any measures designed to protect the patient, other patients, and the office staff were declared discriminatory. Dentists were fined, at times over $10,000, and the money given to the person who brought the complaint to the agency. The fines, not covered by professional liability insurance, were out-of-pocket expenses for the dentists. However, some professional liabilities companies paid their legal fees.

Although appeals were available to these dentists, few took advantage of them because of their cost and uncertainty of outcome. Those few who did based their defense on the grounds that the antidiscrimination laws invariably targeted "places of public accommodation"; and therefore not the private office of a dentist. Dentistry was under the jurisdiction of the professional licensing agency and not that of the human rights agency.

A case typical of these was brought against a dentist in New York for refusing to treat a patient who informed him that he suffered from AIDS. New York City had enacted a law prohibiting discrimination in "places of public accommodation"; its Commission on Human Rights brought an action against the dentist for having violated this law. After a hearing, the dentist was found in violation of the law, and fined. The dentist appealed.

The Appellate Court, in deciding the case stated,

> After the complainant, who tested positive for the HIV virus, filed a complaint against the petitioner, Dr [X], a dentist, with the New York City Commission on Human Rights (hereinafter the Commission), a hearing was held to determine whether Dr [X] did in fact discriminate against the complainant in violation of Administrative Code of the City of New York former §§ 8-107(2) and 8-108. The administrative law judge who heard the case and whose findings were adopted by the Commission, determined that certain statements Dr [X] made to the complainant during a telephone conversation constituted a refusal to treat him based on his status as a person infected with the HIV virus.
>
> Under Administrative Code former §§ 8-107(2) and 8-108, it was unlawful for a "place of public accommodation" to discriminate against an "otherwise qualified physically handicapped" individual. No issue has been raised on this appeal with respect to whether an HIV-infected person constitutes an "otherwise qualified physically handicapped" individual. The dispositive issue in this case is whether the petitioner's one-chair dental practice was a "place of public accommodation" as defined in Administrative Code former § 8-102(9) as that law existed when the alleged discrimination occurred.

The court found it was not: "since the petitioner's practice was not a 'place of public accommodation,' it follows that there was no violation of Administrative Code former § 8-107(2)." The decision of the administrative law judge was reversed, and the dentist found not in violation of the law in refusing to treat the patient.[3]

[3]580 NYS2d 35 (1992).

The determining issue in all such cases in the early period of the enactment of antidiscrimination legislation was whether private dental offices were "places of public accommodation." Appellate courts repeatedly ruled that they were not, and so physicians and dentists were free to decide whom they wished to treat, except that states' practice acts prohibited them from refusing to treat patients because of their color, creed, national origin, religion, etc. The were free to ignore the human rights laws, which prohibited a much broader range of grounds for discrimination: race, color, religion, sex, national origin, ancestry, age, marital status, sexual preference, physical or mental handicap, and the presence of infectious disease—officially termed a disability. The City of San Francisco included "body size" (obesity) in the list of disabilities.

In opposition to these court rulings, the moral consensus among the general population and health officials was that persons charged with the responsibility to guard the health of patients should be made to treat them regardless of disability, notwithstanding the risks.

Centers for Disease Control and Prevention (CDC)

8.3.2   During this period of turmoil, the Centers for Disease Control and Prevention (CDC), a federal agency charged with tracking the outbreak of diseases and their causes, issued guidelines to prevent their spread. On July 12, 1991, the CDC issued specific guidelines related to the control of infectious diseases in private health professional's offices and in hospitals. The guidelines were called "universal precautions." They were to apply to all patients being treated, whether or not they were known to suffer from an infectious disease. The goal was to prevent the transmission of HIV and hepatitis B virus (HBV) to patients during exposure-prone invasive procedures. The publication of its recommendations followed months of investigation by the CDC and extensive public hearings.

The CDC recommended that all health care workers follow universal precautions to prevent the transmission of infectious disease: they should wear surgical gloves, a surgical mask, a gown from neck to below the knee, and protective eyewear. It was anticipated that these guidelines would lead physicians and dentists to accept patients with infectious diseases. But they did not. Many practitioners did not follow the guidelines; they thought them too expensive, or too radical in changing long-standing practices, or unnecessary.

The CDC also recommended that health care workers who are HIV- or HBV-positive be allowed to perform noninvasive procedures. The guidelines suggested but did not require the testing of health care workers. They also did not require disclosure of health care workers' HIV or HBV status to patients undergoing exposure-prone procedures.

As to dentists, these recommendations make it clear that the universal precautions should be followed during all dental procedures, that infected dentists are not required to inform their patients, that dentists are not required to be tested for viruses, and, because almost all dental procedures are invasive, that infected dentists should retire from active practice.

Occupational Safety and Health Administration (OSHA)

8.3.3   Next into the fray came the Occupational Safety and Health Administration (OSHA), an administrative agency in the Department of Labor of the federal government. Its mission is to protect workers from on-the-job-related injuries, including those due to hazardous chemicals and waste products. Pressured by labor unions, OSHA adopted a new set of standards having the effect of law, and designed to protect workers in the health care field from contracting AIDS or other infectious diseases. In effect, OSHA converted the guidelines of the CDC into law. Workers (employees) in the dentist's private office were required to wear all the protective clothing recommended by the CDC. If they did not, the dentist was subject to a fine.

Despite this protection, the concerned community, professional organizations, and government agencies found four major loopholes in the laws designed to prevent the spread of infectious diseases in the private offices of health practitioners:

1. The owner of a practice could decide not to wear protective clothing.
2. Because the office practices dictated by OSHA were not designed to protect patients, there were no standards that required the sterilization of handpieces, instrument, etc.
3. Patients had no official standing to complain if they felt the OSHA standards were being violated, eg, gloves were not being worn by an employee during their treatment. OSHA *could* respond to the complaint of a patient, but it was not *required* to.
4. The penalty imposed against a dentist whose employees did not comply with the law or whose office practices were in violation was usually limited to a fine; there was no provision for taking action against the offender's license.

Furthermore, private offices were still not subject to the antidiscrimination laws. Employees were protected from contamination, patients were not, and dentists were still permitted to refuse care to the disabled. The private office was not a "place of public accommodation." This was addressed through the enactment of two federal laws: the Americans with Disabilities Act of 1990 and the Postal Workers and Transportation Appropriation Act of 1991. With their passage, the remaining loopholes were closed (see chapter 2).

Americans with Disabilities Act of 1990

8.3.4   In 1990, President Bush signed into law the Americans with Disabilities Act. The act was designed to ensure that all barriers to services, transportation, communication, and physical facilities impeding the care of the disabled would be removed. The act declared the private offices of health providers "places of public accommodation." Dentists' private offices thus became subject to the provisions of the act, and so all barriers to equal access to care in the dental office were removed. Under the services provisions of the act, dentists are required to treat, in exactly the same manner as all other patients, all disabled persons, including those who have AIDS, who are HIV-positive, who have other infectious diseases, eg, TB, and who belong to a high-risk group, eg, homosexuals. All antidiscrimination law applies to them, including San Francisco's concerning discrimination against the "obese."

In addition, the Americans with Disabilities Act requires dentists to satisfy a host of other requirements concerning, eg, the physical facility and communications. The rules governing the adjustment of physical facilities and the new construction of dental offices are extremely complex; dentists should contact their local building inspector or a local architect for guidance. The communications section of the law may require dentist to have all complex written instructions and consent forms printed in braille. Dentists who employ 15 or more employees must comply with the hiring regulations of the act. For details of the

Table 3 Americans with Disabilities Act Telephone Numbers	
Nature of call	**Telephone number**
General Information	202-514-0301
Justice Department for Legal Questions	202-307-2222
Employment Questions	800-526-7234
Office and Building Facilities	202-653-7848
Communications	202-634-1816 (4855)

act, it is best to contact the offices that administer it. Their telephone numbers are listed in Table 3.

Special confidentiality laws relating to AIDS patients or those who are HIV-positive are strictly enforced, and many apply to health practitioners. In some jurisdictions a dentist is prohibited from inquiring whether a patient has AIDS or is HIV-positive. In others, New York for example, a dentist may inquire about the HIV status of a patient, but only if all patients are asked the same question. In some jurisdictions a dentist may not require a patient to be tested for the presence of the AIDS virus. If a referral by a dentist is made to another health provider, and the referring dentist is of the professional opinion that the information about the presence of the infectious disease, including AIDS or HIV, is essential to the treatment of the patient, the referring dentist may include the information in the referral. However, it is prudent to discuss with the patient the need to include the information and mention this discussion in the patient's record.

Dentists are urged to determine the local laws that relate to AIDS and HIV, and how the laws affect their management and treatment of patients.

Postal Workers and Transportation Appropriation Act of 1991

8.3.5   The Americans with Disabilities Act of 1990, then, imposed the final limitation on the right of the dentist to select patients. But a problem still remained—ensuring that dentists employ the CDC's universal precautions designed to prevent the spread of disease in the dental office. The Postal Workers and Transportation Appropriation Act of 1991 did that, through a provision requiring each state to include in its regulations a penalty against the license of a health care professional who was in violation of the universal precautions contained in the guidelines of the CDC. States were given until October 1992 to comply, or risk loss of federal public health funds. States could ask for an extension to comply, and many did; however, within a few years all did comply. New York complied within 6 months of the passage of the law and amended its Rules of the Board of Regents to include the failure to use universal precautions in the treatment of all patients as unprofessional conduct punishable by loss or suspension of the license to practice.

Summary on the Limitation of Dentists' Right to Restrict Their Practices

8.4 The erosion of the absolute right of health practitioners to select patients, as defined in the decision of 1901, began with statutes prohibiting health practitioners from refusing treatment of patients because of their race, religion, heritage, etc. Next came the Americans with Disabilities Act, which declared the private offices of health practitioners "places of public accommodation," thus placing them within the jurisdiction of the human rights agencies of the states, local jurisdictions, and the federal government. Aside from these restrictions, however, dentists were still permitted to refuse to treat patients for any reason they chose. For example, in World War II, when dentists were drafted, they could elect not to serve as dentists. Dentists who enter contracts to treat a selected population, however, lose their freedom to refuse to treat members of that specific population; if they do refuse, they are in violation of their contract and subject to civil sanctions.

Courts Define Discrimination

8.5 Early court cases dealt with the jurisdictional issue of whether a dentist's office is a "place of public accommodation," and thus subject to laws related to the prohibition of discrimination against persons with disabilities, such as local human rights laws. The question of whether a dentist's office is a "place of public accommodation" was settled with the enactment of the Americans with Disabilities Act, in which all offices of health professionals were declared places of public accommodation. What had yet to be decided was what specific acts were discriminatory if performed by a dentist in relation to patients suffering from AIDS or infected with HIV. A series of cases decided by the New York appellate courts addressed that issue.

Case 1. Hospital uses drapes for HIV patient

8.5.1 The Supreme Court, Appellate Division in upstate New York held that a health center had not discriminated against a patient by draping all exposed surfaces of the treatment room that might have become contaminated with blood during treatment. The health center followed all infection control universal precautions for all patients. Personnel wore gloves, masks, goggles, and gowns. When the staff became aware that the patient was HIV-positive, they took the additional precaution of draping all exposed surfaces. The State Division of Human Rights brought an action against the health center alleging the center had violated the state antidiscrimination laws and had exposed the patient to "public humiliation." The Commissioner of the State Division of Human Rights ruled that the health center was guilty of discrimination and ordered the center to pay $10,000 compensatory damages to the patient for "hurt, humiliation, and mental anguish." The center appealed, and the appellate court annulled the determination of the Commissioner:

The proof adduced at the fact-finding hearing demonstrated that the draping of surfaces that might become contaminated by blood or saliva is an acceptable precaution against the spread of HIV infection. It was also established that the treatment rooms are not visible from the waiting area, that the doors to the treatment rooms are kept closed except when staff members go in and out, and that no one but the patient and clinic staff members were aware that the precaution of draping had been utilized. The Commissioner's conclusion that this patient was exposed to public humiliation has no foundation in the record.

Although OSHA guidelines suggest that dental care providers treat every patient as if he or she were infected, in our view it does not rationally follow that a dental care provider that takes an extra precaution in the privacy of the treatment room in the case of an identified HIV positive patient has unlawfully discriminated against that patient.[4]

[4]604 NYS2d 406 (1993).

Case 2. HIV patient treated in "isolation room" and draped with orange drapes

8.5.2
A patient visited the dental clinic of North Shore University Hospital on several occasions without incident. Then, during one visit, he was asked about his sexual orientation in order to determine whether he might present a higher-than-normal risk of infection with HIV virus. He became upset and left. He returned at a later date. He was treated in a room reserved for patients who present a risk of being infected with the HIV virus. Unlike other patients, these were treated with "strict isolation techniques" in an "isolation room." The room was marked with an orange "X," and the contents of the room draped with orange plastic. Based upon these facts, the commissioner of the New York State Division of Human Rights determined that the hospital violated the patient's civil rights as protected by the state's human rights law, and that as a result of these actions, the patient suffered mental anguish; it fined the hospital $25,000. The hospital appealed.

The Appellate Division annulled the decision of the Commissioner. The court stated:

> The only "privilege" denied to the complainant was the privilege of being treated without the precautions dictated by the clinic's 1985 infectious disease protocol. *We hold that where such a protocol is based on sound medical judgements which were reasonable when made, as part of a bona fide effort to protect both patients and staff*, the complainant is entitled to no such "privilege." (Emphasis added.)

The court concluded:

> Because the petitioner's infectious disease protocol was based on a *reasonable medical judgment*, the complainant had no right to be exempted from its application. The determination of the Commissioner erroneously recognizes such a right and should, therefore, be annulled.[5] (Emphasis added.)

[5]600 NYS2d 90 (1993).

The decision of the Apellate Division was affirmed by the Court of Appeals of New York, the court of last resort.[6]

[6]633 NYS2d 462 (1995).

Case 3. Dentist refers patient to hospital for root canal therapy

8.5.3   In April 1992, after nearly a 3-year gap in treatment, a patient visited Dr S.'s office for a scheduled appointment. In view of the interval since the patient's last visit, a dental hygienist asked the complainant to complete an updated medical history form. During his session with the hygienist, who cleaned his teeth and took X rays, he disclosed the fact that he had tested positive for HIV.

After the hygienist completed the treatment, the complainant was examined by Dr S., who reviewed the patient's X rays and determined that root canal therapy was necessary. He then referred him to a local hospital for root canal treatment. Explaining this decision, Dr S. testified that neither he nor the other dentist who was present at the time performed root canal therapy, that Dr T., the dentist in the practice who performed 30% to 40% of the practice's root canal work, was away on vacation, and that the patient was in immediate pain. Further, Dr S. remarked that he believed that the hospital, which had recently received a grant for the treatment of AIDS patients, was the best place for the patient to receive treatment in view of the risk of secondary infection inherent in root canal therapy. Although the patient contacted Dr S.'s secretary for additional referrals when he was unable to secure a prompt appointment at the hospital, there is no evidence that he ever again sought treatment from Dr S., or that he requested an appointment with the dentist in the practice who provided root canal services upon his return from vacation.

The patient filed a complaint with the State Division of Human Rights, alleging that he had been discriminated against by Dr S. This agency found that Dr S. had "refused to assist and denied him advantages and privileges offered to other patients, ie, a referral to Dr T. or some other dentist for prompt root canal work, because of his HIV status," and that Dr S. and his associates had therefore unlawfully discriminated against the patient in violation of the Human Rights Law.

Dr S. and his associates appealed the agency's determination to the appellate court, which annulled it:

> The record demonstrates that Dr S. performed a complete oral examination of the complainant, and concluded that further treatment, in the form of root canal therapy, was needed. It is undisputed that Dr S. did not perform root canal work, and that his associate Dr T., who performed root canal work on only 30% to 40% of the practice's patients, was away on vacation. Although the agency emphasized the fact that Dr S. did not advise the complainant of the option of seeking treatment from Dr T. upon his return from vacation, it was Dr S.'s professional judgment that the complainant needed immediate treatment because he was in pain, and that the dental unit of the hospital would best provide that treatment in view of the risk of secondary infection. In this regard, we note that patients infected with HIV are not exempt from "those precautionary measures which are based on sound medical judgments," and no evidence was presented at the hearing to establish that Dr S.'s exercise of medical judgment in advising the complainant to seek immediate treatment in a hospital setting was inappropriate or medically unsound. Finally, although the record establishes that the complainant contacted Dr S.'s secretary to request additional referrals, he sought no further treatment from Dr S. or his associates. Thus, there is no evidence that Dr S. or the members of his practice denied the complainant further treatment.[7]

[7]658 NYS2d 70 (1997).

Case 4. Dentist refers patient for extraction of a molar

8.5.4 Informed that a patient tested positive for AIDS, a Dr P. performed an examination and advised the patient that she required the extraction of a molar tooth, that he did not extract molar teeth, and that she should see an oral surgeon. Dr P.'s group's surgeon was not available at the time and was in the office infrequently. The patient filed a complaint against the dentist, Dr P., and his dental group, with the New York State Division of Human Rights, claiming that the Dr P. refused to treat her because she had tested positive for the HIV virus.

A hearing was held to determine whether Dr P. did in fact discriminate against the patient in violation of law. Dr P. explained that he offered the patient referrals to certain clinics which specialized in the treatment of HIV-positive patients because, in his professional judgment, these clinics offered precautions and accommodations beyond the minimum standards prescribed by the Center for Disease Control. Specifically, he explained that the "state-of-the-art" methods of these clinics, including special sterilization techniques and specially adapted facilities, reduced the possibility of cross infection among patients and staff.

The administrative law judge who heard the case determined that certain acts of Dr P. constituted a refusal to treat the patient based on her status as a person who was perceived to be at risk for HIV infection, found Dr P. and his group guilty of violating the antidiscrimination law, and levied a fine. Dr P. and his group appealed the decision to the appellate court, which annulled it: "Significantly, it has been held that while HIV positive patients have the right to be free from irrational discrimination, they have no legal right to be exempt from the application of those precautionary measures which are based on *sound medical judgments*."[8] (Emphasis added.)

[8]654 NYS2d 822 (1997).

Case 5. Dentist drapes patient and appoints at end of day and week

8.5.5 The Human Rights Commission accused a dentist in New York of discriminating against a patient based on the patient's HIV status by draping all surfaces of the operatory when treating him, scheduling his appointments at the end of the day and week, and charging him an extra fee. The Commissioner of the New York State Division of Human Rights awarded the patient $7,500 in compensatory damages for mental anguish and humiliation. The decision was appealed to the Appellate Division of the Supreme Court, which found that the extra fee charged the patient was discriminatory, but the other acts were not:

> The record, however, does not support the finding that petitioner discriminated against complainant by draping all surfaces of the operatory when treating him. The experts agreed that some professional judgment must be exercised in implementing appropriate barriers for surfaces that might become contaminated by the blood of an HIV-positive patient. Additionally, the scheduling of complainant's appointments at the end of the day and week is justified by the additional precautions with respect to the draping of surfaces of the operatory.[9]

[9]684 NYS2d 738 (1999).

Summary of Cases

8.5.6   In many cases in which dentists appealed human rights agencies' decisions that they had violated the antidiscrimination laws, the appellate courts found that the act of the dentist that was the basis of the complaint was not discriminatory. Dentists who took the necessary precautions to prevent the patient from contaminating others, or who acted to protect the infected patient from further injury, were not found to be discriminatory provided what they did was based upon *sound medical judgment.*

Employees and the Treatment of AIDS Patients

8.6   Situations may arise in which employees in a dental office refuse to assist dentists while treating a patient suffering from AIDS or infected with HIV. The Americans with Disabilities Act states that such employees are in violation of federal law prohibiting discrimination.

Employees Who Have AIDS or Are HIV-Positive

8.7   The law requires that employees in a health provider's office who have AIDS or are HIV-positive must be not be discharged from employment in the office, but must be given a position that will not expose patients to the disease or condition. Thus, a dental assistant with AIDS may act as a receptionist or office manager.

Other Problems Related to AIDS

8.8   Other serious questions have been raised in relation to AIDS.

1. *Mandatory Testing: Should all health practitioners be tested for the presence of AIDS or HIV?* Despite much public clamor for testing all health practitioners, cooler heads in the health agencies and health associations have prevailed. Some felt the cost was too great, considering that the pathogenesis of the disease would require frequent testing. Others felt such testing violated human rights. However, though none have required it, many public health agencies have suggested it.

2. *Duty to Inform: If practitioners have AIDS or are infected, have they a duty to inform their patients?* While no BLLs require health practitioners to inform patients about their health status, one may yet ask whether an infected health provider has an affirmative *duty to inform* a patient on whom he is to perform an invasive procedure that he suffers from an infectious disease like AIDS, or is infected with HIV. In addressing the issue, there are four things to keep in mind:

a. Black letter law does not require a health provider to reveal his health status.
b. A duty to inform is affirmative, which means the patient does not have to ask.
c. Not fulfilling a duty to inform violates a patient's right to know, a tort.
d. Most procedures a dentist performs result in bleeding, and all are performed in the presence of saliva.

A New Jersey court ruled that in the process of obtaining a patient's consent, the doctor had a duty to inform the patient whether his health condition posed a risk to the patient:

> The obligation of a surgeon performing invasive procedures, such as plaintiff, to reveal his AIDS condition, is one which requires a weighing of plaintiff's rights against the patient's rights. New Jersey's strong policy supporting patient rights, weighed against plaintiff's individual right to perform an invasive procedure as a part of the practice of his profession, requires the conclusion that the patient's rights must prevail. At a minimum, the physician must withdraw from performing any invasive procedure which would pose a risk to the patient. Where the ultimate harm is death, even the presence of a low risk of transmission justifies the adoption of a policy which precludes invasive procedures when there is "any" risk of transmission. In the present case, the debate raged as to whether there was "any" risk of transmission, and the informed-consent procedure was left in place. If there is to be an ultimate arbiter of whether the patient is to be treated invasively by an AIDS-positive surgeon, the arbiter will be the fully-informed patient. The ultimate risk to the patient is so absolute—so devastating—that it is untenable to argue against informed consent combined with a restriction on procedures which present "any risk" to the patient.

In a footnote [FN20] included in the decision it stated:

> While the chances of a patient acquiring HIV from an infected provider are small, infected patients have transmitted HIV to a dentist and other health-care providers when small or inapparent quantities of blood are transferred during clinical procedures. Presumably, small blood transfers from the provider to patient likewise could cause transmission. One infected surgeon may perform many operations, increasing the opportunity for transmission. As small as the risk to any individual patient may be, the aggregate risk thus becomes significant enough that patient safety and prudent risk management dictate restricting infected providers from performing invasive procedures.[10]

[10]592 A2d 1251 (1991).

In a case decided in Illinois, the court stated:

> The first certified question asks this court to decide "[w]hether an HIV positive physician has a duty to disclose his or her HIV status to a patient when seeking the patient's consent to perform an invasive medical procedure which exposes the patient to the risk of HIV transmission." The trial court found that such a duty to disclose exists as a matter of law and we agree.[11]

[11]690 NE2d 1012 (1997).

In a case decided in Maryland, the trial court found that neither the surgeon who performed the surgery, nor the hospital in which the surgery was performed had a duty to inform the patient that the surgeon had AIDS. The patient appealed, and he appellate court reversed the decision:

> Under the allegations of the appellants' complaints, taken as true, it was foreseeable that Dr [A.] might transmit the AIDS virus to his patients during

invasive surgery. Thus, we are unable to say, as a matter of law, that Dr Almaraz owed no duty to the appellants, either to refrain from performing the surgery or to warn them of his condition. This is so even though the medical literature indicates that, with proper barrier techniques, the risk of HIV transmission during surgery is extremely low, for legal scholars have long agreed that the seriousness of potential harm, as well as its probability, contributes to a duty to prevent it. . . . While it may be unlikely that an infected doctor will transmit the AIDS virus to a patient during surgery, the patient will almost surely die if the virus is transmitted.[12]

[12]329 Md 435 (1993).

3. AIDS-phobia: Can a patient be compensated for fear of contracting AIDS?
If dentist is aware that he either suffers from AIDS or is HIV-positive and has not informed his patients of the fact, and the fact later becomes known, a patient whom he has treated before the disclosure might enter suit against him alleging that between the time he learned that the dentist was infected and the time he received his own negative test results, he suffered mental anguish, or AIDS-phobia.

A relevant case took place in New York, where a patient who had undergone a blood transfusion brought an action against a hospital for medical malpractice to recover for damages caused by fear that the blood had been contaminated with an infectious disease. After the jury returned a verdict awarding the patient $500,000, the trial court denied the hospital's motion to set aside the verdict but reduced the award to $150,000. The hospital appealed the decision and award, and the appellate court reversed it:

> It was also error to grant plaintiff an award for disease-phobia and indeed, the claim is legally insufficient. The record indicates that the blood plaintiff received tested negative for HIV and hepatitis C as well as other diseases, and that the blood donors and plaintiff have also subsequently tested negative. Thus, in the absence of objective medical evidence of a likelihood of contracting the diseases alleged by plaintiff, his claim is "too remote and too speculative, and not compensable as a matter of law" [quoting a prior case].[13]

[13]635 NYS2d 8 (1995).

Thus in New York to recover from a suit based upon AIDS-phobia, one is required to show by objective evidence that there was a likelihood of contracting the disease. For example, in the case of AIDS-phobia related to dental care, the patient might show that there was some break in the universal precautions, eg, a tear in a glove and some bleeding by the dentist during the treatment of the patient, in addition to the fact that it was later revealed that the dentist was HIV-positive. However, such requirement may not be required in other states for a patient to recover based upon AIDS-phobia.

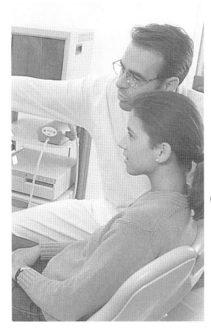

CHAPTER NINE

Consent, Informed Consent, and Informed Refusal

Background: Consent

9.1 The failure to obtain a valid consent for treatment appears as a complaint in almost all allegations of dental malpractice. Knowing how the courts have dealt with a variety of such complaints will help you make decisions the courts will uphold.

Legal History of the Need to Obtain Consent

9.2 Though there had been many earlier assertions of the individual's right to exercise control over what is to be done to his or her person, as for example in John Stuart Mill's 1859 essay "On Liberty," a major appellate court case did not surface in the United States until 1891, when a Massachusetts court was faced with the complaint of a ship's passenger who had joined a line of other passengers receiving vaccinations as a condition to enter the United States. The court ruled that the passenger gave implied consent to the injection by remaining in the line, knowing what would take place, and not objecting.[1] Implied consent will be discussed in detail later in the chapter.

Two cases decided in Illinois and Minnesota in the same year, 1905, dealt directly with the issue of consent. In the first, a doctor in Chicago conducted a sanitarium, in which he had treated a patient about 40 years of age who had been subject to epileptic seizures. The doctor found that her uterus was contracted and lacerated, and that the lower portion of her rectum was diseased.

[1] 154 Mass 272; 28 NE 266 (1891).

He operated to correct these difficulties. Thereafter, she remained in the sanitarium without improvement for several weeks and then returned home. Her brother-in-law, at the request of her husband, took her again to the sanitarium, and the physician performed a second surgical operation upon her, removing her ovaries and uterus. Neither operation improved her health. She grew gradually worse mentally, and on August 25, 1898, was adjudged insane and sent to the state asylum. She was not a witness in the trial of this case. The cause of action was based on the allegation not that the operation was unskillfully performed or unnecessary, but only that it was performed without the authority or consent of the patient, and constituted a trespass to her person (battery). The court ruled that it did.[2]

[2]224 Ill 300; 79 NE 562 (1905).

In the Minnesota case, the patient consulted a surgeon concerning a difficulty with her right ear. The surgeon examined the ear and advised an operation, to which the patient consented. The surgeon administered anesthetics, and after the patient was unconscious, examined the left ear and found it in need of an operation. The patient's family physician attended the surgery at the patient's request and did not object to surgery on the left ear. However, the patient had not previously had any difficulty with her left ear, and was not either informed about or given the opportunity to consent to the operation. Subsequently, on the claim that the operation seriously impaired her sense of hearing and was wrongful and unlawful, the patient brought an action to recover damages for an assault and battery (see chapter 4).

In deciding in favor of the patient, the court stated:

> The patient must be the final arbiter as to whether he will take his chances with the operation, or take his chances of living without it. Such is the natural right of the individual, which the law recognizes as a legal one. Consent, therefore, of an individual, must be either expressly or impliedly given before a surgeon may have the right to operate.[3]

[3]Kinkead on Torts, § 375.

The court continued:

> There is logic in the principle thus stated, for, in all other trades, professions, or occupations, contracts are entered into by the mutual agreement of the interested parties, and are required to be performed in accordance with their letter and spirit. No reason occurs to us why the same rule should not apply between physician and patient. If the physician advises his patient to submit to a particular operation, and the patient weighs the dangers and risks incident to its performance, and finally consents, he thereby, in effect, enters into a contract authorizing his physician to operate to the extent of the consent given, but no further. . . . The methods of treatment are committed almost exclusively to his judgment, but we are aware of no rule or principle of law which would extend to him free license respecting surgical operations.[4]

[4]95 Minn 261; 104 NW 12 (1905).

A landmark case decided in New York in 1914 stated what has become the definitive rule in all cases that followed: "Every human being of *adult years* and *sound mind* has a right to determine what shall be done with his own body; and a surgeon who performs an operation without his patient's consent commits an assault, for which he is liable in damages."[5] (Emphasis added.) The judge in the case referred to the Illinois and the Minnesota cases reported above.

[5]271 NY 125 (1914).

To summarize what has become the rule: for consent to health care to be valid, it must be obtained from an adult of sound mind. To qualify as an adult, the patient must have reached the 18th birthday, and to qualify as of sound mind the patient must be free of any mental disability or impairment and free of the influence of drugs at the time of granting consent. Finally, a physician or dentist who provides care without a valid consent is guilty of a battery (trespass to the person), or, later, of negligence. The rules apply notwithstanding that the service is provided gratuitously and benefits the patient.

A case in Pennsylvania suggests the importance of consent. A patient sued a dentist for a great many things; the informed consent allegation, though buried in a long list of other allegations, was the only one supported by the court. Here is the list:

a. Failing to properly diagnose the condition of the Plaintiff
b. *Failing to inform the Plaintiff of the potential danger of the injection of anesthesia* [a consent requirement]
c. Injecting and puncturing an artery and/or vein in the Plaintiff's mouth
d. Using improper injection techniques, puncturing and/or striking arteries and/or vessels of the Plaintiff's mouth, including the failure to withdraw a needle inserted in an artery of the mouth of the Plaintiff
e. Failing to observe blood in the aspirated needle when withdrawn from the Plaintiff's mouth
f. Failing to promptly withdraw and aid or assist the Plaintiff after becoming aware of extreme pain of the Plaintiff
g. Failing to apply ice or take any other action after becoming aware of the distress of the Plaintiff
h. Failing to provide follow-up treatment or check for infection in the mouth and face area
i. Failing to take any action with regard to substantial swelling from fluids gathering in the face and mouth area
j. Failing to give antibiotics to prevent infection
k. Failing to advise the Plaintiff to obtain the services of a physician
l. Was otherwise negligent under the circumstances[6] (Emphasis added.)

[6]583 A2d 1205 (1990).

Is Lack of Consent Assault and Battery or Negligence?

9.3   The early cases treated lack of consent as an unlawful, nonpermitted touching of a person; and thus a battery. In 1976, a case in New York dealt with the issue. The question before the court was whether to apply the 3-year statute of limitations for malpractice (since reduced to 2½ years) or the 1-year statute for assault and battery (see chapter 4):

> A cause of action against a physician for lack of informed consent with respect to surgery performed by defendant for the removal of a cataract from plaintiff's left eye is based on negligence or malpractice and is governed by the three-year Statute of Limitations, rather than the 1-year statute for assault and battery. Intent to do injury is an essential element in an assault and battery action and plaintiff makes no such allegation.

The court went on:

> A breach by a doctor of his professional duty to properly inform his patient is more akin to malpractice, even though the uninformed consent might

[7]51 AD2d 381
(1976).

lead to the commission of a technical assault and battery, for which the Legislature has fixed a 1-year Statute of Limitations.[7]

The court made two major precedent statements in its opinion:

1. If the action brought by the patient is based upon faulty consent, the statute of limitations for malpractice applies; the doctor was negligent in not informing the patient properly, but there was no intent to harm.
2. A lack of consent may lead to an action for assault and battery.

Another case followed in 1980 in which the court further discussed the relationship of consent and assault and battery:

> The theory of lack of informed consent in medical malpractice actions presents conceptual difficulties arising from the awkward mixture of assault and battery in a suit based upon negligence. A brief look at their ancestry clarifies their differences. Assault and battery is a descendant of the early English common law action of trespass. Negligence, on the other hand, traces its ancestry back to another ancient common-law writ titled an action of trespass on the case. Originally they were related to each other. The older action of trespass developed new variations which became separate forms of action. One variety was "upon a special case" or, later, simply "trespass on the case." Trespass was the remedy for direct injuries and trespass on the case for indirect injuries. These common-law actions have now been abandoned in modern practice, particularly the artificial classification of injuries as direct or indirect. The law today looks instead to the intent of the wrongdoer or to his negligence. In their evolution the action of trespass remained as the remedy for all intentional wrongs and action on the case was extended to include injuries which were not intended but were merely negligently inflicted. Trespass on the case had become distinct from trespass by 1390, and as early as the sixteenth century had evolved as the remedy for libel and slander, negligence and deceit. Battery remains by definition an intentional tort, just as its progenitor trespass. One is subject to liability to another for battery if "(a) he acts intending to cause a harmful or offensive contact with the person of the other . . . , and (b) a harmful contact with the person of the other directly or indirectly results." Negligence as the direct descendant of trespass on the case has a different conceptual basis than battery because negligence includes those unintended wrongs which one actor causes to another.[8]

[8]72 AD2d 231
(1980).

And so, it is firmly settled that lack of consent brings an action for negligence or malpractice rather than for assault and battery (see chapter 4). However, a patient who does not consent, and yet is not injured and therefore cannot succeed in an action in malpractice or negligence, may nonetheless succeed in an action in trespass to the person, a battery.

It Must Be Informed

9.4

As the years passed and more cases came before the courts on the issue of consent, it underwent further refinements. A federal court, in a landmark case decided in the District of Columbia in 1972 by a United States Court of Appeals, ruled that consent had to be "informed" to be valid. In a series of footnotes, the court spelled out what information must be given to a patient for the consent to be informed. Footnote 27 reads:

> The discussion [between doctor and patient] need not be a disquisition, and surely the physician is not compelled to give his patient a short medical education; the disclosure rule summons the physician only to a reasonable explanation. *That means generally informing the patient in nontechnical terms as to what is at stake: the therapy alternatives open to him, the goals expectably to be achieved, and the risks that may ensue from particular treatment and no treatment.* So informing the patient hardly taxes the physician, and it must be the exceptional patient who cannot comprehend such an explanation at least in a rough way. (Emphasis added.)

Footnote 36 reads:

> We discard the thought that the patient should ask for information before the physician is required to disclose. Caveat emptor [let the buyer beware] is not the norm for the consumer of medical services. Duty to disclose is more than a call to speak merely on the patient's request, or merely to answer the patient's questions; it is a duty to volunteer, if necessary, the information the patient needs for intelligent decision. The patient may be ignorant, confused, overawed by the physician or frightened by the hospital, or even ashamed to inquire. Perhaps relatively few patients could in any event identify the relevant questions in the absence of prior explanation by the physician. Physicians and hospitals have patients of widely divergent socio-economic backgrounds, and a rule which presumes a degree of sophistication which many members of society lack is likely to breed gross inequities.[9]

[9]Ibid.

Thus, the court added that for consent to be valid the practitioner has an *affirmative duty* to provide the patient with enough information about the recommended treatment for the patient to make an informed decision as to whether to reject the treatment, accept it, or postpone it. To make the decision the court stated that the patient must be told of:

1. The risks and benefits of the recommended procedure
2. The anticipated outcome (prognosis)
3. The alternatives to the procedure, along with their risks and benefits

The discussion with the patient must be in language the patient understands, the patient must be given the opportunity to ask questions and have them answered, and the consent must be given freely, without coercion.

How Much to Tell of the Risks?

9.4.1   The problem of how much information the patient must be given about the risks has given the courts some difficulty. In deciding the case above, the court stated:

> Once the circumstances give rise to a duty on the physician's part to inform his patient, the next inquiry is the scope of the disclosure the physician is legally obliged to make. The courts have frequently confronted this problem, but no uniform standard defining the adequacy of the divulgence emerges from the decisions. Some have said "full" disclosure, a norm we are unwilling to adopt literally. *It seems obviously prohibitive and unrealistic*

to expect physicians to discuss with their patients every risk of proposed treatment—no matter how small or remote—and generally unnecessary from the patient's viewpoint as well. Indeed, the cases speaking in terms of "full" disclosure appear to envision something less than total disclosure, leaving unanswered the question of just how much [to tell]. (Emphasis added.)

Two different standards have evolved. The *professional community standard* requires the doctor to tell what other doctors in the community tell their patients in the same or similar circumstances. The *reasonable person standard* requires doctors to tell their patients enough to enable them to make intelligent decisions as to whether to proceed with the proposed treatment. When the professional community standard is used, as it is in New York, experts from the community must appear for the plaintiff-patient to inform the jury as to their standards. The reasonable person standard requires no expert testimony and so places less of a burden on the plaintiff-patient. In applying the reasonable person standard, some courts apply an *objective standard*—Is the information provided sufficient for a reasonably intelligent person to make an intelligent choice?—while others apply a *subjective standard*—Was this person in particular given enough information to make an intelligent decision?

In the reasonable person standard, the risks to be communicated to the patient are described as *material.* In the professional community standard, they are described as *foreseeable.* The prudent practitioner, without knowing the laws of the state, should follow both standards and inform the patient of the material and the foreseeable risks. In other words, tell it all!

Black Letter Law on Consent

9.5   On the general issue of consent, the New York Public Health Law, Chapter 45, Article 28–Hospitals contains in Section 2508d the following:

1. Lack of informed consent means the failure of the person providing the professional treatment or diagnosis to disclose to the patient such alternatives thereto and the reasonably foreseeable risks and benefits involved as a reasonable medical, dental, or podiatric practitioner under similar circumstances would have disclosed, in a manner permitting the patient to make a knowledgeable evaluation.
2. The right of action to recover for medical, dental, or podiatric malpractice based on a lack of informed consent is limited to those cases involving either (*a*) nonemergency treatment, procedure, or surgery, or (*b*) a diagnostic procedure which involved invasion or disruption of the integrity of the body.
3. For a cause of action therefore it must also be established that a reasonably prudent person in the patient's position would not have undergone the treatment or diagnosis if he had been fully informed and that the lack of informed consent is a proximate cause of the injury or condition for which recovery is sought.
4. It shall be a defense to any action for medical, dental, or podiatric malpractice based upon an alleged failure to obtain such an informed consent that:

a. The risk not disclosed is too commonly known to warrant disclosure; or

b. The patient assured the medical, dental, or podiatric practitioner he would undergo the treatment, procedure or diagnosis regardless of the risk involved, or the patient assured the medical, dental, or podiatric practitioner that he did not want to be informed of the matters to which he would be entitled to be informed; or

c. Consent by or on behalf of the patient was not reasonably possible; or

d. The medical, dental, or podiatric practitioner, after considering all of the attendant facts and circumstances, used reasonable discretion as to the manner and extent to which such alternatives or risks were disclosed to the patient because he reasonably believed that the manner and extent of such disclosure could reasonably be expected to adversely and substantially affect the patient's condition.

Consent Implied by Law: Emergencies

9.6   In the 1914 landmark case cited above (see section 9.2), Justice Benjamin N. Cardozo stated:

> In the case at hand, the wrong complained of is not merely negligence. It is trespass. Every human being of adult years and sound mind has a right to determine what shall be done with his own body; and a surgeon who performs an operation without his patient's consent commits an assault, for which he is liable in damages. *This is true, except in cases of emergency where the patient is unconscious, and where it is necessary to operate before consent can be obtained.*[10] (Emphasis added.)

[10]271 NY 125 (1914).

Only if a true emergency exists at the time the service is provided can the practitioner proceed at no risk without the consent of the patient. Most jurisdictions hold that an emergency exists when care must be rendered at once to protect the life or health of the patient; under such conditions, consent is implied by law. Most courts also apply two other tests:

1. Would consent have been given if the patient was able to grant consent?
2. Would a reasonable person in the same situation have granted consent?

Consent granted by a spouse is not valid. However, in emergency situations where consent of the patient cannot be obtained, it is wise to obtain the *assent* of the spouse.

The Good Samaritan Laws present in all states have an element of consent implied by law. They preclude the victim of an accident from entering suit against a physician and, in many states, against a dentist or other health practitioner who renders aid at the scene. However, the relief from suit applies to ordinary or simple negligence and not to gross negligence (see chapter 4). In order to qualify for protection:

1. The care must be rendered at the scene, not in an office, health center, or hospital.
2. The care must be rendered with no expectation of being paid.

Consent Implied by the Action(s) of the Party

9.7 Consent may also be implied by the actions of the patient. For example, a patient enters a dentist's office and, after reporting a health complaint, asks to be examined. The patient is told by the doctor that radiographs of the teeth will be taken. The patient allows the radiographs to be taken without objection. Consent is thus implied by the action, or non-action, of the patient. The key elements are:

1. The patient was aware of the nature of the problem or the need for the treatment (examination) being provided.
2. The patient made no objection when the treatment began.

Minors and Consent

9.8 By common law, minors may be *emancipated* and may consent to health care without the consent of the parent. Generally, a minor who is financially independent of parental support and control is emancipated. Many states, such as New York, have codified common law and may list the conditions under which a minor becomes emancipated. The New York law on consent, Public Health Law §2504, lists the following conditions:

1. Any person who is eighteen years of age or older, or *is the parent of a child or has married, may give effective consent* for medical, dental, health and hospital services for himself or herself, and the consent of no other person shall be necessary.
2. *Any person who has been married or who has borne a child may give effective consent for medical, dental, health, and hospital services for his or her child.*
3. *Any person who is pregnant* may give effective consent for medical, dental, health, and hospital services relating to prenatal care.
4. Medical, dental, health, and hospital services may be rendered to persons of any age without the consent of a parent or legal guardian when, in the physician's judgment, *an emergency exists* and the person is in immediate need of medical attention and an attempt to secure consent would result in delay of treatment, which would increase the risk to the person's life or health.
5. Anyone who acts in good faith based on the representation by a person that he is eligible to consent pursuant to the terms of this section shall be deemed to have received effective consent. (Emphasis added.)

In some cases, the courts have stated that a minor may grant a valid consent if the minor understands the nature of the treatment and the risks. This is known as the *mature minor rule.* The youngest age at which it has been applied is 14. In some jurisdictions, a minor of any age may consent to care for treatment of venereal diseases, for sex-related advice and treatment, and for abortions without the consent of the parent. In many jurisdictions, disclosure of this information to the parent places the practitioner at legal risk of criminal action by the state and civil action by the child for breach of confidentiality.

The adult sibling or grandparent of a minor cannot grant a valid consent for the minor, even if the minor lives with the adult, and the adult pays the dentists' fees. Consent granted by an adult child for a parent is not valid. A legal guardian or any parent may grant a valid consent for a minor.

Telephone Consent

9.9   Telephone consent, properly executed, is acceptable to the courts. It must, however, contain all the elements that constitute a valid consent. In addition, it should be properly documented. In the case of a minor, when neither parent nor guardian is present, the parent or guardian should be contacted by phone and told that a third party is listening on an extension. The parent should be told of the situation and the need for treatment, including all the information that would be required to meet a valid consent. Appropriate notes should be made on the patient's chart, signed by the one who obtained the consent and countersigned by the listening third party. A follow-up letter should be sent to the parent or guardian containing all the information about the need for the care, what was said to the parent, and the details of the parent's response.

Exculpatory Terms

9.10   Exculpatory terms appear both in contracts and consents. In both, the legal issues are the same: Both are against public policy (such clauses in doctor-patient contracts have been fully discussed in chapter 3, section 5). So, for example, a consent is ineffective that contains the following provision: "I accept this treatment with the understanding that I will hold the doctor harmless for any negligence in the performance of the treatment." Although people are able to bargain away their rights to merchants, they cannot do so to health providers. Further, such clauses in contracts and consents have been ruled *adhesion contracts*; the parties were not in an equal bargaining position: "Either you agree not to sue me should I be guilty of negligence and you are injured as a result of my negligence, or I will not provide the services you need" (see chapter 3).

Who May Obtain Consent

9.11   Who in the dentist's office can obtain a valid consent: the treating dentist only, an employee of the treating dentist, a hygienist, an assistant, or a secretary-receptionist? The case that decided the issue in New York drew on a Pennsylvania case in which a dentist had removed a patient's maxillary and mandibular left and right third molars. On losing in the trial court, the patient appealed on the grounds that "the trial judge erred in failing to charge the jury that a patient cannot formulate a valid, informed consent to a surgical procedure when disclosures of the risks of surgery are made by a nurse assistant and not by the operating surgeon." The court stated:

At trial, the appellant testified that any information that she received concerning possible complications came only from Mrs [M.] who was the nurse/assistant to her dentist/husband. The appellee, through his deposition, however, testified that he explained the risks of surgery to the appellant. In addition, Mrs [M.] testified in detail as to the substance of the pretreatment information she communicated to the appellant. The appellant asserts that only the appellee, as operating physician, can effectively relate all the information necessary for an informed consent. Our reading of Gray [a decision in a former case], discloses that the holding of the Court in that seminal case was based upon the scope of the information which plaintiff had been given, rather than the identity of the person making the communication.[11]

[11]467 A2d 1353 (1983).

Taking its lead from this decision, the New York Appellate court concluded:

Plaintiff's motion to set aside the jury's finding on informed consent on the ground that there was no effort by a physician to obtain informed consent. Denied. Plaintiff asserts, but offers no authority for such assertion, that a nurse may not act as a physician's agent in obtaining informed consent. Nothing in Public Health Law § 2805-d expressly precludes the use of an agent to provide information to a patient and to obtain that patient's consent. . . . [I]f a nurse were to provide improper information in the course of obtaining the necessary consent, the result would be to make her principal liable under the statute.

And a head note to the case states, "Nurse trained in obtaining informed consent to particular procedure could act as agent for treating physician in obtaining informed consent."[12]

[12]562 NYS2d 479 (1990).

Although the appellate courts of two states, Pennsylvania and New York, have thus ruled that an office worker may obtain a valid consent to care of a patient, a doctor should consider two caveats that before delegating the responsibility. First, the office worker should be trained in obtaining informed consent. Second, the degree to which the procedure is invasive or the degree of risk attached to the it should dictate who should answer the patient's questions. The treating doctor should in all cases be available to answer questions.

Is a Written Consent Necessary?

9.12   In general, consent need not be in writing to be valid. However, in some jurisdictions, written consent is required for surgical procedures. New York requires written consent for some surgical procedures, ie, donation of human organs, acupuncture, and abortion in minors, but not for any dental procedure. A good rule of thumb is to have written and signed consents for any procedure involving either surgery or significant risks. One state, Pennsylvania, has ruled that a written consent is necessary in cases of endodontic therapy as in all surgical procedures. In effect, the court found that endodontic therapy is a surgical procedure:

Certainly no one would argue that the excision of a malignant tumor or even a benign cyst that was causing a patient discomfort is not a surgical or operative procedure. We discern no difference between the removal of diseased nerve tissue in the root of a tooth and diseased cell growth in some other part of the body. The trial court places undue emphasis on the fact that the gum was not cut into in order to accomplish the desired result of alleviating the patient's pain. [The trial court ruled that root canal treatment was not surgical.] The dentist must gain access to the affected area by one means or another. The fact that a dentist would use the least invasive method of treatment available does not diminish the nature of that treatment. Regardless of whether the dentist goes through the gum or the top of the tooth, we clearly have an invasion into the body involving the use of a surgical instrument to make an excision in order to relieve discomfort or restore the patient's health. As such, we find the procedures here involved fall within the definition of surgical. . . . Accordingly, the Appellants presented a viable informed consent claim, and the trial court erred in removing said claim from the jury's consideration.[13]

[13]736 AD 608 (1999).

The court noted that this was a case of *first impression*, meaning that the court never before ruled on the issue of whether root canal treatment was surgical and fell within the rules of the state that require informed consent.

Habit Evidence and Consent

9.12.1 An oral consent is subject to challenge as to whether it exists and what it includes. However, in a case decided in New York, the court applied the *habit evidence rule*. The facts and testimony in the case as reported by the court were as follows:

On February 4, 1984, pursuant to the recommendation of her dentist, the plaintiff visited Dr [L.], a specialist in oral and maxillofacial surgery, for treatment of a lump on the right lower part of her gum. Dr [L.] diagnosed the plaintiff's condition as pericoronitis of the lower right wisdom tooth. . . . On the basis of an X ray and his clinical examination, Dr [L.] determined that the plaintiff's impacted wisdom tooth should be removed. The tooth was extracted that same day. As a result of the surgical procedure, the plaintiff suffers from a permanent condition known as paresthesia which can only arise by the severing or injuring of a nerve within the oral cavity.

The plaintiff testified at trial that Dr [L.] advised her that the surgical procedure might cause her to experience some pain and numbness for a week or two. She claimed that she was not otherwise apprised of the dangers of the procedure and was told that extraction of the wisdom tooth was the only course of treatment for her condition. . . .

Dr [L.] admitted that he had no independent recollection of specifically what he told the plaintiff regarding the risks associated with the removal of an impacted wisdom tooth. The court permitted Dr [L.] to testify, over objections from the plaintiff's counsel, as to his routine practice developed over 19 years of practice in the specialized area of oral and maxillofacial surgery and followed in every instance of the thousands of extractions of wisdom teeth he had performed in his career. Invariably, he asserted, he tells his patients prior to the removal of an impacted wisdom tooth of the risks and complications of the procedure, including the possibility of permanent numbness of the tongue, chin, and lip. He also tells those patients that no alternative to extraction exists to alleviate the condition but that he could treat the condition with antibiotics or by cleaning the infected area. Lastly, he testified that he would then follow the course of action the patient requested. Although Dr [L.] could not recall the specifics of the conversation he had with the plaintiff prior to performing the extraction, he remembered that he had delivered a warning to her concerning the dangers attending oral surgery.

The dentist's assistance corroborated his account of his habitual practice, and the trial court ruled for the dentist. The patient appealed:

> On this appeal, the plaintiff complains that the admission into evidence of Dr [L.]'s habit or custom of routinely advising patients about to undergo surgery for removal of an impacted wisdom tooth of the potential risks attending such surgery constituted error. We disagree.
>
> As a general rule, evidence of habitual behavior or custom is admissible as circumstantial proof that the habit was followed on the occasion in question.[14]

[14]543 NYS2d 983 (1989).

Thus, according to this decision, if you are able to convince the jury that it is your habit to do what you are accused of not doing, you may prevail.

Basic to the issue of oral or written consent is the question of how much risk are you willing to take. The dentist, in the case noted above, took considerably more risk than if he had had the consent in writing and signed by the patient, in which case there would have been less controversy at the trial. It is even possible that an attorney would refuse to take as a client a patient who had signed a consent agreement where the risks were clearly spelled out. You must weigh the risk are you willing to take against the effort you must expend to avoid it (see chapter 17).

Summary of the Elements Needed for a Consent to Be Valid

9.13   The trend in the courts and the legislatures during the past 25 years has been to demand that the health care provider disclose ever more information to the patient; thus, whereas consent used to suffice, now informed consent is necessary. Both the courts and the legislatures, in most jurisdictions, have provided specific guidelines as to the elements required in informed consent. In general:

1. The consent must be freely given.
2. The proposed treatment and its prognosis must be described.
3. The patient must be informed of the risks and benefits of the proposed treatment, including the prognosis if no treatment is provided.
4. Alternative treatment(s) to the one suggested, including their risks and benefits, must be described.
5. The patient must be given an opportunity to ask questions and have them answered.
6. All communication with the patient must be in language the patient understands.
7. The consent must be obtained from a patient authorized to grant consent.
8. The person who obtains the consent must be the treating doctor or one trained in obtaining consent.
9. If the doctor is not the person obtaining the consent, he must be available to answer any questions the patient may have.
10. The consent must be in writing in some jurisdictions.

In summary, when the treatment is invasive or the risks are significant, the details of the risk need to be spelled out in detail and the consent should be in writing, even if local law does not require it. The courts have noted that patients undergoing a surgical procedure may not pay careful attention to what is being said or to the details of what they are signing; therefore, unless the need for the invasive procedure is immediate, the patient should be given the consent form to take home to read. When the patient returns at the time the invasive procedure is scheduled, he should be advised to ask questions and then sign the form. The fact that the act upon which the suit is brought may have been necessary and of benefit to the patient, or that it was provided gratuitously, does not affect liability.

Informed Refusal: A New Caution

9.14   A new legal concept appears to be developing in the arena of malpractice litigation as an outgrowth of informed consent: informed refusal. In a medical malpractice case a woman was advised to undergo a PAP smear test. She refused. Later she developed cervical cancer and died. The physician was sued for failing to inform the patient sufficiently of the consequences of her refusal. Although in the minority, several members of the court agreed that the patient must be told of the possible consequences of refusal in order to make an intelligent decision in refusing a recommended course of treatment. There follow excerpts of the court's discussion on the issue of what the doctor informed the patient and what he should have informed the patient:

> Applying these principles, the court in Cobbs [a prior case], stated that a patient must be apprised not only of the "risks inherent in the procedure (prescribed, but also) the risks of a decision not to undergo the treatment, and the probability of a successful outcome of the treatment." This rule applies whether the procedure involves treatment or a diagnostic test. If a patient indicates that he or she is going to decline the risk-free test or treatment, then the doctor has the additional duty of advising of all material risks of which a reasonable person would want to be informed before deciding not to undergo the procedure.
>
> The duty to disclose was imposed in Cobbs so that patients might meaningfully exercise their right to make decisions about their own bodies. Further, the need for disclosure is not lessened because patients reject a recommended procedure. Such a decision does not alter "what has been termed the 'fiducial qualities' of the physician-patient relationship," since patients who reject a procedure are as unskilled in the medical sciences as those who consent. To now hold that patients who reject their physician's advice have the burden of inquiring as to the potential consequences of their decisions would be to contradict Cobbs. It must be remembered that Dr [T.] [the defendant] was not engaged in an arms-length transaction with Mrs [T.] [the plaintiff]. Clearly, under Cobbs, he was obligated to provide her with all the information material to her decision.[15]

[15]611 P2d 902 (1980).

Although the court, by a majority of one, did not require the doctor to tell all about the risks of refusal, the legal concept was accepted by the court. This was an important legal innovation.

Informed refusal is like informed consent. A patient who refuses to follow the recommendation of a treating dentist must be advised of the consequences of the refusal. For example, if you recommend that a patient undergo endodontic therapy, and the patient nonetheless elects to have the tooth extracted, you should make an entry to what has taken place in the patient's record, which should also state that the patient was informed of the risks of not complying with the recommendation. The most frequent dental recommendation that patients ignore is to seek the services of a periodontist. An entry in the patient's record of the recommendation, and the patient's refusal, may not be enough to satisfy the courts should the patient sue because of tooth loss due to periodontal disease. A form to document that the refusal was informed is easy to design (see chapter 17).

Abandonment and Dismissal of a Patient

Abandonment

10.1 The dentist-patient contract includes an implied duty to complete the services agreed to in the contract. A dentist who discontinues care without the approval of the patient is guilty of abandonment and becomes liable to the patient in a civil suit for damages (see chapter 3). As early as 1891, a judge in his charge to the jury stated:

> When a physician [dentist] engages . . . to attend a patient without limitation of time, he cannot cease his visits except, first, with the consent of the patient, or secondly upon giving the patient timely notice so that he may employ another doctor; or thirdly, when the condition of the patient is such as no longer to require medical treatment—and of that condition the physician must judge at his peril.[1]

In a 1962 case, a Kansas court stated:

> It is the settled rule that one who engages a physician . . . to treat his case impliedly engages him to attend throughout the illness or until his services are dispensed with. In other words, once initiated, the relationship of physician and patient continues until it is ended by the consent of the parties, revoked by the dismissal of the physician, or until his services are no longer needed. A physician has a right to withdraw from a case, but if he discontinues his services before the need for them is at an end, he is bound first to give due notice to the patient and afford the latter ample opportunity to secure other medical attendance of his own choice. If a physician abandons a case without giving his patient such notice and opportunity to procure the

[1] 15 NYS 675 (1891).

[2]369 P2d 238 (1962).

services of another physician, his conduct may subject him to the consequences and liability resulting from abandonment of the case.[2]

A case involving a dentist was decided some years later in the same state, in which the court made several comments related to abandonment. A Mrs G. had had a complete restoration of her teeth, complicated by "jaw thrust, a temporal mandibular joint abnormality, and peculiar physical sensitivity to the electrolytic interaction of some materials ordinarily used in dental repair and construction of dental appliances." She visited her dentist, one Dr D., complaining of "toothache"; he found "stress fractures in the metal core of the bridgework" and advised a complete restoration. He took impressions of her teeth to prepare for this on March 20 and 25, 1979. The case went on as follows:

Mrs [G.] continued to be in discomfort and able to ingest a soft-foods diet only. Her husband personally delivered a letter to Dr [D.] on March 27. She and her husband made telephone calls to the doctor's office on two or three later dates. The purpose of these communications was to seek relief from Mrs [G.'s] discomfort and commencement of a complete restoration program. Dr [D.] did not respond. He testified he had no personal knowledge of the telephone calls and he had not decided upon a restoration treatment program plan. Such a program requires numerous treatment procedures and steps over an extended period.

In late April, approximately one month following the delivery of her husband's letter and without notifying Dr [D.], Mrs [G.] contacted another dentist, a Dr [Z.]. Dr [Z.] first saw Mrs [G.] on May 1; the movement in the bridgework was observed, and a diagnosis of metal fractures in the bridgework was made. Dr [Z.] next saw her sometime in July when he instituted a comprehensive treatment program that was completed in December.

Mrs [G.] relied on other trial evidence to buttress her claim. She and her husband testified that her dental work "broke up" in late December 1978, or early January 1979, and that from then until the engagement of Dr [Z.]'s services late the following April, a total of 11 to 15 calls to Dr [D.]'s office seeking appointments for examination and care had resulted in only the five mentioned office visits. Mrs [G.] and her husband patently were disenchanted with perceived failure on the doctor's part to attend to Mrs [G.'s] complaints with the promptness and frequency they desired.

The record on appeal reflects no complaint made nor opinion ventured that any diagnoses made by Dr [D.] were erroneous or that any services rendered were deficient. We find the sole dispositive issue on appeal to be whether the trial evidence was sufficient to establish abandonment.

[Quoting a prior case] "*It is the settled rule that one who engages a physician . . . to treat his case impliedly engages him to attend throughout the illness or until his services are dispensed with. In other words, once initiated, the relationship of physician and patient continues until it is ended by the consent of the parties, revoked by the dismissal of the physician, or until his services are no longer needed. A physician has a right to withdraw from a case, but if he discontinues his services before the need for them is at an end, he is bound first to give due notice to the patient and afford the latter ample opportunity to secure other medical attendance of his own choice. If a physician abandons a case without giving his patient such notice and opportunity to procure the services of another physician, his conduct may subject him to the consequences and liability resulting from abandonment of the case.*" (Emphasis added.)

The judge concluded by stating the following:

1. Tortious medical [dental] malpractice includes abandonment.
2. Essence of "abandonment" is unilateral nonconsensual termination by medical [dental] practitioner; if practitioner withdraws from case before need for services is at end, he must give due notice to patient and afford patient opportunity to secure other medical attendance.
3. Nondiligence of dentist, that is, delay, inattention, and untimely rendition of services, is, if anything, negligence, not abandonment of patient.
4. Abandonment and negligence by medical practitioner are not same cause of action.[3]

[3]668 P2d 189 (1983).

In this case, the dentist was found not guilty of abandonment because the patient, on her own, elected to seek the services of another dentist.

In another Kansas case a physician dismissed a patient, suggesting "that he should go home and get help the best way he could; that he, the doctor, was sick of the whole deal and that the plaintiff was sick in his head and no medical doctor could do him any good." The court ruled the doctor was guilty of abandoning the patient.[4]

[4]424 P2d 488 (1967).

In an Ohio case, a dentist attempted to force the patient to surrender the right to sue by withholding treatment. The dentist was sanctioned by the Dental Board and found guilty of, among other things, abandoning the patient by not following up on an extraction, failing to inform the patient of a root tip left in the jaw, and demanding that the patient sign a release from liability.[5] Withholding treatment unless the patient gives up the right to sue is discussed in detail in chapter 3, section 11.

[5]453 NE2d 1262 (1982).

Failure to Follow up, Recall, or Be Available

10.1.1 The fact that no suit has been brought on a specific act that a dentist performs does not mean that such a suit will not be brought in the future. Only recently have suits been brought alleging negligence in the failure of a dentist to follow prescribed treatment protocols for patients who have a history of cardiac problems. And suits related to the health history are currently increasing. Prevention through anticipation is therefore best course.

There are situations in dental practice that may support a case of abandonment, though they have not yet been litigated. Clearly a dentist who completes a difficult extraction of a third molar and does not arrange for the patient to be seen following the extraction is guilty of abandonment. But what about dentists who inform their patients that their office will send out reminder notes for recall and never send one to a particular patient? Or what about dentists who know they will not be available to patients for a period of time and do not inform their patients of this nor make arrangements for them to receive care from a substitute practitioner? (See chapter 17.)

Risks

10.1.2   Dentists guilty of abandonment face two risks:

1. A civil suit brought by the patient for breach of one of the implied duties attached to the dentist-patient contract, or, more likely for malpractice, in negligently abandoning the patient
2. Disciplinary action by the licensing agency, eg, in New York, the rules of the board of regents includes the following as "unprofessional conduct": "abandoning or neglecting a patient or client under and in need of immediate professional care, without making reasonable arrangements for the continuation of such care"[6]

[6]Rules of the New York Board of Regents, § 29.2.

Dismissal of a Patient from the Practice

10.2   Not forgetting the above, in every dental practice, no matter how well run, there comes a time when continuing the treatment of a patient will no longer be in the best interests of either the patient or the doctor. There are times when interpersonal relationships break down, or the patient, because of important noncompliance with instructions, has compromised the success of the dentist's care. "I should have stopped treating the patient a long time ago" is something one often hears from dentists facing malpractice suits. A patient's chronic complaints are signs of trouble soon to come. Knowing when to get out and how to get out is not easy. The rules and advice given below are designed to help in such cases.

Dentists most often terminate treatment before it is complete because:

1. The patient has not fulfilled the payment agreement.
2. The patient has not cooperated in keeping appointments.
3. The patient has not complied with home-care instructions, thus jeopardizing a successful outcome of treatment.
4. The patient lied in completing the health history.
5. Interpersonal relationships between dentist and patient have broken down, despite reasonable attempts to restore them.

Any of the above is ample justification for terminating treatment and breaking the contract (see chapter 3). It is best also to discontinue treatment of patients who become antagonistic, seem litigious, or make unreasonable demands on the office staff's or your time and attention. When the time finally comes, you should hold a meeting with the patient, informing him that for any of the reasons listed above, and those that might be unique to the situation, you feel that a change in dentists would benefit him. It is important to convey to the patient that the benefit is the patient's, not yours. Include in the discussion that:

1. Until a new dentist agrees to treat the patient, you will provide emergency care related to any treatment you have provided.

2. You will cooperate by making the patient's records, radiographs, and other diagnostic aids and reports available to the succeeding dentist upon the patient's written request.

The conversation with the patient should be followed by a certified letter for which the patient must sign, recounting this discussion. Patients have been know to delay in such transfers and continue to seek the original dentist's care, but there comes a time when the ties with the patient must be cut.

You must give the patient enough time to obtain the services of a new dentist. The time depends upon the availability of services in the geographic area in which you practice. In an urban area it may be a few weeks, while in a rural area it may stretch into months. An important note for oral and maxillofacial surgeons: Failure to visit your patient in a hospital, when such visits are called for, is a presumption of abandonment.

Some Admonitions

10.2.1
1. The decision to discontinue and dismiss a patient from a practice must not in any way be due to the patient's race, national origin, religion, sex, sexual preference, age, or disability, ie, the presence of AIDS, HIV, hepatitis, tuberculosis, or any other infectious disease (see chapter 8).
2. The decision should not be made at a time when the patient's health may be compromised; for example, during the process of fabricating a fixed partial denture. What has been started must be finished. The dentist has another remedy at law if the patient will not pay: to sue to collect the fee. Holding the patient's health hostage to collect a fee may not be looked upon with favor by the courts.
3. Should the dismissed patient ask you to make a referral to a substitute dentist, you should advise her to make her own choice or to consult with neighbors, family, friends, or the local dental society. Any professional referral link between you and the new dentist may not be in your best legal interest. Should the patient's new dentist be alleged to be guilty of malpractice, you may be drawn into the suit as a codefendant for making the referral.

CHAPTER ELEVEN

Taking the
Medical-Dental History

Courts and the Health History

11.1　　Before examining or treating any patient the dentist must obtain a health history, both medical and dental. Many courts have held dentists to this as a standard of care. Though the history is not required to be written, it almost always is. With an oral history, any dispute at trial about any of the questions or answers will be decided by the jury. A written history in most instances will avert such dispute (an exception is noted in section 11.7).

　　In deciding a dental malpractice case in New York in which a patient contracted subacute bacterial endocarditis as a result of an extraction, a Supreme Court Judge had the following to say about the need for the dentist to complete a health history:

> One of the dentist's fundamental duties is to take a proper and careful medical and dental history of the patient's condition prior to treatment. In order to make a diagnosis, the dentist must first determine the patient's history, and it is an accepted rule of proper dental care that a patient's history must be taken by the dentist. Failure to ask the proper questions necessary to elicit an adequate history or failure to heed the patient's complaints and observations can be as much a dereliction of duty by the dentist as any act or commission in the course of his services.[1]

[1]497 NYS2d 401 (1985).

　　A similar case in Ohio, in which a dentist extracted teeth without taking a health history and as a result the patient suffered subacute bacterial endocarditis, led to a similar ruling. The court found the dentist "guilty of culpable negligence in performing oral surgery . . . without taking . . . any history of plaintiff's past or current condition of health," which omission "was the direct and proximate cause of plaintiff sustaining and suffering a foreseeable [sic] and avoidable complication of the surgical procedures performed by defendant."[2]

[2]223 NE2d 326 (1968).

In another case, a patient sued her doctor for his alleged negligence in prescribing Butazolidin, to which she allegedly suffered an allergic reaction. A jury returned a general verdict in favor of the doctor; the patient appealed. The doctor testified that during his examination he specifically asked the patient whether she had any allergies and that she responded "no." The patient denied that he had asked her this. Basing his treatment on this initial examination, the doctor gave the patient a 2-week prescription of Butazolidin. The patient developed Stevens-Johnson syndrome, possibly because of an allergic reaction to the Butazolidin. The doctor testified that a second history was taken from the patient upon her admission to the hospital for treatment of Stevens-Johnson syndrome and that she reported on this occasion a long history of allergies to numerous medications and contact substances. He further testified that he would not have prescribed Butazolidin if he had known of her history of allergies.

The appellate court upheld the decision of the lower court in favor of the doctor, stating that the following charge given to the jury was correct:

> I charge you that under the law of this state that a patient for his or her own safety must exercise ordinary care to give an accurate history to his or her treating physician. If a patient is aware that the physician is unaware of some aspect of the patient's medical history which may involve risk of harm to the patient, then ordinary care requires that the patient volunteer this additional information to the treating physician. Now, if the patient fails to make such a disclosure, he or she may be deemed to have voluntarily and unreasonably encountered a known risk.

The court went on to state, "the record contains evidence from which the jury could have concluded that appellant did not disclose to appellee all known information concerning her history of allergies. Such nondisclosure of relevant information may constitute contributory negligence on the part of the patient." In the same case, the court stated that the doctor was responsible for knowing all there is to know about the medication the patient is taking and the drugs he prescribed.[3]

[3]164 Ga App 236 (1981).

Another court ruled that a dentist is required to take a patient's blood pressure before administering an anesthetic and to know the information provided in the *Physicians' Desk Reference* (*PDR*). In this case, a man was brought to a dentist for the extraction of an impacted wisdom tooth. Without first taking his blood pressure, the dentist injected the man with "xylocaine, a local anesthetic containing epinephrine, which is a vasoconstrictor," and then removed the tooth. Afterwards, the man suffered a stroke and died. His wife sued the dentist for his failure to test the patient's blood pressure, given that the *Physicians Desk Reference* warns against the use of xylocaine containing epinephrine with patients suffering from hypertension. The court concluded:

> Here, a simple test of a few minutes' duration which [the defendant] presumably was capable of administering, would have informed the defendant that [the plaintiff] had high blood pressure. Clearly . . . plaintiff was entitled

[4]621 P2d 787 (1980).

to be informed of this "simple" test which possibly might have prevented his stroke, and subsequent disability and death.[4]

Common Errors in History Taking

11.2   The errors most commonly associated with medical histories are:

1. Failure to discover a potential drug incompatibility
2. Failure to learn of a drug allergy, or potential drug allergy
3. Failure to discover a medical condition that may result in a serious injury to the patient as a result of treatment, eg, cardiac problems or diabetes

Errors most commonly associated with dental histories are:

1. Failure to determine that the patient presented with a history of problems associated with temporomandibular dysfunction
2. Failure to discover that the patient exhibited a reaction to the administration of a local anesthetic, or other drugs or medications administered in the course of treatment
3. Failure to discover problems associated with periodontal disease

There are a host of other problems associated with failures in history taking, but none appear in court cases as frequently as these.

Errors in taking the patient's health history have emerged as one of the more serious legal risks in dental practice. Patients may die or suffer significant and permanent injury; dentists may lose a malpractice suit the award in which may exceed the level of their insurance. Injuries caused by such errors have resulted in some of the largest awards and settlements against general dentists. But even if the insurance policy covers the financial loss, the dentist will still suffer a loss of reputation, the stress associated with an uneasy conscience, and allegations of substandard care and consequent injury, all exposed to the public, other patients, and the dentist's colleagues.

The Problem

11.3   The basic problem is that many dentists believe all they need do is have the patient complete a self-administered form; that if all the patient's written responses appear negative, treatment may then begin. By contrast, the prudent dentist knows that this is only the first of many steps that must be taken to secure an accurate and complete health history.

Matter of Documentation

11.4   We can quickly dispense with the notion that an unrecorded oral history will meet the test of a adequate care. It will not! The history must be written. Keep in mind that you must document each step in the history-taking process: who completed the history form; who supervised the patient during the process if not the dentist; who reviewed the form and discussed it with the patient; and when each step was completed. Notes that the form was completed and reviewed should be entered on the treatment record. Only when the process of history-taking is complete can the dentist arrive at a definitive diagnosis and, after consultation with the patient, a treatment plan.

The Process

11.5   Obtaining a complete health history is a three-step procedure. First, the patient should complete a medical-dental history form. Second, the doctor should interview the patient. Third, health information should be secured from third-party sources as described below.

Keep in mind that the history form is primarily objective and provides the dentist no conclusive means of learning all there is to know about the patient's previous dental experiences, oral habits, fears, and expectations. An interview should elicit information that is both objective and subjective. It should include questions whose answers generate discussion. Because these questions depend to a large extent on the answers to questions on the history form, it is not possible to provide the dentist with a set that can be asked of all patients.

A dentist has a professional and legal duty to obtain from all available sources health information essential to the safe provision of dental care. The initial source of information is the patient or, for a minor, the parent or guardian. But information may also be obtained from a physician, another dentist, a public health nurse, etc, with the permission of the patient or parent, and in accordance with the administrative rules of the agency or facility that has custody of the health information. Under special circumstances, schools, teachers, and school nurses may be a source of additional health information about minors; but these sources should not substitute for the parent or guardian.

The completed health history form—supplemented by a discussion with the patient, a review of consultation reports when indicated, a study of the results of tests and radiographs, and a clinical examination—will lead to an accurate evaluation of the patient's health status.

Before presenting the self-administered form to the patient, a member of the office staff specially trained in obtaining an initial health history should tell the patient:

1. The dentist and other provider personnel need to know specifics of the past and present health history and medical status of the patient, if they are to provide care that is compatible with the patient's health status and do nothing to compromise the patient's health.
2. All questions must be answered, and answered truthfully.
3. If the patient is confused by any question, or if uncertain about an answer, the patient should ask for assistance.
4. The doctor will discuss the patient's responses to the heath history questions and any other matter related to health history and status that the patient wishes to discuss.

5. All this information will remain confidential, unless the patient grants permission to release the information—except that if the patient agrees to visit a specialist at the request of the dentist, there is an implied waiver of confidentiality of the information held by the referring dentist. If the information relates to AIDS or HIV status, the patient should be told that sharing this information with the specialist is important in the continued provision of care (see chapter 8).

The patient should be given the blank form and told to read the instructions carefully, complete all the answers using a pen supplied by the office (use black ball point), and ask for help if there is a problem in answering any question. The dentist should make certain that someone is available to help the patient. Most important, whoever administers the form should be sure that there are no blanks when the form is completed!

The Form

11.6   At the very top of the form there should be a place for the receptionist to type the patient's name and any other identifying information. It is not uncommon for pages to be misfiled or become separated from the patient's folder.

    Next, the following statements should appear at the beginning of the history section:

> I understand that honest answers to the questions stated below are important to the provision of my dental care, and I will answer them to the best of my ability.
> I understand that if I am uncertain about the question or how the question relates to my health status, I must discuss the problem with the doctor or a member of the office staff.
> I understand that all questions must be answered.
> I understand that the information I provide will not be released without my express permission.

And at the end of the form:

> I understand that should there be a change in my health during my dental treatment, I am to inform the dentist at the earliest possible time. (This statement does not obviate the need for histories to be updated.)

Space should be left for the patient's signature, the date, and the signature of a witness. If someone other than the patient completes the form, that person should sign her name and indicate her relationship to the patient. Finally, at the very end of the form the following should be included:

> Reviewed and discussed with the patient by Dr _____, Date _____.

Faulty Forms

11.7   In the following case the history form played a critical part. The court described what had taken place as follows:

In this dental malpractice action, the plaintiff is a young man with a history of rheumatic fever with complications. He alleged that he sustained serious injuries due to an infection that followed the extraction of a tooth without appropriate special precautions by appellant, who was not aware of plaintiff's medical problems. Liability was premised on appellant's purported failure to take a proper medical history, and resolution of this issue turned upon several disputed questions involving the circumstances under which a medical history form was completed.

Before extracting the offending tooth, the dentist took X rays of the infected area and gave the history form to the patient, asking him to complete it while the dentist developed the films. A friend of the patient testified that he partially completed the form in the waiting room, but answered no questions related to the health history of the patient. The patient, a minor, stated that he was in too much pain from the infected tooth to complete the form himself; he did, however, sign the form. When the form, the standard American Dental Association health history form carrying the association's seal, was presented to the court, all answers to the health history questions were negative; a line was drawn under the "No" space on the form following each question, including the question about heart conditions. The friend, the patient, and the dentist all denied completing the form. So who did it? At the time of the trial, the friend was in the Navy. The jury believed the friend.[5]

[5]497 NYS2d 401 (1985).

Clearly, history forms that simply require a patient to place a check mark in a "Yes / No" column, to circle a "Yes / No" answer, or to underline a "Yes" or "No" do not conform to good risk management practice. Recent court decisions, including the one reported above, have depended upon a determination of who made the check mark, circle, or underline, and each side may deny making such simple marks. Open-ended questions, which require the patient to write out answers subject to analysis by handwriting experts, will avert such doubts. Dentists should therefore use such questions on their forms.

There are additional types of faulty history forms on the market, as the following case shows. A patient brought suit against her dentist and other medical providers for negligent treatment, and, additionally, a brought products liability claim against defendant "Unknown Seller of Medical Form," alleging that this unknown seller sold a defective medical history intake form to her dentist, which he used in her treatment. She alleged that the form was defective in that it failed to inquire whether she had a history of heart murmur, cardiac valvular disease, or mitral valve prolapse, and that as a direct and proximate result of this failure, plaintiff suffered bacterial endocarditis, coma, brain artery aneurysm, and hemiparesis. Attached to the complaint was the affidavit of plaintiff's attorney stating that the name of the seller of the medical form was unknown and could not be determined at that time.

In deciding, the court stated:

Given these considerations we find that the medical form in question was a service provided to the dentist rather than a product subject to strict liability. Defendant's form merely supplied the dentist with a short list of general questions to be answered by the patient. Specifically, the form asked, under the subtitle "Health Questions," the following yes/no questions: "Do you feel you are now in good health?" "Are you presently under a doctor's care?" "Have you ever been told you had high blood pressure?" "Have you had heart trouble, rheumatic fever, diabetes, or hepatitis?" "Have you ever had trouble with bleeding from injuries, or after surgery or extractions?" "Are you allergic to, or have you had an unusual reaction to, any drug or local anesthetic?" In addition, the form asked what pills or medication the patient was presently taking, the name and address of her physician, and the date of her last dental visit.

Given the generality of the questions and the brevity of the form, we find that it would be unreasonable to expect that the form was intended to be a comprehensive inquiry as to a patient's medical history, and there was no evidence presented that defendant represented it as such. Rather, the apparent function of the form was to provide dentists with a list of broad questions to be answered by patients and then supplemented by the dentist as deemed appropriate. It thus appears that the gravamen of plaintiff's complaint is not the form itself; rather, it is the dentist's alleged negligent conduct in his use or reliance on the form. Such errors of professional judgment are held to the standard of reasonable skill under the concept of negligence, and strict liability simply does not come into play.[6]

[6]554 NE2d 773 (1990).

Health-Related Questions

11.8   Questions related to the health history of the patient conveniently fall into two categories, medical and dental, though these areas overlap.

The medical portion of the form should include time-dependent questions about prior as well as present illnesses and complaints, such as heart conditions, bleeding problems, and infection status. It should also include psycho-social questions eliciting attitudes toward general health care and dental health care, and questions about habits that may affect health. It must be particularly thorough in establishing drug history, past allergic reactions, and current drug use because anesthetics and other medications that may be necessary to complete dental treatment may interact—sometimes fatally—with prescriptions, over-the-counter drugs, and illicit drugs. Patients must be told of the crucial importance of informing the doctor of all drugs and medications they are currently taking, of whether they are recovering alcoholics or drug users, current or past, of whether they have AIDS or are HIV-positive. In most jurisdictions, all patients must be asked the same questions: Dentists are advised to check local law. Patients must be reassured that this information will remain confidential. The form should also include the name, address, and phone number of the patient's current physician.

The dental portion of the form should include, in addition to the usual questions about dental history, questions that would raise suspicions about the patients' periodontal and temporomandibular status. It is important to document not only patients' current dental complaint but also their general habits. Questions about smoking, diet and nutrition, attitudes toward dental care, and sexual-social habits may be included in the questionnaire or reserved for the interview and discussion. However, if not included in the questionnaire, they should be documented in a space provided on the form or in the patient's treatment record.

History Updates

11.9   The patient's medical and dental status should be monitored at intervals appropriate to the patient's age and medical and dental histories. There is no rule about how often it should be done; this is a professional judgment the dentist should make based on the individual patient's health history and status. For example, if the patient is 20 years of age with no apparent health problems, an update may be completed at each recall visit with the simple question, "Have there been any changes in your health since your last visit?" If the answer is *yes,* it may be prudent to have the patient fill out a complete history form.

However, if the patient is 60 years of age and has a history of cardiac problems, a more thorough update at each recall visit may be necessary. At the appropriate time the patient should be given a copy of his most recently completed self-administered history form for review. If there are no changes, it should be noted in the patient's record or on a form specially designed for that purpose. If the patient indicates that changes have taken place, it may be advisable to have the patient complete another history form and for the dentist to repeat the entire history taking process.

To lessen health risk to the patient and legal risk to the dentist, it is best to err on the side of needless effort.

Drug and Medication Log

11.10   A separate drug and medication log should be kept for each patient. This is in addition to entries made on the patient's record of the drugs and medications the dentist applies or prescribes. Both entries should include any adverse reactions the patient experienced as a result of taking the drug or medication. The entry of this information in a separate log makes it easy for the dentist to review it without having to go through many pages of the patient's record.

Summary Guide in History Taking

11.11   1. Without exception, a health history should be completed on each patient treated or examined in the office.
2. The history form must remain a permanent part of the patient's record.
3. It should be part of the regular office procedure.
4. Questions should be limited to those that are essential to the diagnosis and care of the patient.
5. There should be evidence that the patient understood the questions and the importance of providing accurate answers. There should be someone specially trained in the office to assist patients who are confused about any question.
6. All questions should be answered; there should be no blank spaces on the completed form.
7. The patient should be required to write something in answer to each question. This will avert any doubt about who entered the responses. Forms with simple "yes / no" columns should be avoided.

8. The answers on the history form should be written with a black ballpoint pen supplied by the office, and never with a pencil.

9. A drug and medication log should be kept.

10. There should be an open-ended, catch-all question about the patient's health status.

11. The patient should be instructed that changes in health must be reported to the office at the earliest possible time.

12. The history must be signed and dated by the patient, or if the patient is a minor, by the parent or guardian.

13. Releases to request and provide health information from and to appropriate sources should be obtained from the patient.

14. The history must be reviewed by the treating practitioner and documented in the record that it was reviewed.

15. If someone other than the patient completed the questionnaire, that individual and his relationship to the patient should be recorded on the form.

16. History updates should be completed on each patient at intervals consistent with the general health of the patient. The decision as to their frequency is professional, not legal.

17. The name, address, and phone number of the patient's current physician must be included on the history form.

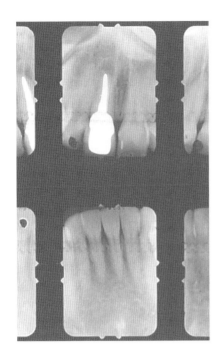

CHAPTER TWELVE

Patient Records

Why Keep Patient Treatment Records?

12.1

[1]38 Cal App 3rd 558; 11 CalRptr 296 (1974).

[2]453 NYS2d 836 (1982).

[3]Rules of the Board of Regents, § 29.2 (6).

[4]Louisell DW, Williams H. Medical Malpractice. New York: Matthew Bender, 1998.

[5]Rules of the Board of Regents, § 29.2 (3).

Legal experts agree on the importance of accurate and detailed patient records. A California judge, in deciding a case against a physician, stated, "the inability of the physician to produce the original of the clinical record concerning his treatment of the plaintiff creates a strong inference of consciousness of guilt."[1] A judge in New York stated, "a patient record so sparse as to be accurate and meaningful only to the recording physician fails to meet the intent of the requirement to maintain records which 'accurately reflect the evaluation and treatment of the patient.'"[2] The judge was quoting the law on record keeping under the Rules of the Board of Regents of the state.[3] The author and editor of a major text on medical and dental malpractice wrote the following about dentists and their record-keeping habits, "Dentists seem to be among the worst record keepers. It is not unusual for the complete dental records to consist mainly or solely of a billing chart. Such scant records should be considered malpractice in and of themselves."[4]

One of the professional responsibilities of all health practitioners is to keep accurate records of the treatment they provide their patients. Such records may prove the best defense in a malpractice suit, while poor records are almost certain to result in the settlement of a claim, or the loss of a suit. In many states, New York among them, maintaining a record of patient treatment is legally required. The New York Rules of the Board of Regents list as Unprofessional Conduct: "failing to maintain a record for each patient which accurately reflects the evaluation and treatment of the patient."[5]

Note the word *accurately* here. A doctor found guilty of maintaining inaccurate records appealed the decision of the licensing agency. The appellate court stated:

> The purpose of the record-keeping requirement is, at least in part, to provide meaningful medical information to other practitioners should the patient transfer to a new physician or should the treating physician be unavailable for any reason. Petitioner's records certainly do not meet this standard of objectively meaningful medical information. Even petitioner's own witness, Dr [M.], when asked if petitioner's method of record keeping reflected the evaluation and treatment of a patient, replied that if he were just to look at one of petitioner's records, without any explanation or interpretation from petitioner, "I don't think I'd get too much information from it." Furthermore, unprofessional conduct is also defined as including failure to make a patient's records available to succeeding practitioners, after a proper request (8 NYCRR 29.2[6]). Inadequate records clearly would make this requirement to provide records to other medical personnel meaningless. Thus, for the foregoing reasons, a patient record so sparse as to be accurate and meaningful only to the recording physician fails to meet the intent of the requirement to maintain records which "accurately reflects the evaluation and treatment of the patient" (8 NYCRR 29.2[3]).[6]

[6]453 NYS2d 836 (1982).

For a record to be meaningful to another practitioner it must be legible and use only abbreviations that are universally understood by practitioners from the same school of practice.

A Brief History of Dental Records

12.2   At first, dental records were designed to record charges for service, payments, and balances. Treatment was recorded primarily to explain the charges. Usually, such records were kept on 5 × 8–inch cards, with the patient's name at the top and the financial information beneath. In the late 1940s and into the 1950s, dentists began to recognize that systemic pathology and diseases manifested themselves in the oral cavity, and that they participated in the treatment of a "whole patient." Printed dental-records systems were offered for sale to the profession, and dentists added sketchy medical histories to their treatment and financial records. In the 1960s and 1970s, practice-management packages became popular. These included extensive record-keeping systems, with medical (health) history forms, diagnostic charts, treatment planning forms, recall records, and periodontal charts, as well as the usual treatment records. As in the past, financial information remained an integral part of the form. With third-party payment plans came forms to note information necessary for third-party participation.

Meanwhile changes in the courts and legislatures were underway that would have a major effect on these forms and systems. The crisis in dental malpractice of the early 1980s revealed major problems in record keeping. Because the forms themselves often omitted essential matters, or were designed so that dentists commonly omitted essential information, and because dentists were not guided in completing them, documentation of diagnosis, treatment planning, treatment, outcomes, consents, etc, was often lacking. (For problems related to the medical history form, see chapter 11.) Today, courts and legislatures view dental records as no less important to patient care than the treatment itself; the patient record has emerged as a legal document. Informal notes made on 5 × 8–inch cards, once universal and still in use in some places, cannot serve the purposes now expected of such records.

Ownership

12.3   For many years, dentists and physicians considered the records they kept relating to the care of their patients their exclusive property. They seldom if ever gave these records or copies of them to their patients. If patients requested that records be sent to other doctors, they could, and often did, refuse. All this changed radically over a period of approximately 10 years, and this change can be traced in a series of New York court decisions.

In a 1968 case, a deceased physician had directed his executor in his will "to burn and destroy all of his office records and files without opening or examining them." The purpose, it was thought, was to maintain the confidentiality of what was contained in the records. However, several patients demanded that the executor deliver their medical records to them, and, when he refused, brought an action against him. The court in its ruling stated:

> The records are medical and technical, personal and often informal. Standing alone they are meaningless to the patient but of value to the physician and perhaps to a succeeding physician. The patient, however, or one responsible for him, is entitled to know the nature of the illness and the general course or regimen of therapy employed by his physician. The patient's dental record is treated by the courts and government agencies as a legal document. It serves many purposes in the judicial process. It contains information about the patient's complaint, health history, the basis for the diagnosis, and it reports all treatment rendered, the patient's reaction to treatment, and the results of the treatment. Case law requires that health practitioners keep accurate records of the diagnosis and treatment of their patients. They constitute an essential part of patient care. *Treating a patient without maintaining accurate records is considered a serious departure from an acceptable level of care as defined by the courts.* Some jurisdictions require that accurate records be kept as part of the rules and regulations of administrative health or licensing agencies. (Emphasis added.)

The court, however, ruled against the patients:

> It is, accordingly, the decision of this Court that the specific relief demanded by the petitioners be denied in that the records and notes requested by petitioners will not be delivered to petitioners personally. The executor should make available the records and notes pertaining to the petitioners to the succeeding physician of the petitioners upon the authorized request of the petitioners.[7]

[7]292 NYS2d 806 (1968).

The outcome was clear: The records must not be destroyed and need not be given to patients; they must be sent to physicians identified by the patients.

Compare this case with one decided 9 years later, in 1977, in the same state. The facts were as follows: A patient retained an attorney "to investigate injuries she sustained after undergoing dental treatment" by her dentist over a period of years and to "bring suit against the person or persons responsible in the event that our investigation should disclose evidence of malpractice." She "complains that after receiving treatment from the dentist for a period of over two years she still experiences great pain in her mouth and jaw area"; that "after consulting with other dentists, she was advised that she is suffering from periodontal disease which is in an advanced stage so as to require either extensive dental reconstructive work or in the alternative removal of her teeth"; and that her lawyer has been advised "by several periodontists that in order to render an opinion as to whether the diagnostic and dental care rendered to his client, the patient, was properly administered it would be necessary to review the treatment and dental records including x-rays kept by the dentist in connection with his diagnosis and treatment." Her lawyer stated that he made a written request to the dentist for access to his client's dental records and that, in response, he received a telephone call from a representative of the Public Service Mutual Insurance Company, the dentist's insurance carrier, who told him "that inspection of respondent's records would not be permitted."

The dentist's lawyer claimed that he was aware of "no provision in the law that requires the doctor to turn over copies of his records at this time." In reply, patient's lawyer expressed dismay, a sentiment shared by the Court: In "this day and age when members of the Bar are being criticized for bringing non-meritorious actions in medical malpractice, counsel for [the defendant] would deny [the patient's] attorneys the ability to verify the merits of [the patient's] complaint prior to commencement of an action." The problem faced by the patient's attorney was that only once a suit was filed could he obtain, under the rules of discovery, a copy of the records of the patient held by the dentist; and yet he could not bring suit without reviewing these records to discover if there were sufficient grounds for one. The courts had not faced this problem before (see chapter 13). In deciding, the court began by calling attention to the current law:

> Before an action is commenced, disclosure to aid in bringing an action . . . may be obtained, but only by court order. . . .
>
> It has often been held that the foregoing provisions authorize disclosure to aid in the framing of a claim for a known cause of action, but . . . may not be used by a potential claimant to determine whether he has a cause of action.
>
> More importantly, although a doctor or dentist may well have the *primary custodial rights* to the treatment records of his patients, it does not follow that his rights are exclusive and that the patient has no rights with respect thereto. To the contrary, in my view, the patient has a *"property" right* sufficient to afford her the privilege of reasonable access to her medical and dental records.[8] (Emphasis added.)

[8]399 NYS2d 584 (1977).

The court granted the patient the right to obtain the information in her dentist's record of her care. And so it was established by case law that the practitioner has the *custodial right* to the patient record, while the patient has the *property right* to the information contained in the record. The doctor owns the paper on which the information is recorded; the patient owns the information itself.

As a result of case law and patient rights' advocates, the black letter law of all states now includes a provision entitling patients to the information contained in their records. In some states, such as New York, the law requires a health practitioner to provide the patient, upon written request, with a copy of the record or to have the record forwarded to whomever the patient wishes. A duplication fee may be charged ($0.75 per page—there is no standard fee for the duplication of radiographs), but the copies may not be withheld should the patient owe a fee for a past service, and if the patient is not able to pay the fee, the copies must be provided at no charge. In jurisdictions where the patient has a right to obtain the record, the right is limited to a *copy*, not to the *original* record (see chapter 17). In other states, the practitioner is required only to provide the patient with a detailed summary of the treatment the patient received. In those states in which the patient has a right to a copy, dentists must keep in mind that whatever they write on the record may be seen by the patient and the patient's attorney (see chapters 2 and 13).

All dentists must know the local law concerning their patients' right to their records or to the information contained in their records.

Purpose and Contents of the Treatment Record

12.4   All states, by black letter law, require that health practitioners maintain records of their patients. The same is required in case law. All third-party payers require that records be kept; some go so far as to indicate what information the records must contain.

Of course, the first and most important reason to keep such records is good patient care, but they may serve a number of other purposes, such as:

1. Recording the health status of the patient at the time of the initial examination
2. Recording the treatment provided to the patient
3. Providing legal documentation on behalf of the patient, the courts, third-party payers, or the patient's heirs
4. Providing legal documentation in the defense of legal claims made against the dentist
5. Fulfilling the laws regulating professional practice
6. Advancing medical research
7. Contributing to quality assessment and assurance
8. Providing communication among health practitioners
9. Helping identify victims of a mass disaster

The dental records of a patient should provide logical, clear, concise documentation of what took place during the treatment of the patient's dental problem or disease. The records should include all the essential information related to the care of the patient:

1. Specifics, in detail, of the treatment provided
2. Reactions to treatment, adverse and positive
3. Doctor and patient comments
4. Radiographs
5. Prescriptions
6. Laboratory authorizations

7. Correspondence
8. Consultations requested and reports
9. Consents
10. A drug and medication log
11. Financial information and agreements
12. Demographic information
13. Medical and dental history
14. Waivers and authorizations
15. Insurance information and claims submitted
16. Contact persons in case of emergencies
17. Other information unique to the specific patient's needs

Maintaining a good patient record is essential to the defense of a case of alleged malpractice, breach of contract, or lack of informed consent. The information contained on the patient's record is often the critical point in the trial of a case against a dentist. If the record is poor it may serve to undermine the defense. If you are aware of an impending lawsuit against you, you must not add to, delete, or modify information on a record; you may, however, write on a separate page what you recall about the case, enter the date you write the information, and sign the entry. For example, suppose during the process of filing a canal during endodontic therapy the tip of a reamer fractures, you decide to allow it to remain in the canal, and you inform the patient orally of this but do not enter it on the record. After a suit is filed against you, it is good practice to enter your recall of this on a separate page. During the trial you will be asked if you told the patient about the event, and reminded how long ago the event took place and how difficult it is to remember accurately over such a long period of time. If you recall and record the incident between its occurrence and the trial, that period will be shortened.

Financial information has no place on the treatment record; keep track of financial agreements, charges, and payments elsewhere. During a malpractice trial, the jury will view the whole record entered into evidence, and may be influenced by what the dentist charged for his services, especially if they think it excessive.

The treatment record should be written in black ink or black ballpoint pen. It should be neat, well organized, and easily read. A sloppy record implies a sloppy dentist and has a negative effect upon the jury and judge. The record should not include any abbreviations unique to the office; all abbreviations should be easily understood by any dentist. Courts require such legibility to ensure that if the original dentist is not available, or if the patient chooses to change dentists, whoever cares for the patient will have no difficulty understanding that dentist's records. Moreover, a well organized, legible, complete record, which bears no evidence that it has been tampered with following notification that a suit is contemplated, will have a positive effect upon the judge, jury, and the patient's lawyer. Often a well-kept, accurate, and complete record will avert a potential lawsuit.

Retention of Treatment Records

12.5   Records should be kept as long as possible. At the very least, they must be kept as long as the local law requires. The law in New York about keeping patient records is in Section 29.2 of the Rules of the Board of Regents:

> a. Unprofessional conduct shall also include, in the professions of: . . . dentistry, dental hygiene,
> 3. Failing to maintain a record for each patient which accurately reflects the evaluation and treatment of the patient. Unless otherwise provided by law, all patient records must be retained for at least six years. . . . [R]ecords of minor patients must be retained for at least 6 years, and until 1 year after the minor patient reaches the age of 21 years; . . .

Other states have similar rules, but the retention times vary. You are advised to check the law in the state in which you practice.

However, a lawsuit may well be brought after the date at which time the legal requirement has expired. Even the statute of limitations is not a sure guide because many cases have been brought after the statute has been thought to run. In discovery states, like Massachusetts, it does not begin to run until the patient discovered, or should have discovered, the act that produced the injury; and even in occurrence states such as New York, where the statute begins to run at the time the act occurs, there are exceptions in cases of fraud, foreign bodies, and continuous treatment (see chapter 5). A good rule is to retain the records of adults for 10 years following their last visit and of minors for 10 years after they reach majority. A better rule is to keep them forever. The death of a patient or dentist should have no effect on these rules because the heirs of a deceased patient may sue the heirs of a deceased dentist.

Never surrender the original of a record or radiograph to anyone, except by court order. Keep in mind what the California judge stated about the need to produce the original of the patient's treatment record as noted above.[9]

[9]38 Cal App 3rd 558; 11 CalRptr 296 (1974).

Confidentiality

12.6   Copies of patients' records, or information about patients and their treatment, should not be given to anyone without the patients' express written authorization. To reveal the information or supply the records, even copies or oral statements, may form the basis of a civil suit for breach of confidentiality or invasion of privacy. In most jurisdictions it is against the law, as it is in New York, where the Rules of the Board of Regents in Section 29 list Unprofessional Conduct as "revealing of personally identifiable facts, data or information obtained in a professional capacity without the prior consent of the patient or client, except as authorized or required by law." Also, it is a violation of professional ethics as contained in the Principles of Ethics and Code of Professional Conduct of the American Dental Association, Section 1B, which states, "Dentists are obliged to safeguard the confidentiality of patient records. Dentists shall maintain patient records in a manner consistent with the welfare of the patient." Courts often take judicial notice of a profession's code of ethics in determining the standard of conduct to which a member of that profession is to be held.

If you receive a letter from an attorney, or from any other source including another dentist, asking to be sent a copy of a patient's record, do not comply unless a permission to release the record, signed by the patient, accompanies the request.

Signatures on Treatment Records

12.7   Anyone authorized by the owner of the practice may enter information on the patient's record. If more than one person in the office does so, each entry should be signed or initialed. A dentist who is uncertain about the source of an entry will not seem credible at a trial. To avoid the problem, the office should keep a sample of the signature and initials of each person in the office permitted to make entries on the patients' records.

Spoliation of Records

12.8   Spoliation is defined as the intentional, reckless, or negligent destruction, loss, material alteration, or obstruction of evidence that is relevant to litigation. To engage in such activity with patients' records is a serious violation of trust and may bring seriously unpleasant consequences. As noted previously, patients' treatment records are legal documents. To tamper with them for the purpose of depriving patients of a fair and honest appraisal of their rights in court may constitute a crime for which the punishment may be severe. A record that has been altered, no matter how slightly, in anticipation of a trial damages a dentist's credibility irreparably.

Records at the Trial

12.9   In all jurisdictions, once a suit has been brought against you, the patient's attorney may obtain a copy of the patient's record, or may view the original in your presence and that of your attorney. During the course of a trial, the judge and jury will view the original record, and the defendant dentist will be called upon to explain each entry, and any notation, no matter how insignificant it may appear. The same is true during the course of an examination before trial (EBT). If it is discovered during the trial or the EBT that the record has been altered in any way following notification of a suit, all other entries on the record become suspect, and the defendant's testimony, wherever it conflicts with that of the plaintiff, will not be believed by the jury.

The outcome of many suits against dentists are decided on the content and quality of patient records. For the treating doctor, the record is the only documentation of the entire course of treatment. Memory alone is often viewed as self-serving, and, as one court put it, "the shortest written word lasts longer than the longest memory." In cases in which the doctor and patient disagree on what took place and there is no written documentation of the event, the question may be settled in court by deciding who seems most believable. This can be risky for the doctor (see chapter 13).

Here are three examples of how not to handle records at trial:

1. A defendant-dentist submitted his records to his attorney, and what was thought to be a copy to the patient's attorney. At the EBT it was discovered, when both were compared, that they were different. Under pressure the dentist admitted that he made some self-serving changes on the copy he submitted to the plaintiff's attorney. The insurance company for the dentist rushed to settle the claim, and the company did not renew the dentist's policy.
2. Following notice of a suit, a dentist submitted to his attorney a patient's treatment record that appeared to cover 8 years of treatment; however, all the entries appeared, even to a casual observer, to have been made by the same person and at the same time; the handwriting was the same throughout the years; and the ink was identical in color and appearance. Under questioning by his attorney the dentist admitted having written the entire record the night before their meeting. He stated that he kept no treatment records on any of his patients but was able to reconstruct the treatment on the subject patient from the insurance claim forms submitted to the patient's insurance company. The dentist in this case suffered the same fate as the dentist in the one above.
3. The third case involves the lack of the health history rather than a treatment record. Following the filing of a suit against an oral and maxillofacial surgeon, the attorney assigned by his insurance company asked him to submit a copy of the patient's records. The attorney discovered that no health history was included. When questioned, the surgeon admitted he had never completed a written history on any patient he treated. He took his patients' histories orally, and never made any notes of them on the treatment record. To become an oral and maxillofacial surgeon he had gone through years of training in a hospital where the taking of a written health history is mandatory. His decision to take a short-cut in his private office was as unfortunate as it was strange: His policy was not renewed, and the suit was settled for an excessive amount.

12.10 Advice to Employee-Dentists and Those Selling a Practice

Employee-Dentists and Patient Records

12.10.1 Employee-dentists face unique circumstances as to patient records. Courts have determined that the original records kept by an employee-dentist belong to the practice and not the employee. Should the employee leave the practice, whether voluntarily or by termination of employment, the employee's patient records must remain with the employer. The parties may agree to modify these rules, however, and there is one modification essential to the employee-dentist's legal protection. As noted above, the original of a patient's treatment records are essential in the defense of a claim, assuming the records meet acceptable standards. Therefore, employee-dentists should have the following terms included in the employment contract:

1. The original treatment records of all patients treated by the former employee shall be maintained for a period of 10 years by the employer following the termination of the employment of the employee.
2. Should the former employee need the original treatment record of any patient treated by her during the period of his employment for any judicial proceeding, the employer shall deliver the original record to the former employee within 10 days of his written request.

Records and the Sale of a Practice

12.10.2   It is customary in the sale of a dental practice to transfer the patients' records to the purchaser; but this act may invite many legal difficulties. Unless they have given their consent to this transfer, patients may sue for breach of confidentiality. In those states where health practitioners are required by law to retain patients' records for a specified time, the transfer may be illegal. Perhaps the most important consequence is that which arises if a seller-dentist is sued by a former patient. The records, without which the suit will undoubtedly be lost, may be difficult to obtain from the buyer-dentist. The solution to the problem is not simple. The contract of sale should include a provision that the original (not just a copy) of a patient's record shall be delivered to the seller in the event it is needed to defend a lawsuit or in any other judicial proceeding. However, this will not recover records that are lost or destroyed. To prevent the buyer from destroying the records of patients who have not elected to be treated by the buyer, the agreement of sale should require the buyer to retain the originals (not copies) of all patient records for a period of 10 years following the transfer of the practice.

Computer Records

12.11   Computer-generated records are admissible into evidence in judicial proceedings. However, the weight given to them by judge and jury will depend upon their appearance of validity. A hard copy, signed by the provider of care and dated at the time the service was rendered will have the same weight as a traditional record. A hard copy produced expressly for the judicial proceeding will have less weight. Though technology is being developed that will allow computer-entered data that cannot be altered once entered, or that will lock in entries at a fixed time and thus prevent alterations at any later time or date, a well-written record is still the best evidence. You must balance the benefits of a computer record system with the risks (see chapter 17).

Appointment Book

12.12   The appointment book kept in the dental office has taken on new meaning in the law; it is an official record of the practice and should be maintained in the same manner as the patient treatment record. Its importance in the trial of malpractice should not be underestimated. One of the important factors in a trial in which a dentist is found guilty of negligence is to the degree to which the patient contributed to the injury. Often, if it can be shown that the patient was guilty of no-shows, repeated broken appointments, frequent change of appointments, and/or consistent late arrivals, the jury may be told by the judge that the patient was guilty of comparative or contributory negligence, and that the plaintiff's award should be reduced by the percentage the jury feels the patient contributed to his injury (see chapter 4).

The following case report demonstrates the importance of the appointment book. A doctor submitted his patient's records during the discovery period of a medical malpractice action. The patient's lawyer wished to examine the office appointment book as well as the original or carbon copies of the telephone message pad book. He filed a motion to obtain them. The book that the lawyer sought was for 3 years before the time the motion was made. The court stated the book should be made available, with all names other than the patient's stricken.[10]

[10]464 NYS2d 191 (1983).

The lessons to be learned from the case are:

1. Treat the appointment book just as you would the records of your patients—entries made in ink with no erasures—and maintain the book for as long as your office maintains patient records. It is a usual practice to record treatment appointments in pencil so that if the patient cancels or changes it, the original appointment can be erased. These habits should changed.
2. If a patient cancels, changes an appointment, or is a no-show, make a note in the book as well as in the patient's treatment record.

Drug and Medication Log

12.13   Prescriptions, drugs, and medications administered to the patient should be kept in a log in addition to the information placed in the chronological patient treatment record. The log should include the drug and medication history of the patient as well as any allergic reactions, both before and since treatment was begun. Having all this information in a convenient place in the patient's folder will not only save the dentist's time in looking for the information, but will prevent the dentist from prescribing or administering a drug or medication to which the patient has suffered an adverse reaction or allergy.

Summary

12.14   A well-documented record of the diagnosis and treatment of your patient is an essential part of good patient care—as important as your skills at diagnosis, treatment planning, technical ability, and overall care of the patient. It may also influence the attorney of a litigious patient to advise his client of the unlikelihood of success in a malpractice suit against you (assuming you were not guilty of substandard care). In addition, should the suit against you find its way into the courtroom, your records may be your best defense, or, if badly maintained, your downfall. The presumption by a reasonable person is that a sloppy record is kept by a sloppy dentist, while a neat, accurate, and complete record is kept by a careful dentist. Poor and inadequate records are a major contributor to *loss without fault* (see chapter 17).

Summary Rules on Record Keeping

12.14.1

1. Keep a record for all individuals who appear in the dental office for either diagnosis, treatment, or emergency care.
2. Make all entries legible.
3. Make entries in ink or ballpoint pen, never in pencil.
4. If more than one person is authorized to make entries on the record, have all entries signed or initialed (and maintain a record in the office identifying the signature or initials of employees authorized to make entries).
5. Keep records as long as possible.
6. Never relinquish original records, radiographs, reports, test results, etc, unless ordered by a court or other government agency authorized to demand their release.
7. Always make entries on the lines, and never in the margins, or below the last line at the bottom of the form, where they might be taken as evidence of tampering.
8. Never make entries after there is any evidence that a lawsuit may be considered by the patient. Make additions based upon memory on a separate sheet.
9. Never send copies of any component of the patient's record to anyone, including the patient or other practitioners, unless a demand is made in writing by the patient.
10. Correct errors by drawing a single line through the error so that it can still be read and entering the correction on the next available blank line as a correction.
11. Note all cancellations, late arrivals, and changed appointments on the record.
12. Note all conversations related to the care of the patient held with anyone on the record, except those related to any suit (such notes should be entered on a separate sheet).
13. Keep records in a safe place, preferably in a fireproof cabinet.
14. Guard the confidentiality of information.
15. Should you leave practice, check with the appropriate government agency about any rules or regulations related to what should be done with your patient records.
16. Should any adverse occurrence result from treatment, inform the patient and make a note on the record (if possible, have the patient initial or sign the entry).
17. Note referral(s) recommended, home-care instructions, and things the patient should not do, eg, smoke, drink.
18. Note patient noncompliance with instructions, referrals, etc.
19. Document consents (if you use forms, note that the form was given to the patient).
20. Space entries uniformly on the record (there should be no unusual or blank spaces).

No amount of documentation is too much, and no detail is too small to be included in the record.

What Not to Put on the Treatment Record

12.14.2
1. Do not record financial information on the treatment record. Use a separate financial form.
2. Do not record subjective evaluations, such as your opinion about the patient's mental health, on the treatment record unless you are qualified and licensed to make such evaluation. Record such observations on a separate sheet marked *Confidential—Personal Notes.* Confidential and personal notes can be withheld from the patient and are not discoverable by the patient's attorney.
3. Do not record any correspondence or conversations with your professional liability insurance company, your attorney, or the attorney representing a patient on the treatment record. Use a separate sheet to record these activities and conversations.

Trial of a Suit in Malpractice: *Res Ipsa Loquitur*, Hearsay Evidence, and Contributory Negligence

Introduction

13.1   This chapter will explain some of the trial procedures dentists will encounter if they are unfortunate enough to be sued by a patient for malpractice. From the initial service of the court papers to the case's final resolution, few dentists will find it easy to cope with the experience. They enter a world for which they are totally unprepared, a strange, at times frightening, place in which even the language is different from any they have ever heard. The judicial system is complex and not easily understood by outsiders. Dentists will find themselves out of control of events, forced to rely wholly on the attorneys and the judge. Their records, their professional judgement and ability, the details of their office practices, will all be exposed to persons they believe should not have access to them: attorneys for both sides, the complaining patient and witnesses, representatives of the insurance company; a judge, a jury, and in some cases, the media. Dentists will have to explain to these "outsiders" each entry on the patient's record; the details of their treatment, their office practices, and anything else that comes to the minds of their inquisitors. They will be faced and challenged by a hostile attorney, and not always protected by their own. Their former patients may say things that may not be true, and all will hear about the injury they allegedly caused these patients, who in the past trusted and respected them. It is an experience that all dentists fear. All that takes place during the trial, win or lose, is public. A written record of the trial will last for as long as court records are kept, and be available for all to see. The dentist's other patients may discover that their dentist was sued for malpractice. In short, being a defendant in a malpractice suit is an experience to be avoided at all possible costs.

To understand the following malpractice case, one must understand first the court system (explained more fully in chapter 1), the hearsay evidence rule, *res ipsa loquitur,* and comparative negligence.

Courts and Their Jurisdiction—A Brief Review

13.2   A case brought against a dentist in his professional capacity is heard and decided in a trial court of *original jurisdiction* by a judge and jury, or a judge sitting alone. If an appeal is taken by either party, the case goes on to the appellate court with jurisdiction over the trial court. The grounds for an appeal may be that the judge made a *procedural error* during the trial, eg, by excluding testimony that should have been included, or a *substantive error* in not properly instructing the jury on the law to be applied to the facts as determined by them. Appeal courts make precedent law that lower courts within their jurisdiction must follow. Precedents are state and jurisdiction specific. The same set of facts may lead to different precedents. However, precedents set by the US Supreme Court must be followed by all courts in the country.

The jury decides the facts; the judge instructs the jury on the law applicable to the facts as determined by the jury. There are no juries or witnesses in appellate court cases, because appellate courts accept the facts determined by the lower courts. Rarely will an appellate court permit the introduction of facts not introduced at the lower court trial. The appellate court decides only on whether the trial judge erred in the conduct of the case, or whether the instructions to the jury were in error as to the law. Not all cases in which a party feels that a reversible error was made during a trial are taken to appeal; a losing litigant must consider the time it takes for a decision to be reached, the cost, the uncertainty, and the risk of establishing a new precedent that may adversely affect future cases in which a party (ie, the insurance company) may have an interest.

The court system provides for changes in the law. If in instructing the jury the judge does not follow the precedent for what he believes to be a compelling reason, it is possible that the appellate court might agree, on the grounds that the old precedent was not in keeping with changes in societal values, or that new technology has been introduced since the original precedent was established, or for many other reasons (see chapter 9).

Hearsay Testimony and Evidence

13.3   *Hearsay,* that is, secondhand information, should not be admitted into evidence. The rejection of hearsay is part of the *best evidence* rule in law: Only the best evidence should be entered at trial, not evidence that may be unavailable for examination and cross examination, or tainted by the interest of the party repeating what was said. Litigants may try to introduce hearsay testimony or hearsay evidence that will serve their interests: A patient's attorney, for example, may ask that patient, "What did the dentist say when you told him of your pain?" In such a case, the dentist's attorney may object on the ground that the dentist is available at trial to be questioned directly as to what he said, and this will provide the *best evidence*.

However, there are exceptions to the hearsay evidence rule. One of particular importance to health practitioners is that if the statement is made immediately after the incident took place, and is not in the best interest of the one making the statement, it is a *res gestae* exception to the hearsay evidence rule. And so, if after fracturing and failing to remove the root of a tooth during an extraction the dentist says to the patient, "I made a mistake, I fractured the root of the tooth, and I can't get it out," the patient may testify as to what the dentist said because the statement was made immediately after the incident took place and was not in the dentist's best interest. Thus one should not make statements admitting error in the heat of some problem during treatment.

In one case in which hearsay evidence was admitted, the patient came to the dentist's office for an examination. The dentist discovered several carious teeth and an impacted mandibular third molar that he advised the patient to have extracted. Four days after the first visit the patient returned, and the dentist extracted a crowned tooth which was directly in front of the impacted tooth. He then proceeded to "cut away the gum." His assistant then applied a "hammer and a chisel and after she had tapped with the mallet for some time, defendant allegedly seized the mallet and struck it with such force that it broke plaintiff's jaw." The patient claimed, "I immediately told him that he had broken my jaw. He asked me not to interrupt him and he proceeded to hammer until he got this impacted tooth out. After he had removed it he asked me to bring my teeth together for him, which I did. He said, 'Well, I did break your jaw, I guess I hit you a little too hard.'" The trial court dismissed the complaint at the close of the plaintiff's case based upon the hearsay testimony of the plaintiff. The plaintiff appealed. The intermediate appellate court granted a new trial, stating the plaintiff's testimony about what the dentist had said was admissible as an exception to the hearsay evidence rule. The dentist appealed. The Court of Appeals of New York, the court of last resort in the state, upheld the decision of the intermediate appellate court.[1]

[1] 11 NYS2d 85 (1939).

Hearsay evidence may relate to a doctor's records and to recommendations made in scientific publications and by professional organizations about what should be done in a given situation. A record by itself is hearsay because it cannot be subject to either direct or cross examination. It cannot and should not be accepted at face value. So how do the patient's records find their way into evidence at trial? The person responsible for the records is asked if the record is kept in the usual course of business of the practice. If the answer is "yes," then the person who made entries on the record can be questioned about them, and the record itself entered into evidence. As to recommendations made in scientific publications and by professional organizations, the information contained on the paper in which the recommendations are made cannot be entered directly into evidence; however, people giving testimony can be asked if they have read the recommendation and if they agree with what it states. If they answer in the affirmative they can be asked to read it aloud and then they can be examined and cross examined on it, and it will be entered into evidence. When they agree with what is written, the opinion becomes theirs and therefore they can be questioned about it.

Though rules on the admission of hearsay evidence are strictly applied by all courts, each jurisdiction has its own, as will appear from the following three cases, each dealing with whether *The Physicians' Desk Reference* (*PDR*) may be entered directly into evidence during a trial.

Case 1. The Court of Appeals of New York, in a case decided on Dec. 2, 1999, stated:

> [*PDR*] is hearsay, and cannot, by itself, establish standard of care for a physician in prescribing and monitoring a drug during treatment of patient; rather, expert testimony is necessary to interpret whether the drug in question presented an unacceptable risk for patient, in either its administration or the monitoring of its use.

The court went on to state:

> [The] [m]edical malpractice plaintiff whose expert witness testified that *Physicians' Desk Reference* represented standard of care for physicians in use and administration of prescriptions drugs, and had described risks of prescribing drugs in question in light of plaintiff's medical condition, could offer testimony concerning expert's professional evaluation of physician's conduct based, in part, on reliance on *PDR*, but could not offer contents of *PDR* as proof, standing alone, of applicable standard of care.

Thus, the New York court declared what was contained in *PDR* as hearsay, and not admissible by itself.[2]

[2]701 NYS2d 689 (1999).

Case 2. The Court of Appeals of Texas, in a case decided on Oct. 13, 1999, offered a different opinion:

> [The] trial court improperly classified the *Physicians' Desk Reference* (*PDR*) as a learned treatise . . . instead of as a market report or commercial publication. . . . The difference in treatment between these classifications is significant. A market report or commercial publication is received for the truth of the matter asserted, which permits the jury to take the document into the jury room. . . . A learned treatise, on the other hand, is admissible only in conjunction with an expert's testimony and may not be taken into the jury room.
>
> We believe the hearsay exception . . . is not intended for a compilation such as the *Physicians' Desk Reference*. One commentator on the identically worded federal rule noted that this exception was developed for information that is readily ascertainable and about which there can be no real dispute.[3]

[3]12 SW3d 501 (1999).

This Texas decision that the *PDR* could be entered directly into evidence is directly contrary to the case decided in New York less than 2 months later.

Case 3. The Supreme Court of New Jersey, on February 26, 1998, wrote:

> In sum, we hold that the trial court did not commit reversible error in refusing to read to the jury the two warnings in the *PDR*. We further hold that the trial court did not err in refusing to instruct the jury that if Dr [D.] knew of the *PDR* warnings and nonetheless violated them, his conduct was evidence of negligence. Although admissible along with expert testimony on the issue of the standard of care, the *PDR*'s recommendations are not conclusive evidence of the standard of care or accepted practice in using the

[4]152 NJ 563 (1998).

drug. Thus, the *PDR* entries do not, as a matter of law, establish the standard of care or negligence.[4]

This court, then, came to the same conclusion as the court in New York. The *PDR*, without expert testimony in agreement, is hearsay and cannot be entered directly into evidence.

These three cases establish precedent law for the states in which they were decided; they demonstrate vividly that in establishing precedent law courts may disagree, and the precedent laws of each state may differ, though all are bound by the US Supreme Court.

In an administrative hearing conducted by a licensing agency such as the dental board, the hearsay evidence rule may be relaxed.[5]

[5]453 NE2d 1262 (1982).

Res Ipsa Loquitur

13.4   *Res ipsa loquitur* is a phrase that describes a rule of evidence in negligence suits and sometimes in dental malpractice suits. While all attorneys are familiar with the rule, some health practitioners may never have heard of it. And in fact it is of little practical interest to dentists, for although it may play a critical role in deciding a case, the facts that enter into its use in a trial are not under the dentist's control. Still, because it may confuse the dentist at trial, it is useful to introduce it here.

Res ipsa loquitur, translated literally, means "the thing speaks for itself." As it applies to negligence cases, the "thing" is the injury, which, because it exists, creates a presumption of negligence. This shifts the burden of proof from the plaintiff to the defendant, who must rebut this presumption by showing that he was not guilty of negligence, or that his negligence did not cause the injury. Where there is no claim of *res ipsa loquitur*, the burden is on the plaintiff to show that the defendant was negligent, and that the negligence resulted in an injury to the plaintiff.

For *res ipsa loquitur* to be applied in a case the plaintiff must show that:

1. The instrumentality causing the injury was under the exclusive possession and control of the defendant.
2. The injury would not have occurred but for the negligence of the defendant (this sometimes requires expert testimony).
3. The injured party could not have been aware of the circumstances under which the injury took place.

A classic example is that of a pedestrian who, while walking along a street, is struck on the head by a cement bag that falls from the roof of a building. The pedestrian has no control or knowledge of what took place on the roof of the building that caused the cement bag to fall; and so no means of proving the workers on the roof were negligent. The plaintiff's attorney must therefore plead that *res ipsa loquitur* be applied to the case, in effect claiming that the very fact of the plaintiff's injury implies negligence. The defendant would then have to present evidence at the start of the trial to show there was no negligence that resulted in the cement bag falling.

An example in medicine is a patient who undergoes an operation to correct an injured knee under general anesthesia in the operating room of a hospital. When he recovers consciousness he finds himself in traction. He is told that his hip was fractured during the operation. Clearly, something took place while he was under the anesthetic that resulted in his injury, and presumably it could not have happened unless someone in the operating room was negligent, though there is no way for him to know what took place, or what caused the injury.

Res ipsa loquitur, however, does not often apply to medical or dental malpractice cases unless the injury was due to an obviously negligent cause, such as the beating of the patient, or the leaving of a foreign object in the body, or the injury of the patient under anesthesia outside the site of an operation. There follow two dental cases, one in which *res ipsa loquitur* was rejected by the court, another in which it was accepted.

Case 1. The plaintiff visited the defendant, Dr [S.], a dentist and oral surgeon to whom she had been referred by another dentist. The defendant examined the plaintiff and concluded that she had an acute periapical abscess involving the mandibular second molar on the left side. He then performed a surgical procedure known as trephination, which involved drilling a hole in the bone below the roots of the tooth to allow the inflamed fluids to escape. Following the surgery the plaintiff was found to be suffering from paresthesia, ie, numbness of the left side of the face.

The plaintiff subsequently commenced the action to recover damages for dental malpractice and lack of informed consent.

At the jury trial, upon the defendant's motion at the close of the plaintiff's case the court dismissed the case to recover damages for dental malpractice, on the ground that the plaintiff had failed to establish a case of malpractice. The jury returned a verdict in favor of the defendant on the remaining complaint to recover damages for lack of informed consent. The trial court denied the plaintiff's motion to set aside the verdict.

In the appeal, the plaintiff contended that the court erred in dismissing the cause of action to recover damages for dental malpractice and that the dismissal thereof prejudiced her case before the jury to recover damages for lack of informed consent.

The appeal court noted that:

> Although the plaintiff's expert, Dr [E.], testified that in his opinion the angle of trephination was such that it caused entrance into the mandibular canal and severed some nerve fibers of the interior alveolar, he did not expressly state that the defendant's conduct constituted a deviation from the requisite standard of care.

Noting that "proof that the defendant's conduct constitutes a deviation from the requisite standard of care could only be adduced by expert opinion testimony," the court concluded:

> [C]ontrary to the plaintiff's contention, we are of the view that the doctrine of *res ipsa loquitur* is inapplicable to the facts of this case. Under the cir-

cumstances, the court properly ruled that the plaintiff failed to make out a prima facie case. Despite the testimony of the plaintiff's expert as to the cause of the injury, *res ipsa loquitur* was not applied; the plaintiff was required to show by direct evidence the negligence of the defendant-dentist—suffering the injury was not enough.[6]

[6]180 AD2d 789 (1992).

Case 2. This is the case reported in section 13.3 above, in which the dentist admitted breaking the plaintiff's jaw. The plaintiff alone testified, and the trial court dismissed the case. According to the appeals court:

> The question presented is whether plaintiff in the absence of expert medical testimony established a prima facie case of lack of ordinary care on the part of defendant. As a general rule, where the exercise of proper skill or care on the part of a physician, surgeon, or dentist is in issue, expert medical testimony is required by plaintiff to show that the untoward results might have been avoided by due care. However, expert evidence is not required where the results of the treatment are of such a character as to warrant the inference of want of care from the testimony of laymen or in the light of the knowledge and experience of the jurors themselves.

The court went on to apply *res ipsa loquitur* to the case: "The rule of *res ipsa loquitur* put upon the defendant the burden of going on with the case."[7]

[7]11 NYS2d 85 (1939).

The effect of *res ipsa loquitur* is twofold. If the doctrine is pleaded and accepted by the court, the normal presumption of innocence is reversed, and the defendant must rebut a presumption of guilt. In medical cases, if it is pleaded on the grounds that the facts relating to the negligence of the defendant fall within the common knowledge of the jury, the defendant will be required to defend the claim notwithstanding that the plaintiff calls no expert to testify (see chapter 6).

Contributory and Comparative Negligence

13.5　At common law if the plaintiff (the injured party) contributed in any way to the injury, the defendant was totally relieved of liability, according to the doctrine of *contributory negligence.* Clearly, such a rule would lead in today's society to injustice. For example, a dentist extracts a patient's tooth negligently, so that the patient later suffers a postoperative infection at the site of the surgery. The dentist prescribes antibiotics, with instructions to the patient as to their use. The patient disobeys the instructions, and the infection spreads. Under the old doctrine of contributory negligence the dentist is relieved from any liability for his negligent act because the patient was negligent in disobeying his instructions.

The injustice in the strict application of contributory negligence has led all jurisdictions to reject that doctrine and apply what is now known as *comparative negligence.* Some courts continue to use the term *contributory negligence,* but apply the principle of comparative negligence. For example, New York converted, as of September 1, 1975, from a traditional contributory negligence state to one applying the legal doctrine of comparative negligence. The text *The New York Pattern Jury Instructions* illustrates this change. In cases of patient negligence, the judge is advised to state to the jury:

If you find that defendant [doctor] was negligent and that defendant's negligence contributed to causing the injury, you must next consider whether plaintiff [patient] was also negligent and whether plaintiff's conduct contributed to causing the injury.

The burden is on defendant to prove that plaintiff was negligent and that his negligence contributed to causing the injury. If you find that plaintiff was not negligent, or if negligent, that his negligence did not contribute to causing the injury, you should go no further and report your findings to the court.

If, however, you find that plaintiff was negligent and that his negligence contributed to causing the injury, you must then apportion the fault between plaintiff and defendant.

Weighing all the facts and circumstances, you must consider the total negligence, that is, the negligence of both plaintiff and defendant which contributed to causing the injury and determine what percentage of fault is chargeable to each. In your verdict, you will state the percentages you find. The total of those percentages must equal 100%.

For example, if you should find that the defendant and plaintiff were equally negligent you would report that each was 50% responsible. If you should find that one party was more negligent then the other in causing the injury, you would assign a higher percentage to that party and a lower percentage to the other, with the total of the percentages equaling 100%.[8]

[8]The New York Pattern Jury Instructions— Civil, Vol 1, ed 2. Cumulative 1996 suppl, § PJI 2:36. Rochester, NY: Lawyers Cooperative: 140.

Thus, in the hypothetical dental case described above, if the jury believed that as a result of the injury the patient should be compensated $100,000, but by not following the dentist's recommendation as to the prescribed antibiotic, the patient contributed 25% to the injury, the jury award would be reduced to $75,000.

The legal doctrine of comparative negligence was applied in the following case decided in New York. In the trial court, the jury found the dentist guilty of malpractice. However, evidence was produced that the patient did not follow the dentist's instruction for a full course of treatment. (The report does not explain what this "full course of treatment" was.) Therefore the award to the patient was reduced by 50%, to $12,500 for pain and suffering, and $10,000 for medical and dental expenses. The dentist appealed to the appellate court, which affirmed the decision of the trial court:

> A review of the record demonstrates that there existed a rational and valid line of reasoning by which the jury could find that defendant Dr [K.] committed dental malpractice and that such malpractice constituted a proximate cause of plaintiff's injuries when he failed to install an upper roundhouse bridge to match the lower roundhouse bridge that had been installed in plaintiff's mouth. . . . The parties' expert testimony concerning the source of plaintiff's jaw pain created a factual issue which was resolved by the jury. *Finally, no basis exists to disturb the jury's finding with respect to plaintiff's comparative negligence, particularly where plaintiff declined to follow the full course of treatment and work recommended.*[9] (Emphasis added.)

[9]582 NYS2d 708 (1992).

Contributory negligence may be of major importance to dentists in the award made by juries as a result of negligence. However, to support a claim of contributory negligence, the dentist must be able to show, by documentation, that the patient did in fact contribute to his injury. Such evidence may include frequent canceled appointments, failure to respond to recall notices, failure to follow home-care instructions, or failure to seek recommended consultative services and/or specialty treatment.

Trial

13.6   This section will describe the legal process that begins when suit is filed against a dentist. Each step will be described and explained in some detail. We begin with the service of the notice to a dentist that a patient has entered suit.

Summons—The Suit Begins

13.6.1   Until some procedures mandated by the courts take place, there is no suit; a letter threatening suit from a patient or a patient's attorney does not begin one, although it must be reported to the insurance carrier. For the legal process to begin, the patient's attorney must file papers with the appropriate court, and the dentist must be served with papers. In New York the statute of limitations in medical malpractice cases runs until the appropriate papers are filed with the court. The dentist must be served with papers within 120 days after the suit is filed in the court, and may know nothing of the case until then.[10] Other states have various rules as to these matters. Following is a scenario illustrating how you, as a dentist, may learn of a suit that has been filed against you.

One day, to your surprise, your receptionist interrupts your treatment of a patient to inform you that there is a person in the waiting room who wishes to see you. When you enter the waiting room this person wishes you a pleasant day, asks your name, and then hands you some papers. You have been served with a summons by a process server. Be pleasant; he is not suing you, just doing his job. The summons may be accompanied with a complaint. If so, it is called a "Summons and Complaint." It simply states that the plaintiff, named on the paper, is suing you, also named on the paper, and includes the general cause of action (negligence, malpractice, or breach of contract), the court in which the suit is being filed, and the date of filing. This date may be important: Should the date you receive the summons fall more than 120 days after this date, your attorney may then file a motion to have the suit dismissed. For this reason you must retain copies of all papers involved in the service, including the envelope. The originals are to be sent to your insurance company by certified mail, a signed receipt requested. (see chapter 14). On the following page is a copy of a summons (names have been changed).

From the date the suit is filed with the court, the clock begins to run. You must notify your carrier as soon as possible after you receive the summons. The attorney assigned to your case will answer the claim. If for any reason you miss a deadline you are required by law to meet, you will not be able to defend the claim; in effect, you will have admitted liability and the only matter to be decided at trial will be the amount of the award levied against you. Though the insurance company assigns you an attorney, his duty to the insurance company is subservient to his duty to you. Should you feel that the attorney does not represent you as you wish—for example, by not returning phone calls within a reasonable time, or making no effort to discuss the matter with you—you should complain to the company. You may go so far as to demand that another attorney be assigned to the case; however, if you employ your own attorney, the insurance company will not pay the fee. If you are sued for an amount in excess of your policy, your insurance company is required to notify you of the

[10] New York Civil Practice Law & Rules, §304, §360-b.

SUPREME COURT OF THE STATE OF NEW YORK   INDEX NO: 1988768/99
COUNTY OF QUEENS

————————————————————————————————x

DATE FILED: 8/10/99

MARY SMALL,   Plaintiff(s) Defendant(s)
         Plaintiff   QUEENS COUNTY
            As Place of Trial

 -against-   Basis of Venue is
                                   Plaintiff's Residence

STEVEN ROBINSON
         Defendant   SUMMONS

————————————————————————————————x
                             Plaintiff's Address is:
                             835 Elmhurst Road
                             Roadside, NY 12875

TO THE ABOVE NAMED DEFENDANT(S)

        YOU ARE HEREBY SUMMONED to answer the complaint in this action and to serve a copy of your answer, or, if the complaint is not served with this summons, to serve a Notice of Appearance, on the plaintiff's attorney within 20 days after this service of this Summons, exclusive of the day of service (or within 30 days after the service is complete if this Summons is not personally delivered to you within the State of New York); and in case of your failure to appear or answer, judgment will be taken against you by default for the relief demanded in the complaint.

Dated: Rockport, New York
       August 6, 1999

Yours, etc.,

_____

Orfano, Maxwell & Orfano
Attorneys for the Plaintiff
222 South Street
Jefferson, New York 12435
(631) 463-8889

Defendant's Address:
Steve Robinson, DDS
347 Baltimore Avenue
Coram, New York 11234

fact that it will only represent you to the limits of the policy, by means of a letter called a *Reservation of Rights.* If you receive such a letter, you should get an attorney of your own, who will assist the attorney assigned by the insurance company in the defense of the claim to the extent of your interest.

Discovery

13.6.2 Once a suit is officially filed, the long period of discovery begins. Its purpose is for each side to learn as much as procedural rules permit about the facts supporting the claim and the defense against the claim. Courts anticipate that the disclosures by each side will lead to an early resolution of the dispute, that a settlement will be reached or the claim withdrawn. Their goal is to avoid litigation in the already crowded courts by having parties settle disputes directly.

The discovery period usually begins with a demand by the patient's attorney for copies of all records relating to the care of his client, including X rays, consultant reports, etc. Once a suit is begun, the insurance company will make a similar request. Shortly thereafter, you will be visited by a member of the claims department of the insurance company who will want to learn about your credibility and the details of your treatment of the patient so that the company can decide whether to defend the claim or attempt a settlement.

Discovery may extend for many months, sometimes years—a period that defendant-dentists find most disturbing as they are haunted for what seems an eternity by fears of the worst outcomes. Discovery ends when the attorney for the plaintiff and the attorney for the defendant notify the court that they are ready for trial. There is no limit on the time for discovery, except that it be reasonable, and a "reasonable" time may extend for years if the case is sufficiently complex.

Verified Bill of Particulars

13.6.2.1 The summons and complaint is general as to the basis for the claim. It does not include the precise details of what you did or are alleged to have done to cause the injury to the patient. For this information your attorney will demand a *verified bill of particulars* (BOP, not to be confused with the BOP mentioned in chapter 19), in which the allegations of malpractice are listed, along with other information that will enable your attorney to prepare a defense. The courts list the information to be included in the BOP. An example of a BOP used in New York is presented on the following pages.

The BOP is a critical document in the litigation process. In reviewing it, many defendant-dentists ask, "How did the attorney for the patient learn of the damages I might have been responsible for?" The answer opens up one of major the risks to which potential dentist-defendants are exposed. Following is what typically takes place.

When a patient believes that the treatment you provided, eg, a fixed partial denture, was faulty and is told by another dentist that it must be redone, he consults an attorney. The attorney, after hearing from the patient about his treatment, will refer him to a dentist, usually one who has provided dental examinations for the attorney in the past. This dentist performs a thorough

* *

SUPREME COURT OF THE STATE OF NEW YORK
COUNTY OF NEW YORK

——————————————————————————————————————x

Mary Jones
      Plaintiff   VERIFIED

     -against-   BILL OF PARTICULARS

Dr Sidney Smith
      Defendant

——————————————————————————————————————-x

    Plaintiff, by her attorney, _____ as and for a Verified Bill of Particulars on information and belief respectfully states as follows:

1. Plaintiff was treated continuously from on or about March 1984 to December 1986. The exact dates of treatment are within the charts of defendant, known to defendant.

2. Defendant rendered dental treatment to plaintiff at the office of Dr. Smith at _____, NYC

3. The malpractice of defendant Dr Smith consisted of, but is not limited to, the following:

    a). Failure to perform the proper diagnostic procedures to determine the extent and nature of plaintiff's dental problems

    b). Provision of provisional restorations which were ill fitting, had defective margins, open contacts, were poorly contoured, did not fit, and had poor occlusion

    c). Installation of prosthetic restorations in the presence of improperly treated teeth and periodontium

    d). Failure to diagnose and adequately treat an ongoing developing and disintegrating periodontal condition

    e). Installation of provisional crowns on teeth he improperly prepared

    f). Failure to refer plaintiff to a qualified periodontal specialist

    g). Failure to refer plaintiff to a qualified prosthodontic specialist h). Failure to diagnose a developing and disintegrating occlusal condition

i). Failure to provide the proper occlusal relationship

j). Failure to evaluate her temporomandibular joint problem

k). Failure to refer plaintiff to a temporomandibular joint expert

l). Provision of restorations that were ill fitting and overcontoured and had poor marginal integrity and improper embrasures

m). Failure to inform plaintiff of risks and consequences of prescribed treatment, of the severity of her dental problems and of the temporary nature of such treatment

n). Indiscriminately prescribed antibiotics

5. The accepted medical practices that were violated were in not performing a proper diagnosis, not referring to competent specialists, and proceeding with the treatment in the manner discussed in answer 3.

6. The departures are listed in answer 3.

8.   a). Ignored complaints and signs and symptoms of periodontal disease, of ill-fitting restorations, of occlusal inharmony, and of TMJ.
     b). Defendant should have made the diagnosis in the beginning of treatment and throughout his treatment.
     c). Outlined in 3.
     d). Indiscriminate use of antibiotics; the exact antibiotics are known to the defendant.
     e). Lack of proper X rays, proper occlusal analysis, proper TMJ exam, proper clinical periodontal examination.

10. a). As a result of defendant's malpractice, plaintiff has lost teeth, lost tooth structure, and she can anticipate the early loss of her other teeth; she has bone loss; periodontium destruction, temporomandibular joint problems, and neuromuscular disturbance; all of her teeth as well as the surrounding neuromuscular system have been adversely affected; she has experienced anguish, and her normal habits and pattern of life, including her ability to chew properly, have been varied since the start of defendant's treatment; she was rendered disabled and deformed; and she has experienced much pain and suffering and continues to do so because she must still undergo comprehensive dental treatment. Additionally, plaintiff has suffered monetary damage in the amount paid to defendant as well as approximately $35,000, which must be paid for subsequent periodontal, endodontic, restorative, surgical, and implant dental work, as well as approximately $15,000 for medical problems caused by the negligence of the defendant.

Additionally she has suffered emotionally to a point of requiring medical help and has lymph, sinus, and allergy problems, Epstein-Barr virus, and severe insomnia.

b). Plaintiff's permanent injuries include, but are not limited to, loss of tooth structure, loss of natural teeth and anticipated loss of more natural teeth, loss of bone, destruction of periodontium, temporomandibular joint and neuromuscular problems, and monetary damage. Severe pain and mental anguish may be permanent.

11. Plaintiff was confined to,
    a). Bed and/or
    b). House and presently goes out only to her physicians and dentists.
    c). Not applicable, not confined.

12. Special damages to be incurred are as follows:

    Dr Henry periodontist . . . .$7,000.
    500 _____ Avenue

    Dr Ronald Thomas, endodontist . . . .$400.
    30 _____ Street

    Dr Stanley, oral surgeon . . . .$150.
    200 _____ Street

    Dr Gerald Klein, psychiatrist . . . .$3,000.
    200 _____ Street

13. Occupation: Consultant
    self-employed, address 200_____ Street

14. Date of Birth: 7-17-55

15. Address: _____ Street

16. Social Security #123-45-6789

17. Collateral reimbursement. [Collateral payments are those made by a third party as a result of treatment received related to the injury alleged to have been caused by the defendant. They include any monies received by the plaintiff from medical insurance policies. This amount, in most jurisdictions, is deducted from any award made by the court (jury) to the plaintiff.]

    Dental & Medical Insurance, King Life Policy #1222222, Baltimore, MD.

Dental, $1,000 per year maximum, implants not included.

Psychiatric, $1,000 per year maximum.

Plaintiff has received about $2,500 reimbursement for Dr B's treatment at or about $10,000 worth of treatment.

Plaintiff reserves the right to amend her answers upon discovery of new and/or different information.

Dated: New York, New York
November 23, 1999

Yours etc.
(Attorney for the plaintiff)

To: Williams, Pimms & Muller (Attorneys for the defendant)
20 _____ Street

****

examination that includes a complete periodontal examination: pocket depths, bleeding points, and mobility on all surfaces of all teeth. More often than not, an examination of the TMJ is included. All the foregoing is in addition to the specific complaint of the patient, which may have been limited to the faulty fixed partial denture that the patient wants replaced. The examining dentist sends his report to the patient's attorney. While this is taking place, the attorney obtains a copy of your records, by means of a demand accompanied by a release authorization signed by the patient. He discovers that nowhere on your records is there any evidence that you completed a periodontal examination, nor an examination of the TMJ. The attorney then includes this in the suit against you. In this way, what began as a complaint related to a faulty fixed partial denture ends up in multiple claims.

There is another reason that the BOP includes as many allegations as the attorney for the patient has any reason to believe may be applicable: Courts do not like litigants to be taken by surprise during trial. Therefore, attorneys are held to prove only what is contained in the original BOP, though a judge may, at a later date, allow an attorney to amend the BOP should new evidence be discovered about an injury that was included in the original. However, to avoid the risk of not being allowed to amend the BOP, the plaintiff's attorney tries to include all possible claims in the original document. The extent of the claimed injuries and allegations of malpractice often shocks the defendant-dentist.

Next, the dentist's attorney must respond to the allegations enumerated in the BOP with either a general denial, or specific denials of each allegation. The general denial is by far the most frequent. From this point, additional discovery may be carried out by each side, including documentation of loss of wages, subsequent examinations, reports by health practitioners, hospital records, and other information and facts related to either the plaintiff's allegation of malpractice or the defense against it. For the most part, the results must be shared between the parties. Experts are recruited by both sides, along with their reports. The degree to which this information is shared depends upon local law. In addition, some jurisdictions require that a *merit of claim* be submitted by the plaintiff and completed by another practitioner. A merit of claim demonstrates to the court that another practitioner believes the claim to be meritorious and is designed to protect against frivolous suits. Third parties may be brought into the suit by both the plaintiff and the defendant. For example, if a general dentist is sued and an oral and maxillofacial surgeon also treated the patient, and it appears to the general dentist that the oral and maxillofacial surgeon caused or contributed to the injury suffered by the patient, the oral and maxillofacial surgeon may be brought in as a third-party defendant. The same opportunity to implead third parties is available to the plaintiff.

Credibility

13.6.2.2   One of the most important factors in a suit's outcome is the credibility of the litigants. Credibility relates to the weight the trier of facts (in jury trials the jury, in bench trials the judge) will give to the evidence. In most malpractice cases there is disagreement about what took place while the patient was undergoing treatment. Facts in dispute become major elements in the outcome of a case. Who will be believed depends upon who appears most credible and whose claims are best supported by the evidence (see chapter 15).

The issue of credibility surfaces shortly after a suit is filed. When the attorneys for both parties view the records of the defendant-dentist, each may make an initial judgment as to the credibility of the dentist. Records that are illegible, sloppy, or incomplete, or that appear to have been altered following the notice of suit, serve to destroy at the outset the credibility of the defendant-dentist. When the representative of the claims department of the insurance company interviews the dentist about the facts that led to the suit, he also evaluates the credibility of the dentist, eg, his general appearance and demeanor, how he answers questions, his professional background, and his knowledge of the subject matter. The claims representative will report to the insurance company on the dentist's credibility and the merits of the claim.

Examination Before Trial

13.6.2.3   Under the rules of practice, each side in the lawsuit has the right to take a discovery deposition, an examination before trial (EBT), of the opposing party. Thus, when you become a defendant in litigation, the opposing party has the right to require you to appear at a specified time and place (usually an attorney's office) to give oral testimony under oath. Plaintiffs and other parties to the suit may be called to appear. There is little difference between testimony at a deposition and testimony at trial except that there is no judge to rule over legal questions as they arise; however, your attorney may object to the questions asked by the opposing attorney, and a judge may rule on them later.

The testimony will be recorded either in shorthand by a stenographer present at the EBT, or by mechanical means. It is then transcribed and distributed to the attorneys, and through yours to you, for correction. Under your signature, witnessed by a notary, it becomes an official record in the case. Should you make statements at the trial that conflict with those you make at the EBT, the EBT may be entered into the trial record; your testimony may be impeached and your credibility compromised, and you may be charged with lying under oath, a felony.

After the EBT, each attorney then further evaluates the merits of the claim and the credibility of the dentist. A suit may be lost by the dentist long before it goes to trial; many are settled or withdrawn as a result of what takes place at this stage. The EBT may result in a *loss without fault*: the loss of a case of alleged malpractice when you have not been guilty of malpractice, but nonetheless your attorney feels the case cannot be successfully defended. The saddest part of the entire field of dental malpractice is the dentist who loses a case when he has done nothing wrong (see chapter 17).

The EBT is often postponed several times, sometimes late in the afternoon of the day before it is scheduled. Despite how this may make you feel, it is not always done for the purpose of harassment. EBTs are usually conducted by trial lawyers, and the ends of trials cannot be exactly predicted. If your attorney feels that harassment is the purpose of the postponements he will ask a judge to set a date, after which no excuse for delay will be accepted.

The EBT has three purposes:

1. The attorneys want to find out what facts you have in your actual knowledge and possession regarding the issues in the lawsuit. They want to know what happened during the treatment of the patient, to pin down your story, and make sure you tell the same story at the trial.
2. The attorneys want to evaluate your credibility on the basis of how you conduct yourself when under examination, eg, are you arrogant, evasive, forgetful, or unprepared?
3. The plaintiff's attorneys hope to catch you in some discrepancy, so that at the trial they can show that you are not a truthful person and therefore your testimony should not be believed on any of the points, particularly the crucial ones.

These are legitimate purposes; the opposing side has every right to take your discovery deposition for these purposes and in this fashion. Correspondingly, your attorney has the same right to take the discovery deposition of the opposing litigant, the patient. Other witnesses may be called by either side to an EBT. An EBT thus can take many hours to complete, at times over a period of several days, depending upon the complexity of the case and its potential for a large award.

Your deposition, properly given, can go a long way in assisting your attorney in handling the litigation, either by way of settlement or trial. What you do at the deposition can help you or hurt you, depending upon your preparedness for the examination, your attitude, you truthfulness, and your appearance: your credibility. The following information and instructions are offered in an effort to better acquaint you with what is expected of you, and how you can be an effective witness at discovery deposition time. Many of the recommendations apply to both an EBT and a trial.

Your Physical Appearance

13.6.2.3.1   You should remember that usually the first opportunity that the opposing counsel has to see you comes at the time of the giving of the discovery deposition. It is important that you make a good impression upon opposing counsel. You should appear at deposition time dressed as you would expect to dress if you were actually going to court to appear before a judge and jury. Men should dress in a traditional business suit, shirt, and tie. Women should dress conservatively.

How to Act While Giving Testimony

13.6.2.3.2   1. Tell the truth. The truth, in the deposition or on the witness stand, will never really hurt a litigant. A lawyer may be able to explain away the truth but there is no explaining why a client lied or concealed the truth.
2. Never lose your temper.
3. Don't be afraid of the lawyers.
4. Speak slowly and clearly.
5. If you don't understand the question, ask that it be explained.
6. Answer all questions directly, giving concise answers to the questions, and then *stop talking*. Never volunteer any information. Wait until the question is asked—answer it and *stop*. If you can answer "yes" or "no," do so and *stop*. However, if a question cannot be answered with a "yes" or "no," then by all means give the answer in your own words.
7. Stick to the facts and testify only to those you personally know or what your dental records indicate; use them to refresh your recollection. If you don't know, admit it. Some witnesses think they should have an answer for every question asked. It is imperative that you be honest and straightforward in your testimony.
8. Don't try to memorize your story. Justice requires only that a witness tell his story to the best of his ability.
9. Listen carefully to the questions asked of you. No matter how nice the other attorney may seem, he may be trying to hurt you as a witness. Understand the question. Have it repeated if necessary; then give a thoughtful, considered answer. Do not give a snap answer without thinking. You must not be rushed into answering.
11. Be serious at all times and avoid laughing and talking about the case with your opponents. At the deposition do not chat with the opponents or their attorneys. Remember they are your legal adversaries.
12. Certain questions that will be asked of you may be legally objectionable; you are not expected to know which ones. If such a question is asked, your attorney may voice an objection. In order for him to have an opportunity to do so, he must have time to hear the question and determine whether or not it is objectionable. So wait for at least 30 seconds before answering any question; this will also give you time to think about the question and your answer.

The fact that a question is objectionable does not mean that the question or its answer will be harmful to your case. It merely means that at this time and at this place your counsel feels that the plaintiff is not entitled to this information. On occasion, your attorney may object to a question and then permit you to answer the question subject to that objection.

13. If your answer is wrong, correct it immediately.

14. If your answer is not clear, clarify it immediately.

15. Don't say, "That's all of the conversation," or "Nothing else happened." Say, "That's all I recall," or "That's all I remember happening." It may be that after more thought or another question you will remember something important. When asked questions concerning conversations between you and the patient or any other possible witness to this lawsuit, respond to the best of your ability. If you do not recall verbatim conversations, indicate that you are testifying as to the sum and substance of those conversations.

16. Always be polite, even to the other attorney. Always address a man as "sir" and a woman as "ma'am." Do not let the opposing attorney get you angry or excited. This destroys the effect of your testimony and you may say things that may be used to your disadvantage later. It is sometimes the intent of attorneys to get a witness excited during his testimony, hoping that he will say things which may be used against him. Under no circumstances should you argue with the opposing attorney. Answer him in the same tone of voice and manner you use to answer your own attorney's questions. The mere fact that you get emotional about a certain point could work to your opponent's advantage in a lawsuit.

17. Do not exaggerate.

Avoid Persistent Mannerisms

13.6.2.3.3

1. Don't act nervous. Avoid mannerisms that will make the opposing party think you are frightened, not telling the truth, or withholding information.

2. Testifying for an extended length of time is trying. It causes fatigue. You will recognize fatigue by certain symptoms: *(1)* tiredness, *(2)* crossness, *(3)* nervousness, *(4)* anger, *(5)* carelessness, and *(6)* willingness to say anything, or answer any question, in order to complete your examination. When you feel these symptoms, recognize them and ask for a few minutes' suspension of the examination.

3. Talk loud enough so that everybody can hear you. Don't chew gum, and keep your hands away from your mouth. Give an audible answer so the court reporter and the jury at the trial can hear and understand you. Don't nod your head to indicate a yes or no answer.

Need for Self-Reliance

13.6.2.3.4

1. Don't look at your attorney for help in answering a question. You are on your own. If the question is improper, your attorney will object.

2. Don't hedge in your answers.

Trick Questions

13.6.2.3.5

1. There are questions known as "trick questions." That is, if you answer them the way the other attorney hopes you will, he can make your answer sound

bad. For example, "Have you talked to anybody about this case?" If you say "no," that isn't right because good lawyers always talk to the witnesses before they testify. If you say "yes," the lawyer may try to imply that you were told what to say. The best thing to do is to say very frankly that you have talked to whomever you have talked to, and that you just answered questions about the facts and nothing more. Simply tell the truth.

2. You may also be asked something in reference to insurance. Be careful not to mention insurance in your examination before trial or at trial. Except in a few situations, an insurance company cannot be joined as a defendant, and if anything is said that will let the judge know that an insurance company is actually defending the case, the judge will declare a mistrial—the jury will be discharged and the case retried at a later date with a new jury. The lawyer assigned by the insurance company to represent you becomes your lawyer, and you are the client, not the insurance company.

What to Bring with You to Your Deposition

13.6.2.4   It is of the utmost importance that you bring all the patient's records to the deposition to assist you in your testimony. You will be permitted to review your records before answering each question. The attorney for the opposing party has a right to review these records and mark them as exhibits in the lawsuit. You should bring:

1. Histories, medical and dental
2. Treatment records, including your appointment log
3. Radiographs
4. Study casts
5. Correspondence between you and the patient
6. Any prostheses in your possession
7. Financial records of the patient
8. Laboratory notes and prescriptions
9. Consultation reports
10. Any evidence of the patient's noncompliance in, eg, your records, correspondence, or your office appointment log
11. Any and all other records made during the course of treatment referable to the patient's treatment or diagnosis

Correspondence or materials that you prepared for your insurance company or your attorney are not records for the purposes of the EBT or at trial. Do not confuse correspondence between you and the patient with correspondence or materials prepared for litigation. The latter material and correspondence are not subject to discovery nor are they required to be submitted to the opposing attorney.

Among the questions that will be asked of you at the deposition and at trial, some will refer to your educational and professional background. It is always helpful to have prepared a curriculum vitae or résumé including:

1. Your educational background
2. The degree(s) you hold

3. Continuing dental and medical education courses you have taken
4. Study groups to which you belong
5. Hospital training you have received
6. Faculty and hospital positions you have held
7. Seminars you have attended
8. Conventions you have attended
9. Professional and scientific publications to which you subscribe
10. Hospitals with which you are affiliated
11. Articles, chapters, and texts you have published
12. Specialty training you have received, and whether it is board certified
13. Professional associations or organizations to which you belong and your status in the group, eg, member, associate, or fellow
14. Clinics you have attended
15. Professional talks or lectures you have given
16. Any other of your professional activities you feel would add to your credibility

Additional Helpful Hints

13.6.2.5 The attorney for the opposing party may not be well versed in the field of dentistry, and may ask questions that to you as a dentist appear inarticulate. If you do not understand a question, or a question is asked in such a manner that it is impossible for you to respond, simply ask the attorney to rephrase the question. You are not appearing at the deposition or trial to teach the plaintiff's attorney dentistry, and it is always best to avoid falling into the habit of lecturing in response to a question that is asked.

Questions about your background will usually be followed by questions about your knowledge of the patient's dental and medical history. You will be asked about your diagnosis of the patient's problems and the diagnostic tools that you used in making it. Be prepared to answer questions as to alternative treatment for this patient's particular problem, and also be prepared to explain how you and the patient determined which treatment plan to follow.

At times an adverse event may take place during the course of proper treatment. A dentist who has failed to advise the patient of this in advance can be found culpable. Questions about the adverse event should be anticipated. Assuming that you did advise the patient of possible adverse events, you may anticipate you will be asked what actions and/or treatment you took after the adverse event.

You may also anticipate being asked about any medications that you gave or prescribed for the patient, and the reasons for such medications, as well as the extent of your knowledge concerning the composition, side effects, contraindications, etc, of these medications. Home-care instructions given to the patient may become important.

On occasion attorneys have been known to use dental and medical books, treatises, and articles in the prosecution of their lawsuit. If you are unfamiliar with a particular book, treatise, or article, this is not necessarily fatal to your defense. The attorney who will appear with you at the deposition will discuss this matter with you before your testimony.

Needless to say, questions will be asked of you at your examination before trial or at your trial that neither you nor your attorney can anticipate. Remember that you are testifying under oath and all that is asked of you is to testify to the best of your knowledge and to tell the truth. A deposition is merely a formal procedure for eliciting the truth. Remember that perhaps the most important aspect of your lawsuit is you and the appearance you make. If you give the appearance of earnestness and fairness, this will go a long way toward a decision in your favor.

You will find there is really nothing at all to be apprehensive or nervous about in testifying. You may ask your attorney about anything you don't understand. If you relax and remember that you are simply telling your side of the story, you will get along without a problem. Most of all, remember *loss without fault*. You don't want to lose a case in which you did nothing wrong in treatment merely because of what you said or did at an examination before trial or during the trial.

After the Examination Before Trial

13.6.2.6   Shortly after the EBT ends, your attorneys will advise the insurance company about whether they think the claim can be successfully defended, given the facts and your credibility as a witness. They will also judge the credibility of the patient, as will the patient's attorneys. These judgments will determine whether the claim is withdrawn, settlements are sought, or the suit goes to trial. Below are excerpts of letters written to an insurance company by the claims representative after his interview with a defendant dentist and an attorney after the EBT. Such comments are never seen by the defendant-dentist; they are intended for representatives of the insurance company.

1. Dr [R.] is a friendly individual who does not appear terribly anxious about the suit. Although he answered all questions candidly, he did not appear to fully appreciate the importance and potential harm of some of his answers. Additionally, his records and treatment charts (copy enclosed), are illegible in most instances, and those that are legible lack important information, such as examination findings that may explain why a particular procedure was performed.

2. Dr [B.] presents a very nervous and agitated appearance. He is clearly angered by this lawsuit and this may affect his credibility with the jury. If he can learn to control his emotions, I believe he will make a good witness.

3. In this case we have a major problem with the credibility of our defendant. He was uncertain as to the facts that led to the lawsuit, and his records reflect his uncertainty; they are sketchy about what he did and when he did it. It will be trouble for us.

4. The case will come down to a battle of credibility between the dentist on one side and the plaintiff and her daughter on the other side.

5. Dr [M.] is a 51-year-old, professional-looking man who comes across as extremely self-confident, which may be viewed as somewhat arrogant by a jury.

Bringing in Third Parties

13.6.2.7   During the discovery period, and often after the EBT, each side may learn that third parties may have played a role in the patient's injury. The plaintiff's attorney may learn that a dentist in addition to the one sued may have contributed, either directly or indirectly, to the injury sustained by the patient. Or the defense attorney may have discovered that a dentist not named in the suit by the patient's attorney played a part in contributing to the injury suffered by the patient. Each side has the opportunity to join another defendant in the suit as a third-party defendant. Keep in mind that each jurisdiction has its own rules about how this is to be done, though the principle is generic.

Physical Examination

13.6.2.8   One of the essentials during the discovery period is for each side to have the patient-plaintiff examined to determine the current status of the patient's oral health, and specifically to have the injured site and/or the complaint evaluated. Naturally, each side in the litigation will select for the physical examination a practitioner who is not only credible, but inclined to favor the side that referred the patient. However, despite what might appear as bias in selecting the dentist(s) to conduct the evaluations, each side needs to be aware of the merits of the claim. In most jurisdictions, the reports are required to be shared; there are to be no secrets and no surprises at trial.

If you should be called upon to conduct a physical examination, here are some suggestions.

1. You are not asked to decide if the defendant dentist was guilty of malpractice; that is for the jury to decide. You can state that you believe the care did not meet the standard as you see it.
2. Your examination should be thorough and adequately recorded.
3. You should take radiographs if you feel they will contribute to your evaluation of the patient's complaint. If the plaintiff-patient refuses to permit you to take radiographs, make a note of the refusal on your record and have the patient sign or initial next to the note; then go on to do the best you can, but state what took place in the report.
4. If the plaintiff's attorney insists on being present during the examination, you may not be permitted to bar him; local court rules may apply. If you are in doubt, contact the attorney who made the referral and ask what you should do.
5. Questions may arise as to whether the patient-plaintiff is entitled to a copy of the report. Court decisions have gone both ways, and the question is unsettled in many jurisdictions. It is best to contact the referring attorney and ask for his opinion. It might be best to inform the patient that if he asks for a copy, the request should be directed to the attorney.
6. As to your fee, you may charge for the "visit" and any additional amount to compensate you for the review of any test results (eg, radiographs) and the preparation of the report. It is best to keep a record of the time you spend Before conducting the examination you should contact the referring attorney

and tell him what you expect the fee to be, keeping in mind that it is an estimate.

7. It is axiomatic that you retain a true copy of your report for your files, and that no person other than the referring attorney have access to a copy. If the opposing attorney requests a copy, notify your attorney of the request.

8. In writing the report, keep in mind that you may be asked, on the witness stand, to explain all you have written, and to justify any of your opinions relating to the care provided by prior dentist(s).

9. There is a distinction made in procedure between a written report submitted by a dentist who treats or will treat the patient and a dentist whose responsibility is limited to the examination and provision of a report. An examining dentist may not report any conversation held with the patient that may be self-serving about the alleged injury he received at the hands of the defendant-dentist; however, such information given to a treating dentist may be included. The presumption is that a patient whose care may be dependent on information given to a treating dentist is likely to be true, and not necessarily invented for the purpose of bolstering the patient's claim.

Trial Procedure

13.7   When each side completes its process of discovery, the court is informed that the case is ready for trial. The rules on whether or not there will be a jury are a matter of local law. However, in all jurisdictions if either party claims a jury there will be a jury. In some jurisdictions a jury is automatic unless waived by both parties. In New York it is necessary to claim one. If the case is to be heard and decided by the judge without a jury, it is called a *bench trial*. If a jury is necessary, it is selected by way of a complex process. Then the court sets a trial date. The number of jurors used in civil trials may vary among jurisdictions. In civil trials in New York there are six jurors, and five are needed to decide a case (see chapter 1).

Before evidence is offered, the attorneys for each party have a separate right to make an opening statement of what they hope to prove by the evidence they will present; first the plaintiff, then the defendant. At the conclusion of the opening statements the presentation of evidence begins. At the close of all the evidence, each side, in reverse order, may make a closing argument, stating why the trier of the case should decide in its favor.

The presentation of evidence begins with the plaintiff, who must show by a preponderance of the evidence (more than 50% certain) the following:

1. A duty was owed by the defendant to the plaintiff. *The duty was a result of a dentist-patient relationship* (see chapter 3).
2. There was a standard of care to which the defendant should have adhered. *To establish the standard, the patient is required to present testimony by experts* (see chapter 6).
3. The defendant departed from this standard of care. *Experts are required to present this testimony.*
4. The patient suffered an injury. *Experts are required to describe the injury and its extent—whether temporary or permanent, and the cost of repair.*

5. A proximate, or direct, cause of the injury was the defendant's departure from the standard of care owed the plaintiff.

If the plaintiff-patient does not present evidence of an expert as to the standard of care to which the defendant-dentist is held, the case against the dentist will be dismissed on motion by the defense attorney at the conclusion of the plaintiff's case. Keep in mind, however, that if the claim is negligence and not malpractice, no expert testimony by the plaintiff is required; a jury of laymen without assistance is able to decide the standard of care to be exercised by the defendant. For example, should a dentist extract the wrong tooth, no expert is needed (see chapter 4).

The burden is on the plaintiff to prove all of the above by a preponderance of evidence, from testimony of witnesses, including the patient and experts if called for, and from demonstrative evidence such as patient records, radiographs, and photographs. The plaintiff's attorney will call his client to the witness stand and, by direct examination, establish that a doctor-patient relationship did exist between the dentist and the patient, and so a duty was owed to the patient. If the defendant feels that there was no doctor-patient relationship, the patient will be cross-examined in an attempt to show that there was no doctor-patient relationship, and therefore, no duty owed to the patient by the dentist. The plaintiff's attorney will go on, by the testimony of "friendly" experts, to establish the standard of care to which the defendant-dentist should be held, and to show that the defendant departed from that standard. These experts may be, and usually are, cross-examined by the defense lawyer. During the plaintiff's case, demonstrative evidence may be, and usually is, presented to the jury, eg, the patient's treatment records, radiographs, casts, etc. At the end of the plaintiff's case, the defense attorney is likely to ask the judge to direct a verdict for the defendant, on the grounds that the plaintiff has not shown by a preponderance of the evidence that the defendant was guilty of malpractice. Rarely will the judge direct a verdict, and so the case goes on.

It is now time for the defense to present its evidence to rebut the allegations of the plaintiff with its own witnesses, experts, and demonstrative evidence. The defense may show that the patient contributed to the injury by not cooperating in his care (see section 13.5). In a civil trial, unlike a criminal trial, the defendant-dentist must take the witness stand to undergo direct examination by his attorney and cross examination by the patient's attorney. The process is never pleasant (see chapter 15). At the conclusion of the evidence, attorneys for each side make a closing statement, summing up their case and letting the jury know what it should decide.

Following the closing statements, the judge takes over center stage. The jury decides the facts and the judge instructs (charges) the jury as to the law to be applied, depending upon the facts as determined by the jury. The judge may say, "If you find the following to be true, the law to be applied is . . ." In addition, the judge may provide the jury with legal definitions of terms used in the case, eg, malpractice, comparative negligence, and standards of care. After the judge's charge, the jury retires for its deliberations, and subsequently presents its verdict. If the dentist is found culpable, the jury makes an award for damages. The damages may be general, special, but rarely punitive.

Case Report 2

Title: Dental Malpractice—Failure to Premedicate Patient with Heart Murmur—Endocarditis and Subsequent Valve Replacement—Defense Verdict

[C. P]

v

[S.T.], DDS; [C.R.], DDS; [G.W.], DDS; [T.S.], DDS; and Oral Surgery and Implant Center of [X]

Facts: Plaintiff-patient, a 42-year-old social worker at the time, presented to Deft Oral Surgery and Implant Center for oral surgery on 10/28/91. Pltf claimed that Deft was negligent in failing to premedicate him prior to performing the surgery. Pltf testified that he informed the employees of the Center that he had a heart murmur that required him to be premedicated prior to any dental procedure. At trial, Deft produced a medical history card, signed by Pltf, which indicated that he did not have a heart murmur. Pltf claimed that he was called to the treatment room before he was able to complete the history card, and contended that he signed a blank history card and someone from the Center filled in the negative answers.

Pltf claimed that as a result of Deft's failure to premedicate him, he contracted bacterial endocarditis, which necessitated a 6-week hospitalization and treatment with intravenous antibiotics. Pltf claimed that he then suffered a gradual deterioration of heart function as a result of the endocarditis, requiring mitral valve repair surgery in 7/96. Pltf's oral surgery expert testified that Defts were negligent in failing to take a proper medical history. Pltf's infectious disease expert claimed that the endocarditis was related to the surgery performed by Dr [T.]. Pltf's cardiologist testified that the valve repair surgery was a consequence of the endocarditis.

Defts contended that Pltf was at fault in failing to provide a complete and accurate medical history before the oral surgery. Defts further claimed that a therapeutic dose of penicillin provided by the referring dentist, co-Deft Dr [R.] coupled with a therapeutic dose given postoperatively by Dr [T.], was sufficient to eliminate any bacteria from the blood stream that could cause the endocarditis. Defts further argued that the normal incubation period for bacterial endocarditis related to dental treatment is 2 to 4 weeks, and that the 12-week incubation period in this case was too long to be causally related to the dental treatment. Deft's cardiology expert testified that the heart surgery performed in 1996 was the result of a degenerative condition, and was not related to the endocarditis.

Demonstrative evidence: color visuals of a normal mitral valve, a prolapsed mitral valve, and a myxomatous mitral valve.

No offer; demand: $2,000,000.

Pltf experts: Oral surgeon, cardiologist, infectious disease specialist.

Deft experts: Oral surgeon, cardiologist; internist, infectious disease specialist.

2-week trial. Jury deliberation: 4 hours. All female.

[11]New York Medical Malpractice 1998; 12(2):12.

[12]New York Medical Malpractice 1998; 11(11):12.

Awards made by the jury may be reduced by the trial judge if he feels that the amount of the award was not supported by the evidence. At times, if the decision is against the dentist but the award seems excessive, his attorney may ask the appellate court to reduce the award. Case Reports 1[11] and 2[12] describe jury trials reported in *New York Medical Malpractice* (see chapter 1; for additional cases of reported jury trials, see chapter 16).

Case Report 3

Dental Malpractice—Permanent Paresthesia After Extractions—Plaintiff Verdict

[M.B.]

v

[A.K.]

Verdict: For plaintiff. Breakdown: $250,000 for past pain and suffering; $500,000 for future pain and suffering. Subsequently settled for $200,000.

Facts: On 12/15/86, Pltf, a 23-year-old salesperson, presented to Deft's oral surgery office with dental pain and an inability to open her jaw. Deft made a clinical examination and took periapical X rays, and determined that the extraction of three molars was required. After the extractions, Pltf complained of paresthesia in the lower jaw. A permanent sensory loss in an area about the size of a silver dollar on the lower right jaw was eventually diagnosed. Pltf contended that Deft was negligent for failing to take a proper preoperative X ray showing the roots of tooth 32 and its proximity to the inferior alveolar nerve. Pltf also claimed that Deft never informed her of the risk of paresthesia.

Deft argued that paresthesia is a known risk in bottom third molar extractions and can occur even when the dentistry is proper; that Pltf could not prove a causal link between the paresthesia and a departure during the surgery; and that a substandard X ray is immaterial to the procedure once the surgeon flaps the gum and makes an intraoral inspection and operative decisions. He claimed that even if Pltf had been fully informed, she would have undergone the procedure because she was in a dental emergency.

Pltf claimed that because of the numbness, she drools and has had to adjust her eating habits. She also claimed that she has a tendency to slur her speech, and claimed that her social life has changed because she avoids interaction with strangers.

Demonstrative evidence: X rays; texts, chart, hooked root tooth anomaly; dental records.

Offer: $25,000; demand: $1,000,000; final demand: $150,000; $550,000 high/low settlement.

Note: We [the publishers] have been advised that this case lay dormant for 7 years at Supreme Court and Civil Court until present counsel substituted in late 1995. [The law in New York requires that patient records be kept for 6 years. Here is a case that was stalled in the judicial process for 7 years. Had the dentist thrown out the patient's records after 6 years he would not have been in violation of the law, but he would have been at a serious disadvantage if he needed the records to support his defense in a civil suit. The admonition to keep patient records forever if possible is based upon situations such as this one.]

Pltf expert: Dr L.R.T., prosthodontist.

Deft expert: Dr F.B., oral surgeon

5-day trial. Jury deliberation: 4 hours. Jury: 4 male, 4 female.

Case Report 4

Dental Malpractice—Orthodontic Work—Malocclusion of the Jaw

[J.S.]

v

Dr [L.S.]

Date of settlement: 12/12/95 Westchester Supreme Court

Pltf Atty: R.D.B., Esq, Manhattan

This dental malpractice action settled for $160,000 after Pltf's deposition [examination before trial]

Facts: Pltf's age was 14 when he first saw Deft Orthodontist, was treated by Deft from 1991 through 1994. Pltf claimed that Deft improperly performed orthodontic work, resulting in the necessity for additional procedures. He contended that Deft created a malocclusion of his jaw and expanded the upper dentition to the point of buccal crossbite. Pltf claimed that he will require future jaw surgery because his jaw has shifted.

Deft contended that Pltf might have required surgery in any case.

Settlements

13.8   At any time following notice of an intent to sue, a claim may be settled. A claims representative, after a discussion with the dentist and a review of the patient's record, may try to negotiate a settlement if in his opinion the suit may not be successfully defended. This is especially likely in extreme cases, such as when a dentist has extracted the wrong tooth. Suits may be settled at any time before, during, or after the trial, even after an appeal is taken and decided. Whether and when a case is settled will depend upon the opinion of the representatives of the insurance company, including the attorney assigned to the dentist, whether the suit can be successfully defended, the estimated cost of the defense, and the demand in money made by the patient's attorney. Parties may agree not to have the settlement amount disclosed. Settlements are required to be reported by the insurance company to the National Practitioners Data Bank (see chapter 2, section 2.11).

Case Reports 3 and 4 describe cases that were settled and reported in the *New York Jury Reporter.*

In many policies of professional liability insurance there is what is known as the settlement clause. It states that the insurance company shall not enter into settlement negotiations, or settle a claim, without the express written consent of the insured. This protects the dentist from a settlement entered into for the benefit of the insurance company based solely upon financial considerations, which leaves the dentist with a mark against his reputation. Most professional liability policies will lower the premium if the dentist gives up the right to pro-

Case Report 5

Dental Malpractice—Failure to Diagnose and Treat Periodontal Disease Necessitating Tooth Extractions

[S.] and [H.S.]

v

Dr [R.D.], PC

Date of settlement: 6/3/96 Nassau Supreme Court

Pltf Atty: W.M.W., Esq, Manhattan

This dental malpractice action settled for $75,000 prior to jury selection.

Facts: Pltf, a 57-year-old salesman, presented to Deft Dr [D.]. For routine dental care between 1986 and 1989. Pltf claimed that over a period of 3 years, Deft and his two associates engaged in a course of treatment that constituted dental neglect. He contended that Deft failed to treat his periodontal disease and failed to refer him to a periodontist in a timely fashion. Pltf required the extraction of several teeth and extensive restorative care as a result of his advanced periodontal disease.

Deft would have argued that Pltf's dental habits were less than acceptable and, therefore, that he caused or contributed to the periodontal disease.

hibit the insurance company from entering into settlement negotiations. Before deciding what to do about the settlement clause, you should be aware that the settlement of a claim is not an admission of guilt. If it were, few cases would be settled and the courts would be crowded beyond belief (see chapter 19).

Appeals

13.9   The losing party in the trial court may take the case to appeal. Grounds for appeal are either that the judge during the trial made a procedural ruling not in keeping with the rules of procedure or a precedent interpreting those rules, or that in instructing the jury the judge informed them of a law that was not applicable to the facts of the case as decided by the jury, or that the judge did not follow the precedent setting laws of the appellate court. Thus appeals may be based upon procedural errors committed by the trial judge, or substantive errors made by the trial judge in instructing the jury. If the appellate court finds that a procedural error was made, the case will be remanded for a new trial. If the appellate court finds that a substantive error was made, the finding of the trial court will be reversed. Should the state have two appellate levels, the case decided in the lower court will be appealed to the intermediate court, and that court's decision to the highest appellate court of the state, the court of last resort (see chapter 1).

Some cases that may be subject to appeal are not, in fact, appealed because insurance companies fear that the appellate court may set a new precedent that would be unfavorable to them. Other factors may influence their decision, such as the cost in time and money and the uncertainty of the result. Recall that there is no way that anyone, not even the most knowledgeable legal scholar, can predict what a court or judge will decide.

CHAPTER FOURTEEN

What to Do and What Not to Do If You Are Sued

What to Do If You Are Sued

14.1 Accept the service, and don't panic! Don't get nasty with the process server. First, make a copy of the papers that have been served. Keep the copy and send the original to your insurance carrier by certified mail, signed receipt requested.

Next, write a comprehensive narrative statement about the incident on a separate sheet, preferably your letterhead. Title the sheet "Confidential Report to the Insurance Carrier." Use your records to refresh your memory. Include any statements you or your office staff made to the patient, or the patient to you or your staff, about the incident. Date and sign the statement. Make a copy and send it to your insurance company. Keep the original in a safe place. The information you provide will be held in confidence and not subject to discovery by the patient or his attorney.

Next, make a copy of the patient's records and radiographs. Store the originals in a safe place. *Do not add or delete any information on the patient's treatment record.*

Tell your office staff that you have been sued. Impress upon them the need to keep the information confidential, and that they are not to provide any information about the treatment of the patient to anyone. If they are asked about the case, they are to report immediately to you.

If you or your staff are asked any questions about the suit or the treatment of the patient, refer the party to the attorney assigned to you by your carrier. If the questions are asked before the attorney is assigned, refer the party to your carrier. Send copies of all letters or requests for information you receive to the attorney, or as noted above, to the carrier.

Keep in mind that your insurance company is bound to defend you, and the attorney selected by the insurance company is your legal representative; therefore, you must make honest and complete disclosures about the patient's care to enable your attorney to make an informed judgment about the merits of the patient's claim and to plan your defense. Tell all to the attorney, and don't distort the facts to make yourself look good. The attorney is to represent your interests despite what you may have done, both good and bad. A surprise at trial about information known to you but not to your attorney may jeopardize your interest in the outcome of the suit. Your cooperation in this matter with your insurance carrier, and the attorney assigned to defend you, is essential.

If you have a personal attorney, inform him about the suit. If you do not have a personal attorney, you may consider retaining one. If the amount of the suit exceeds the limits of your policy, it is essential that you retain one to watch over your financial interests. The insurance company will send you a "reservation of rights" informing you of the fact.

What Not to Do If You Are Sued

14.2   The shock of service may bring a variety of inappropriate responses. Among them are to place the papers in the desk drawer, hoping that the problem will go away. Before you do this, remember that deadlines have to be met.

Another inappropriate response is to phone the patient, either to tell her what you think about her and what she has done, or to try to talk her out of suing you, or, if that fails, to tell her what you intend to do to her in a countersuit. Another is to call the patient's lawyer, thinking you can persuade him to advise his client to drop the suit, or that you can threaten him into dropping it with a suit for harassment. Another is the softer approach of seeking to mitigate the claim against you by informing the patient that you are willing to return your fee, or pay for additional services rendered by another dentist. Do not contact the patient-plaintiff, or her attorney, at all. If the patient calls you, state that you are not permitted to engage in conversation by instruction of your attorney. If you discover that another dentist is involved in any way in the suit against you, do not call her. There is a clause in all professional liability insurance contracts that require the dentist to cooperate with the insurance company and not to engage in any activity that may compromise the suit; all of these activities may do just that. Payments to or for the patient, except for first aid, are prohibited.

Some Additional Don'ts

14.2   1. Don't alter, or add, any notes to the patient's treatment record.
2. Don't lose any of the patient's records, X rays, test results, or reports.
3. Don't make any entries on the patient's record about the lawsuit or any other matter relating to the suit, such as receipt of the summons, demand for records, or communications with the insurance company or your attorney

(these and similar notes related to the case should be recorded on the "Confidential Report to the Insurance Carrier").

4. Don't tell anyone that you are insured.
5. Don't speak to your colleagues about the case.
6. Don't tell anyone except your staff that you are being sued.
7. Don't agree to see the patient, no matter what the reason for the proposed visit. As soon as the patient elects to file suit, the doctor-patient relationship ends, and the adversarial relationship begins; the patient chose to convert the relationship. Once papers are served, treat the patient as an adversary.
8. Don't agree to settle the claim.
9. Don't pay any expenses incurred by the patient that might relate to the injury the patient claims you might have caused.
10. Don't admit fault or guilt to anyone.

Dentist As Witness

Background

15.1   In malpractice suits, plaintiff-patients are required to introduce expert testimony; defendant-dentists, though not legally required, always introduce experts of their own. Thus a witness in a malpractice trial may appear as an expert, or as a nonparty (fact) witness. Expert witnesses offer professional opinions as to whether the treatment provided by the defendant-dentist met the standard of care, whereas nonparty witnesses provide only facts, such as the condition of the restorations, presence of caries, or periodontal status.

Are You Required to Appear in Court?

15.2   Simply because you have treated a patient, you may be asked to testify in court as a fact witness—an unpleasant experience, particularly for those not used to it. Do you have to testify? As to facts, you probably do. A court in New Jersey faced this question: A worker at an industrial plant had been injured on the job and treated by a physician. He sued his employer, and his attorney asked the physician to testify. This attorney repeatedly tried to set a date with the physician, who would always claim he was unable to commit himself. The case was postponed many times; no other physician was available to support the patient's claim of injuries. When at length the trial took place the physician did not appear, though he had promised to do so, and the attorney had tried several times to remind him by phone before and during the trial. Both sides acknowledged that without the testimony of the physician the outcome of the case would be compromised. As a result, the lawyer for the patient was forced to settle the claim before the case came to the jury for an amount he felt was wholly inadequate to compensate his client for the injury.

The patient then entered suit against the physician, claiming negligence and, among other things, "breach of his duty to treat his patient; a duty alleged to include testifying on his behalf if necessary." The court was asked to decide whether a physician who agrees to treat a patient by implication agrees to testify on the patient's behalf. The trial court decided in favor of the patient. The physician appealed. The appellate court commented thus on the trial judge's jury instructions:

> In its ensuing charge to the jury on plaintiff's negligence cause against H., [the defendant physician], the trial judge, without objection from defendant, defined a treating physician's . . . duty to his patient as follows: "A doctor, I charge you, has the duty, when he undertakes to treat a patient, to treat the whole patient unless otherwise agreed, and it can be otherwise agreed when a doctor treats an accident victim, the physician impliedly agrees to appear and testify on behalf of his patient on issues such as the nature, extent and causality of his patient's injuries. This duty, I caution you, is one tempered by reasonableness and fairness; that is, there must be a reasonable notice to the doctor and the obligation must be allowed to be discharged in a reasonable manner with minimal inconvenience consistent with the objects, however, of the testimony being elicited with consideration being given to the physician in matters such as time and place of the appearance, whenever reasonably possible. Fairness generally dictates that the physician should be fairly compensated for his time and the care of the physician's patient may never be put at risk by such an appearance. . . . With all of those considerations in mind, a doctor who fails to respond to Court on behalf of his patient, may be held liable for the damage suffered by the patient because of that refusal. You must find that the standard, as I have described it, was violated by the Doctor and in order to prevail, Plaintiff must prove that failure proximately caused his damage."

The appellate court judge affirmed the opinion of the lower court:

> Our courts have recognized, on contract principles, the enforceability of a treating physician's affirmative undertaking to testify. Although no reported decision in this jurisdiction has dealt with the physician's duty to testify as part of his duty to treat his patient, we are in general concurrence with the view of the trial judge and that expressed in Alexander and Hammonds [a Pennsylvania case]. Thus, we are satisfied that a treating physician has a duty to render reasonably required litigation assistance to his patient. . . . Clearly, a physician who tells his patient from the outset that he will not testify is not thereby absolved from rendering other litigation assistance, including the rendering of reports, consultation with counsel and forensic witnesses, and the like. By the same token, we are not prepared to say that a physician who does not make such an early disclaimer has no choice but to testify.
>
> We recognize the ongoing tensions between the medical and legal professions in respect of required physician testimony. Doctors generally do not want to come to court, and personal-injury plaintiffs cannot try their cases without them. Thus, trial judges as well as opposing counsel are ordinarily extremely indulgent in terms of scheduling adjustments, taking witnesses out of turn, and otherwise accommodating the needs of physician

witnesses. R[ule] 4:14-9 was obviously designed to provide another solution to the problem. Physicians themselves, as we have suggested, may render other litigation assistance short of testifying. But however far the litigation duty may extend at its outer limits, this much at least is clear—a treating physician is not at liberty to ignore with impunity the basic obligation of rendering a reasonable modicum of litigation assistance. Nor is he free, without compelling professional justification, to renege on a promise, reasonably and detrimentally relied upon by his patient, to render specific litigation assistance. This is what the jury here found defendant H. to have done. That finding was clearly supported by the weight of credible evidence and, just as clearly, supported the conclusion of defendant's liability to plaintiff on both tort and contract grounds.[1] (See chapter 3.)

[1]229 NJSuper 430 (1998).

It is clear from the above decisions that, at least in New Jersey and Pennsylvania, and probably in all other states (which, though they may have different rules, will nonetheless, in the interest of justice, allow patients essential testimony), once a dentist accepts a patient for care that dentist has an implied duty to appear in court on behalf of that patient, and to testify when called upon to do so. However, the New Jersey decision accepted the proposition that before accepting a patient a practitioner may enter into an express agreement with the patient not to testify, though such a practitioner must, in the least, provide the patient with a written report of treatment that then can be entered into evidence at the trial. Keep in mind that you may be subpoenaed, in which case you must either appear or face penalties imposed by the court, and that if you fail to inform your patient of your wish not to appear in court, and do not appear, you may be liable to the patient for any loss he may suffer as a result.

Dentist As Nonparty (Fact) Witness

15.3   As a fact witness you may be asked to describe to the jury the results of treatment performed of a previous dentist, or the results of an examination if the patient was specifically referred for that purpose. If you are currently treating the patient you may be asked about the oral condition of the patient at the time your treatment of the patient began. In general, your testimony will be limited to the facts; you will not be asked to assess the quality of care rendered by another dentist. If you are, the opposing attorney may object to the question. When on the witness stand you are permitted to use the patient's records to refresh your memory as to the facts.

You may become a fact witness in one of three situations:

1. If you were, or are, the treating dentist and the patient wants your testimony because of an injury unrelated to dental care, eg, an automobile accident.
2. If you are the dentist currently treating a patient who wishes to sue a previous dentist, and the patient asks you to report your findings on her oral heath at the time you first examined her.
3. If you are asked by the attorney for either side, plaintiff or defendant, before trial, to examine a patient to determine the current state of the patient's oral health.

As a fact witness you will probably be asked to submit a written report of your findings before the trial.

If you testify as a nonparty witness, and are not the treating dentist, you will not be permitted to repeat in court any statements made to you by the patient relative to the care of the defendant dentist, or any other matter related to the suit. These statements are considered self-serving and designed to bolster the patient's claim, and if you should mention them the judge will order the jury to ignore them. However, if you are the treating dentist such information is admissible because of the presumption that a patient's statements will be true when his care depends upon them.

Fee for Appearance

15.4   The fee for your appearance should be negotiated between you and the patient's attorney before you agree to appear. As a nonparty witness you may be asked to submit a written report. You may charge whatever you believe is reasonable, keeping in mind the loss of income from your practice, transportation costs, time spent in preparation for your testimony and a report, and any additional costs of your appearance. The fee must be fair and equitable. In submitting the fee, note the time spent on each activity related to the case and charge by the hour. Keep in mind that you may be subject to subpoena, in which case a minimal fee is set and paid by the court. Most attorneys, however, will not resort to a subpoena because they want a friendly witness, not one forced to give testimony.

Dentist As Expert Witness

15.5   Jurors are lay people. If they have any relationship with dentistry or dentists, other than as patients, they will be excused from serving on a jury in which a dentist is a litigant. It may seem unfair that a dentist, in the exercise of his profession, should be judged by lay people; but the purpose is to avoid bias. To help jurors arrive at a decision that involves the standard of care in technical professional services, experts in the field are called. Unlike fact witnesses, expert witnesses offer opinions. They will give testimony as to the following (see chapter 6 for a fuller discussion):

1. The standard to which the defendant-dentist should be held
2. Whether the dentist, in providing the service that caused the injury, departed from the standard
3. The severity of the injury that was caused by the departure, whether temporary or permanent
4. Whether the departure was the proximate (direct) cause of the injury
5. What treatment will be necessary to restore the patient to optimal health given the severity of the injury
6. How much the restorative treatment will cost

Any licensed dentist may qualify before the courts as an expert in matters relating to dental care. The attorney presenting the expert to the jury is required to qualify him before the court by asking about his professional background, education, experience, and any additional qualities that may add to his credibility as an expert. The purpose of the questions is to enable the jury to determine the weight to be given to the testimony. The attorney asking the questions knows the answers in advance, but wants the jury to hear them. At times the opposing attorney will interrupt by stating that she will stipulate (agree) to the qualification of the witness as an expert. Her motive is to keep the jury from hearing about the qualifications. However, this ploy almost never works; the judge will permit the qualifications to be heard by the jury.

Although, as stated above, any licensed dentist may qualify as an expert, his credibility will be affected by such credentials as years in practice, knowledge of the field of practice that caused the injury, publications, lectures, society memberships, hospital and faculty appointments, and, if the suit is related to one of the specialties of practice, board certification. For example, in a highly polarized set of facts, suppose one expert is a recent graduate and the other a dentist with 30 years' experience, author of 5 textbooks and over 30 lectures on the subject of the case, a clinical professor in a dental school, and the director of a dental department in a local hospital. If the testimony of the experts conflict on the standard of care in the community and whether the defendant-dentist departed from that standard, which expert is likely to convince the jury?

In malpractice suits the plaintiff is required to produce an expert, even, as in the following New York case, on matters such as the sufficiency of a dentist's efforts to communicate:

> Plaintiff [R.P.M.] (hereinafter plaintiff) commenced this action seeking damages for the purportedly unauthorized surgical extraction of his four lower front teeth. The trial record shows that plaintiff had been defendant Dr [G.]'s dental patient since 1980. In late 1984, [G.] advised plaintiff that all 10 of his upper teeth, as well as several lower teeth, had to be removed due to a serious periodontal problem. [G.] referred plaintiff to defendant Dr [S.], an oral surgeon, for a consultation which occurred on January 11, 1985. During the examination, Dr [S.] took two panorex X rays, one of which he sent to [G.]. On February 5, 1985, Dr [S.] conferred with [G.] by telephone as to plaintiff's condition. According to Dr [S.], it was mutually agreed that 18 teeth had to be removed, including the four lower front teeth in question. [G.], however, testified that no agreement was reached concerning the four lower front teeth. [G.] further testified that he thereafter reached a definite agreement with plaintiff to remove only 14 teeth, temporarily preserving the four lower front teeth. [G.] or his hygienist ostensibly telephoned this information to Dr [S.]'s office, but did not provide a written confirmation. Dr [S.], however, subsequently received a predetermination of benefits form, dated March 7, 1985, from plaintiff's insurer, which identified each of the 18 teeth ultimately removed. On May 2, 1985, plaintiff signed a consent to removal form in Dr [S.]'s office, which also listed 18 teeth for removal. Dr [S.] testified that this was the standard consent form utilized in the community at that time. Dr [S.] surgically removed the 18 teeth on May 6, 1985.[2]

[2]150 AD2d 967 (1989).

In deciding, the court stated,

> Initially, plaintiff argues that Supreme Court erred in dismissing the case against [G.] for lack of expert proof as to the qualitative sufficiency of [G.]'s

communication efforts. In a dental malpractice action, expert proof is required to establish matters beyond the experience of the average juror.

Absent competent medical evidence, the jury was not qualified to assess whether [G.]'s communication efforts comported with the standard acceptable for dentists in the community during this time frame.

Expert's Fee

15.6   If called as an expert you may charge whatever you feel the time spent in preparing for trial and the appearance in court is worth, including a report if you are asked to prepare one. Courts appear to place no limit on this amount; whatever is reasonable to the expert is considered reasonable to the court, regardless of the financial status of the litigant for whom the expert is appearing. In submitting the fee, note the time spent on each activity and charge by the hour.

A case decided in 1987 addressed the issue of whether an expert is able to charge whatever she wishes. Divorced parents were arguing before the court for custody of two children. One parent moved to have admitted into evidence two reports, one prepared by a physician, formerly of the court's mental health clinic, who examined the parties for the court, and one prepared by another physician who examined the parents for a court in the divorce proceeding. While both physicians were physically able to testify at the custody hearing, they demanded a fee as expert witnesses. The petitioner (one party to the action) who asked for their testimony could not afford their fees, and thus asked the court to admit their reports instead. The respondent (the other party to the action) objected to the admission of the reports as hearsay, absent the testimony of the doctors at the trial. The court thus summarized the case:

> The court is presented with the unique issue of whether these reports are admissible under certain hearsay exceptions because the witnesses are "unavailable" due solely to petitioner's financial inability to pay the demanded witness fees.
>
> The issue germane to this discussion centers around one of the physicians and his report. His request for an expert testimony fee was more than the petitioner could afford, and he refused to appear at the custody hearing. The question before the court was whether his report could be entered into evidence.

The court continued:

> *It is settled that though this court may compel the doctor to appear via subpoena, it cannot compel him to give expert opinion testimony* which is exactly the type of testimony for which the petitioner seeks his appearance.[3] (Emphasis added.)

In another New York case, the court noted,

> The plaintiff's attorney argues that he cannot produce the doctor who is alive and well simply because he cannot afford to pay the $750 that he has requested for his court appearance.
>
> The court notes that expert testimony may fall into two categories, factual and opinion. An expert may be compelled to testify to "facts" within his knowledge. [Quoting another case] "An expert may not be compelled to give his 'opinion' against his will." The distinction lies in the nature of the

[3]509 NYS2d 527 (1986).

legal process. The function of a witness is to state what he has seen, heard, or knows about the facts in issue, and he is within the command of a subpoena to do so. He is not within command of a subpoena to give an opinion based upon knowledge acquired through study.[4]

The plaintiff, therefore, moved to have the doctor's records admitted under the business records exception to the hearsay evidence rule. The defendant argued that because the doctor was available to testify, his records should not be admitted without his testimony at trial. The court noted that although the doctor could be made to testify about the "facts within his knowledge" (as a fact witness), he could not be compelled to testify as to his "opinion" (an expert witness). The court went on to admit the doctor's records into evidence, but not as to his medical opinion.

It is well to note what the Principles of Ethics and Code of Professional Conduct of the American Dental Association, in §4, 4D has to say about a dentist as an expert witness: "Dentists *may* provide expert testimony when that testimony is essential to a just and fair disposition of a judicial or administrative action." (Emphasis added.)

If you, as an expert, are asked by the opposing attorney during your testimony as to the fee you charged to testify, you should answer that no fee was charged for the testimony; a fee was charged only to compensate you for the time spent in preparing for the appearance and for the time lost from your practice to be present at the trial.

[5]ADA
Principles of
Ethics and
Code of
Professional
Conduct,
§4, 4D1.

Contingency fees, that is, fees dependant upon the winning of the suit by the side you are called upon to testify for, are unethical, and if discovered during the trial will nullify any statements you made or opinions you expressed during the trial.[5] In addition, your credibility will be lost and difficult to regain.

There are times when experts and fact witnesses other than dentists may give testimony in a dental malpractice suit, eg, anesthesiologists, neurologists, and internists, if the attorneys for either side feel that their testimony will assist the jury in deciding the case. The general rules that apply to dentists in court apply equally to all who appear in court.

Forensic Odontology

15.7 Forensic odontology, also known as forensic dentistry, is the application of the science of dentistry to the law. Forensic odontologists assist medical examiners and coroners in the identification of bodies in mass disasters and the police in the investigation of crimes. In addition, dentists may become important in assisting the police and other agencies in the prosecution of cases of child abuse. Dentists may provide critical evidence in the prosecution of crimes or the identification of crash victims.

Dentists and the Crash of TWA Flight 800

15.7.1 On July 17, 1996, TWA Flight 800 from Kennedy Airport in New York took off for Paris. There were 230 passengers aboard. Shortly after takeoff the plane exploded and crashed into the Atlantic Ocean a few miles off the south shore of Long Island in Suffolk County. About 100 bodies were recovered in the first few hours after the crash and transported to the medical examiner's office in Suffolk County.

Several years before the crash, a local dentist, Dr B.K. Friedman, volunteered his services to the medical examiner's office as a forensic dentist. He later was appointed as its official consultant. Shortly after his appointment, he organized a group of local dentists, approximately 45, into what became the Suffolk County Society of Forensic Odontologists. Dr Friedman arranged to have them trained in forensic odontology. The members of the society became part of the medical examiner's staff. After the crash of TWA 800, the members of the society were immediately called to assist in the identification of the victims. On the day following, it became apparent that there were not enough dentists for the work, and local dentists who were not members of the society were called to help. There were still not enough dentists. The dental school at State University of New York at Stony Brook was then called to help, and 11 faculty members and 29 students agreed to go to the medical examiner's office and join the dental team. The identification process took several weeks; some dentists spent over 100 hours on the job. Of the 230 passengers, dentists identified 82 with the aid of dental records, and assisted in the identification of an additional 56.

Crash victims must be positively identified for purposes of insurance and inheritance; a death certificate must be issued for each deceased passenger. Equally important, the families of the crash victims must be notified as quickly as possible of the identities of the victims for obvious personal reasons. The crash of TWA flight 800 provides a striking example of the importance of dentists in this work.

Dentists' Responsibility to the Community

15.7.2   There is no law compelling dentists to assist medical examiners in the identification of crash victims or the police in the investigation of crimes, but they have a strong moral and civic responsibility to make their special services and knowledge available. A dentist who wishes to do this should contact the local medical examiner's office and the local child protective agency.

CHAPTER SIXTEEN

Reports on Jury Trials and Disciplinary Proceedings

Jury Trials: Background

16.1   There is much to be learned about what can go wrong in the practice of the profession by witnessing a jury trial. It is there that cases are won or lost, and the outcomes are not always related to the dentist's guilt. Courtrooms in jury trials are the "trenches of litigation" in which battle is joined between the attorneys for the opposing parties. At the trial, testimony is taken of the dentist and the patient, witnesses appear, credibility is judged, reports of other dentists are submitted, experts appear for each side, and physical evidence is produced. It is not a pleasant time for the defendant-dentist. Her professional judgment and skill are attacked by the patient and other dentists in public and in front of a jury. The patient's attorney tells the jury that because of the dentist's lack of skill his client suffered an injury that could have, and should have, been avoided; that she did what other dentists in the community would not have done, or would have done better. The accused dentist will have sleepless nights, whatever the trial's outcome. The best way to prepare yourself for such an event, aside from witnessing jury trials, is reading case reports about them. In New York, a digest of the jury trials held throughout the state is published regularly.[1] Case Reports 6 to 12 describe some cases in which the dentist was on trial for allegedly committing malpractice. The descriptions are taken verbatim from the reports except that the names have been removed. To find a dentist guilty of malpractice, the patient must show, by a preponderance (more than 50%) of the evidence, that the dentist departed from the standard of care.

[1] New York Medical Malpractice. East Islip, NY: Moran.

Case Report 6

Title: Dental Malpractice—Insertion of Crown—Adjustment of Opposing Tooth—Lack of Informed Consent—Hypersensitivity

[A.B.]

v

Dr [B.]

Verdict: $25,000 for past pain and suffering. A post-trial motion is pending.

Facts: Pltf, a 35-year-old model, presented to Deft Dr [B.] in December 1988 for the insertion of a crown in the lower left molar. She claimed that after he inserted the crown, Deft overfiled the opposing upper molar, exposing the dentin. Pltf claimed the Deft failed to advise her of the extent of the adjustment required on the installation of the crown. She also contended that he failed to warn her of the risks and failed to provide alternative treatment. As a result of the malpractice, Pltf claimed, she has hypersensitivity in that area and has difficulties eating. Deft denied that he deviated from standard dental practice and claimed that he warned Pltf about the need for possible adjustment. He also contended that it is acceptable to adjust the opposing teeth when installing a crown. Deft contended that if any dentin was exposed, it may have been due to the work of the prior treating dentist, who had worked on the tooth in question both before and after Deft's procedure. The jury found for Pltf question of informed consent, but found for Deft on the issue of malpractice.

Demonstrative evidence (physical evidence presented at trial): dental records; impressions of Pltf's teeth; model of tooth.

Pltf experts: Dr [S.L.], retired dentist; Dr [R.B.D.], treating dentist.

Deft expert: Dr [C.F.], dentist.

6-day trial.

Case Report 7

Title: Dental Malpractice—Insertion of Bridge—Defense Verdict

[G.T.]

v

Dr [T.] and Dr [K.]

Verdict: Defense.

Facts: Pltf presented to Deft [T.] in 1989 complaining of pain in his upper front teeth. Deft [T.] examined him and determined that Pltf required a bridge from the upper left canine to the upper right canine. Pltf only had four teeth on his upper jaw. The bridge was installed with temporary cement, with the understanding that Pltf would return and adjustments would be made to better fit his mouth. Deft [T.] claimed that he told Pltf to return in a few weeks so that he could adjust the bridge and install a removable bridge on posterior top and bottom. He contended that Pltf did not return to his office for 6 months and claimed that when he finally returned, he required root canal on several other teeth. Deft testified that he decided to delay replacing the bridge until after the root canals were completed and Pltf had time to recover. Deft contended that he again told Pltf to come back to his office soon to have the root canals done. Pltf did not return for another 9 months. When Pltf returned to Deft's office in February 1991, Deft began treating decay that formed under the top teeth where the bridges were mounted. In May 1991, Pltf stopped treatment with Deft [T.] and presented to third-party Deft [K.] who informed Pltf that his four upper teeth could not be saved, and he extracted them. Dr [K.], testified as Pltf's expert, claimed that Deft [T.] was negligent for failing to properly prepare the teeth for crowns and a bridge, and for improperly performing the root canals. He testified that Deft [T.] should have offered Pltf the option of removable partial dentures. He claimed that the failure to adequately prepare the teeth for the bridgework caused the upper teeth to decay. Deft contended that the upper teeth decayed because Pltf failed to keep up his treatment schedule at a regular interval. He also claimed that Deft [K.] departed from accepted medical practice by failing to refer Pltf to a specialist who could have restored the teeth without surgery.

Demonstrative evidence: X rays; model of the teeth and the bridge; diagram of the teeth and how they are prepared.

Offer: $20,000; demand: $65,000; amount asked of jury: $100,000.

Pltf expert: Dr [R.S.], dentist.

Deft experts: Dr [B.R.P.], periodontist; Dr [E.J.B.], dentist.

2-week trial. Jury deliberation: 2 hours. Jury: 2 male, 4 female.

Case Report 8

Title: Dental Malpractice—Root Canal—Installation of Three-Tooth Bridge

[E.] and [R.N.]

v

Dr [P.]

Verdict: $66,930. Breakdown: $5,000 for past pain and suffering; $1,930 for past dental expenses; $30,000 for future pain and suffering; $30,000 for future dental expenses.

A post-trial motion is pending.

Facts: Pltf, a school teacher in her late 40s, presented to Deft Dr [P.] in Middletown in December 1991 for root canal to the lower right rear tooth. Pltf argued that Deft negligently performed the root canal by drilling a hole that he failed to fill, which later necessitated the removal of the tooth. She subsequently underwent the installation of a three-tooth bridge. Pltf's expert testified that Deft deviated from standard dental practice by drilling the hole in her tooth. Deft testified that Pltf was referred to him by her treating dentist, and that the tooth was damaged before he began treatment. Deft's expert reviewed the X rays and office notes, and testified that there was no deviation from standard dental treatment.

Demonstrative evidence: molds of the lower jaw which were used for the bridge.

Specials (out of pocket costs): $1,930 for past dental expenses for the bridge.

No offer; demand: $50,000.

Pltf expert: Dr [M.S.], treating dentist.

Deft expert: Dr [B.W.], dentist.

3-day trial. Jury deliberation: 6 hours. Jury: 3 male, 3 female.

Case Report 9

Title: Dental Malpractice—Extraction of Wisdom Tooth—Lack of Informed Consent and Negligence

Defense Verdict

[M.S.]

v

Dr [T.]

Verdict: Defense.

Facts: Pltf, a 33-year-old EEG technician, presented to Deft's office for an evaluation of her left lower wisdom tooth in 1990 after being referred to him by her dentist. Deft decided that the tooth could not be saved and had to be extracted. The procedure was performed in Deft's office 2 weeks later. Postoperatively, Pltf developed paresthesia and numbness of the tongue, lip and cheek. Pltf contended that the procedure was done without her informed consent because Deft did not tell her about the risk of permanent impairment as a result of the surgery. Pltf's expert testified that Deft negligently removed the tooth, causing injury to the inferior alveolar nerve and the lingual nerve. He also testified that the consent form used by Deft was obsolete, and the surgical technique employed in the procedure was incorrect, that Deft improperly used anesthesia, and that Deft used the wrong suture method. Deft contended that the consent form was appropriate and that he gave Pltf all the pertinent information regarding the risks of this surgery. He further testified that he had no alternative but to remove the tooth because of its extreme state of decay and the possibility of infection. Deft contended that the absence of any alternative treatment negated the cause of action for lack of informed consent. The court agreed and dismissed that cause of action for lack of informed consent. On the negligence issue, Deft contended that the surgery was done properly, noting that postoperative X rays were indicative of a nontraumatic extraction. Deft contended that injury to the nerve is sometimes unavoidable. Deft's experts testified that some of Pltf complaints of pain were inconsistent with nerve distribution in the area of the injury.

Demonstrative evidence: X rays.

No offer; demand: $400,000.

Pltf experts: Dr [B.R.], oral surgeon; Dr [E.S.], neurologist.

Deft experts: Dr [M.G.], oral surgeon; Dr [R.B.], neurologist.

6-day trial. Jury deliberation: 1.5 hours. Jury: 1 male, 5 female.

Case Report 10

Title: Dental Malpractice—Tooth Extraction—Severed Lingual Nerve—Defense Verdict

[B.L.]

v

Dr [R.]

Verdict: Defense.

Facts: Pltf, a 38-year-old chiropractor, testified that in November 1989, he presented to Deft for the extraction of his upper and lower third right molars. Pltf contended that Deft severed the lingual nerve while performing the extraction. Pltf's expert testified that Deft failed to remove enough bone before removing the teeth. He claimed that, based on the dental X rays, Deft had to exert greater force to remove the teeth because there was too much bone left, thereby damaging the nerve. On cross-examination, Pltf's expert admitted that damaging the lingual nerve was an accepted risk of the procedure. Pltf also claimed that he was not fully informed of the risks of the procedure and that he should have been referred to an oral surgeon. Deft contended that damage to the lingual nerve is an accepted risk of the procedure. He testified that he informed Pltf of this before the procedure was undertaken. He further testified that the tooth came out easily and that there was no need to remove much bone to extract it. He also testified that he removed as little bone as possible to make the procedure less traumatic. Deft's expert testified that the lingual nerve is an aberrant nerve that cannot be found on an X ray. Deft's dentistry expert testified that Deft, given his extensive experience, was qualified to perform the procedure and did not have to refer Pltf to an oral surgeon.

Injuries: paresthesia to the lower right side of the mouth; numbness. Pltf claimed that as a result of the injuries he frequently bites his tongue.

Demonstrative evidence: X rays.

Pltf expert: Dr [L.R.], dentist.

Deft experts: Dr [S.L.], dentist; Dr [A.P.A.], oral surgeon.

4-day trial. Jury deliberation: 2 hours. Jury: 4 male, 2 female.

Case Report 11

Title: Dental Malpractice—Treatment of Malocclusion—Further Dental Treatment Required

[T.W.]

v

Dr [D.]

Verdict: $195,000. Breakdown: $100,000 for past pain and suffering; $5,000 for past dental expenses; $40,000 for future pain and suffering; $50,000 for future dental expenses (59 years).

Facts: Pltf, age 12 at the time of the procedure in 1984, testified that she presented to Deft Dr [D.], a general dentist, with a separation between her two front teeth. This was a heredity trait from her mother. Deft diagnosed the condition as a Class II malocclusion and inserted a full set of brackets and arch wires. Pltf had 38 cavities on 20 teeth when the brackets were removed and was required to undergo root canal therapy on five teeth and the placement of a crown on one tooth. Pltf's expert testified that Deft was negligent for misdiagnosing the initial condition, for failing to properly treat her, for failing to take X rays, and for failing to monitor her teeth during the orthodontic treatment. Pltf's expert also testified that because Pltf had a cosmetic problem Deft should have referred her to an orthodontist. Pltf was ultimately treated by an orthodontist to close the space with brackets on six upper teeth for approximately 9 months followed by a permanent retainer. Deft argued that Pltf failed to exercise good home care and dental hygiene resulting in the subsequent treatment after the removal of the braces. *Pltf denied that Deft made an issue of her hygiene and argued that his office records appeared to be altered about the noncompliance.* Deft's expert testified that he examined Pltf in 1993 and found evidence of poor home care. Pltf's subsequent dentist testified that he treated her for 7 years and found that she did not have poor hygiene. Pltf is now a 21-year-old college student. She has cosmetic laminates on 11 front teeth and a crown on one tooth. Testimony indicated that all 12 anterior teeth must be crowned and these crowns will require replacement during her life, as will multiple composite fillings. (Emphasis added.)

Demonstrative evidence: enlarged office records; model of teeth; Pltf's dental impression.

Pltf experts: Dr [J.A.], orthodontist; Dr [R.P.], treating dentist.

Deft expert: Dr [H.W.], examining dentist.

5-day trial. Jury deliberation: 3.5 hours. Jury: 4 male, 2 female.

Case Report 12

Title: Dental Malpractice—Surgery on Infected Gums Without Antibiotics, Endocarditis Results

[R.D.]

v

Dr [Z.]

Verdict: $600,000 for Plaintiff. Breakdown: $500,000 for past pain and suffering; $100,000 for future pain and suffering

Facts: Plaintiff underwent gum surgery performed by Dr [A.] and testified that Dr [B.] represented himself to be a Diplomate of the American Board of Oral and Maxillofacial Surgeons. Testimony indicated that neither Dr [A.] nor Dr [B.] were board certified at the time of the incident and that Dr B. was not listed by the American Dental Association as an oral or maxillofacial surgeon.

   Plaintiff claimed that Dr [B.] operated on her gums and sutured them, but did not prescribe antibiotics either pre- or postoperatively. Plaintiff's experts testified that as a result, an infection entered her bloodstream and traveled to her heart, precipitating sub-acute bacterial endocarditis and causing permanent heart damage. Plaintiff contended that she will require antibiotics for any dental or surgical care for the rest of her life. Plaintiff had no history of scarlet fever. Plaintiff's experts contended that the tissue was "angry" and "very friable" with three infected teeth and bleeding and oozing gums, and that it was negligent to perform surgery under these conditions. Plaintiff contended that Defendant simply forgot to prescribe antibiotics. Defendant claimed that he called her at home but that she was not there and he assumed she would visit his office the following week. He also argued that he only cleaned Plaintiff's teeth. Plaintiff contended that if that was so, no sutures would have been needed.

No offer; demand: $150,000; amount asked of jury: $2,000,000.

Pltf expert: Dr [B.R.], oral surgeon; Dr [R.T.], dentist.

Deft expert: Dr [V.S.B.], oral surgeon; Dr [C.R.], oral surgeon; Dr [D.S.], dentist.

1-month trial. Jury deliberation: 3 days. Jury: 3 male, 3 female.

Disciplinary Cases: Background

16.2   Each state has disciplinary proceedings against dentists who have been accused of violating one of the laws or the rules and regulations included in its Dental Practice Act. In some states the findings of the disciplinary board are published and distributed by the licensing agency to dentists licensed in the state. In others, although the findings of the disciplinary board are subject to freedom of information acts, they are not published. The current trend is to make public, through the Internet, cases in which a dentist was disciplined by the licensing agency. In New York, such information is available monthly. Other states provide the same information, and some include also the malpractice history of the practitioners, in favor of which there is much public pressure. Currently New York reports only disciplinary findings.[2] Below are reported cases. The dentists' names, addresses, and license numbers have been deleted here, although they are present on the Internet.

The degree of proof necessary to find a dentist guilty of violating one of the rules or regulations of the dental board varies from state to state. One case will illustrate the standard in New York. A dentist who distributed a pamphlet to his patients about his ability to diagnose and treat dental disease as a bacterial infection was accused and found guilty by the licensing agency of "unprofessional conduct" as defined in the Dental Practice Act. He appealed based upon the insufficiency of evidence of his guilt. The appellate court in reversing the decision of the licensing agency stated, "As to the sufficiency of the evidence, a determination of guilt of professional misconduct must be based upon a preponderance of the evidence."[3] Other states use a different standard. California requires a clear and convincing weight of evidence (somewhat more than "preponderance" but less than "beyond a reasonable doubt") to convict. The California Court of Appeals, in deciding a case in which a physician was found guilty of negligence by the state's licensing agency, stated:

> It has been generally recognized that administrative proceedings, including proceedings to revoke or suspend a license, are civil rather than criminal in nature. Generally, proof in civil cases is required by a preponderance of the evidence. However, in a number of situations, a greater degree of proof, usually clear and convincing evidence, is required.

The court went on to state:

> Since it is apparent that the underlying purpose of disciplining both attorneys and physicians is protection of the public, it would be anomalous to require a higher degree of proof in disciplinary hearings involving attorneys or real estate agents than in hearings involving physicians. Accordingly, we hold that the proper standard of proof in an administrative hearing to revoke or suspend a doctor's license should be *clear and convincing proof to a reasonable certainty* and not a mere preponderance of the evidence.[4] (Emphasis added.)

Thus New York requires a lesser level of evidence to convict a practitioner of violating a provision of the Dental Practice Act than does California. The penalties range from "censure and reprimand" at the mildest, through fines of less than $10,000, mandatory retraining, therapy, and public service, to loss or suspension of license.

[2] Internet address: www.op.nysed.gov/ramthly.htm.

[3] 517 NYS2d 599 (1987).

[4] 185 CalRptr 601 (1982).

How does the New York Office of Professional Disciple (OPD), know to investigate a dentist? There are three major sources of information: other dentists, employees (current and past), and patients. Reports to the OPD can be made anonymously. In one case a dentist went to court to force the OPD to provide her with the name of the person registering the complaint. The court ruled that the information should remain confidential. Complaints about physicians must be made in writing and signed, but remain confidential. The State Education Department publishes a pamphlet listing the licensed professions, stating what constitutes professional misconduct, and providing a toll-free telephone number for reporting a licensed professional suspected of professional misconduct. The line is open 24 hours a day.

Disciplinary Reports

16.2.1

Case 1. Licensee was found guilty of charges of prescribing a medication to which he knew, or should have known, that the patient was allergic, and failing to keep accurate patient records.

Board of Regents Action: Censure and Reprimand, $1,500 fine.

Case 2. Licensee admitted to charges of submission of fraudulent insurance claim forms and negligent submission of insurance claim forms.

Board of Regents Action: 3-year suspension, execution of last 2 years of suspension stayed; probation 3 years under various terms; $50,000 fine.

Case 3. Licensee admitted to charges of failing to fill a root canal to the apex, leaving two silver wires protruding through the surface of a tooth, filing two teeth leaving open contacts, failing to diagnose a patient's caries, and filling a tooth which was in need of root canal therapy.

Board of Regents Action: Partial suspension for not less than 6 months and until successfully complies with certain conditions; probation 2 years under various terms; $5,000 fine.

Case 4. Licensee is found guilty of charges of prescribing excessive quantities of controlled substances, issuing prescriptions for a controlled drug for a non-patient despite the fact that this person had no condition requiring the drug; failing to maintain accurate records; delegating responsibility of a suture removal to a nonprofessional; and administering general anesthesia inappropriately.

Board of Regents Action: 3-year suspension, execution of last 2 years of suspension stayed; successful completion of certain course work; probation 3 years.

Case 5. Licensee admitted to charges of billing an insurance company for work he agreed with a patient to do without charge.

Board of Regents Action: 1-year suspension, execution of suspension stayed; probation 1 year; $500 fine.

Case 6. Licensee admitted to charges of writing numerous controlled substance prescriptions in the name of a relative, submitting the prescriptions for himself, charging the cost of the prescriptions to his relative's prescription payment plan, and obtaining controlled substances for self-administration for nondental conditions.

Board of Regents Action: 2-year suspension, execution of suspension stayed; probation 2 years; $2,500 fine.

Case 7. Licensee admitted to charges of willfully filing false Medicaid and insurance claims.

Board of Regents Action: Application to surrender license granted.

Case 8. Licensee was found guilty of fraudulently submitting insurance claims forms on more than one occasion, and signing various prescriptions while his license was suspended.

Board of Regents Action: Revocation; $7,500 fine.

Case 9. Licensee was found guilty of certifying that he had provided certain services to two patients when he had not.

Board of Regents Action: Censure and Reprimand.

Case 10. Licensee did not contest charges of overpreparing a patient's teeth for porcelain veneers, preparing castings that fit poorly for a patient, and using excessive amount of cement when inserting a crown. Licensee admitted to charges of practicing while his ability was impaired by mental disability.

Board of Regents Action: Indefinite suspension until fit to practice—upon termination of suspension, probation for 2 years under various terms to commence if and when return to practice.

Case 11. Licensee was found guilty of submitting an insurance claim form on which he certified that he had rendered dental services that he had not.

Board of Regents Action: 2-year suspension, execution of suspension stayed; probation 2 years; $2,000 fine.

Case 12. Licensee did not contest charges of prescribing drugs for four patients for nondental purposes and ordering drugs at wholesale for nondental purposes.

Board of Regents Action: 2-year suspension, execution of suspension stayed; probation 2 years; $2,000 fine.

Case 13. Licensee admitted to submitting an insurance claim form for work not performed and failing to pay a fine pursuant to terms of probation.

Board of Regents Action: 1-year suspension, execution of last 9 months of suspension stayed; probation stayed 1 year under various terms; 100 hours of public service.

Case 14. Licensee admitted to charges of failing to use required infection prevention techniques.

Board of Regents Action: 2-year suspension, execution of suspension stayed; probation 2 years; $500 fine.

Case 15. Licensee was found guilty of charges of failure to inform a patient that her tooth had been perforated and failure to record the perforation in the chart maintained for the patient.

Board of Regents Action: 1-year suspension, execution of suspension stayed; probation 1 year.

Case 16. Licensee was found guilty of charges of having been convicted of Offering a False Instrument for Filing in the Second Degree, a Class A Misdemeanor.

Board of Regents Action: 2-year suspension, execution of last 21 months of suspension stayed; probation 2 years; $5,000 fine; 100 hours of public service.

Case 17. Licensee was found guilty of charges of having been convicted of Grand Larceny in the Third Degree, a Class D Felony.

Board of Regents Action: 5 years suspension, execution of last 4 years of suspension stayed; probation 5 years; 100 hours of public service.

Case 18. Licensee did not contest charges of failing to adequately treat two teeth.

Board of Regents Action: Censure and Reprimand; $2,500 fine; probation 1 year under various terms to be terminated upon proof of successful completion of certain course work.

Case 19. Licensee admitted to charges of prescribing controlled drugs for herself and family members for nondental purposes and failing to maintain patient records, ordering controlled drugs at wholesale for nondental purposes, failing to maintain records of controlled drugs received, failing to properly dispose of controlled drugs not dispensed to patient, failing to prepare and maintain biennial inventories of all controlled drugs possessed by her between 1987 and 1991; preparing and inserting an ill-fitting fixed bridge in the mouth of one patient and one ill-fitting denture into the mouth of another patient.

Board of Regents Action: 2-year suspension, execution of suspension stayed; probation 2 years; $2,500 fine.

Case 20. Licensee admitted to charges of preparing and inserting an ill-fitting fixed bridge in the mouth of one patient and one ill-fitting denture into the mouth of another patient.

Board of Regents Action: 3-year suspension, execution of suspension stayed; probation 5 years; $2,500 fine.

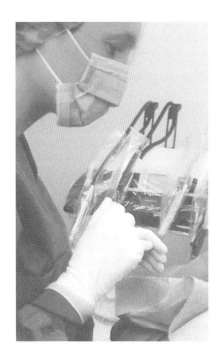

Risk Management in Dental Practice

Background

17.1   This chapter will provide dentists, hygienists, dental assistants, and other office personnel with information about the legal risks of practice and methods designed to eliminate or reduce them. Its goal is to enable dentists and their employees to practice without worry or litigation.

The malpractice crisis of the early 1970s spread from physicians and hospitals to dentists less then a decade later. During that period, both the number of malpractice suits and the amounts of jury awards increased dramatically. The manner in which dentists managed their offices and conducted their practices made them easy targets of patients unhappy with or injured by the results of treatment, and there was no shortage of attorneys willing to represent these patients. The losses were indemnified by insurance companies, who were also paid to defend the claims. To compensate for their losses, they increased their premiums. The situation deteriorated to such an extent that for a short period of time in one state (Massachusetts) there was no insurance company that would insure dentists for malpractice.

However, the problem for dentists did not end with the attacks of patients and their attorneys. Responding to public pressure, government agencies joined in. Licensing agencies scrutinized the office practices of physicians and dentists for professional misconduct. A federal agency, the Occupational Safety and Health Administration (OSHA), adopted regulations that appeared to target dental offices. The result was a major increase in the cost of practice, which now required one to buy surgical gloves, gowns, masks, etc. Then, as some dentists refused the accept patients who had AIDS or HIV, or who fell within a group thought likely to contract the disease, the media seemed to delight in their exposure. Local and state human rights agencies brought criminal actions against dentists who were alleged to have discriminated against high-disease-risk patients. Some court decisions exonerated dentists charged with discrimination, finding that human rights agencies lacked jurisdiction over the practices of dentists in their private offices. To make certain that health providers, including dentists, could be held responsible for their alleged discriminatory practices, the federal government passed a law, the Americans with Disabilities Act, that declared their private offices "places of public accommodation" and therefore subject to the jurisdiction of local, state, and federal antidiscrimination agencies and their laws. As a result, dentists who discriminated in any manner against a widely defined health-risk population group were subject to severe punitive action.

During the years that followed the crisis of the early 1970s, the costs and risks of practice took a dramatic upward turn. Once a stable profession far removed from public concern, dentistry came dramatically into public view and endured some serious criticism. The community and the law began to focus on what dentists did, how they did it, to whom they did it, and to whom they chose not to do it. Patients' rights and the courts pierced the armor of anonymity that had protected dentistry since the early days of the profession. Dentist-patient relationships suffered as many dentists began to view patients as possible adversaries in litigation. The practice of dentistry was forever changed. Dentists practicing after the 1980s even looked different than those who practiced in the 1970s; the short white jacket over a shirt and tie were replaced by a modified surgical gown, surgical gloves, and eye or face shields.

Led by the malpractice insurance companies, many of whom suffered great losses in the 1970s and early 1980s as a result of a dramatic increase in malpractice litigation and soaring jury verdicts, the dental profession took positive action to protect itself from the rising cost of insurance and the loss of professional reputation that resulted from claims of malpractice brought by patients and of professional misconduct brought by government agencies. Borrowing a strategy from industry, the profession adopted programs in risk management. Risk management presentations appeared in almost all continuing dental educational programs, many supported by insurance companies. To entice dentists to attend these programs, many insurance companies rewarded attendance with premium reductions.

Introduction to Risk Management

17.2   The goal of a program in risk management is to protect the financial resources of an industry or business from legal action. For health practitioners, it is designed also to protect the practitioner's professional reputation and license to practice. An effective risk management program includes:

1. Loss identification (exposure to legal claims)
2. Loss analysis (evaluation of loss experience)

3. Loss avoidance or reduction
4. Loss financing (financing claims exposure)

Three activities are associated with risk management:

1. Identifying areas of legal vulnerability
2. Instituting corrective or preventive measures
3. Purchasing liability insurance (see chapter 19)

This chapter will provide information related to the first two activities listed above. It is based on a thorough review of cases brought against dentists and opinions of courts deciding medical and dental malpractice suits. Court cases and decisions reported in previous chapters will not be repeated, though many of the risk management recommendations are based upon such decisions.

The risk management activities included here are designed to help the dentist avoid professional liability, which relates to injuries that result from the treatment of patients, and not general liability, which relates to physical accidents that occur in the office. If, for example, in the course of treatment, a patient's tongue is lacerated by a disk, that is professional liability, which may be covered by malpractice insurance. On the other hand, if a patient falls in the waiting room as a result of tripping over an electric cord, that is general liability, which may be covered by a general liability policy.

An Admonition

17.3   One risk management strategy may not protect you if you fail to follow them all. For example, a dentist is claimed not to have informed his patient that during root canal treatment the tip of a file broke and became lodged in the canal, though he had recorded the facts in the patient's record and they were clearly evident to the jury when the patient's record was entered into evidence. However, it was later shown that the dentist altered another part of the record following notice of the suit, and the entire record therefore became suspect as to its accuracy and truthfulness, including the entry about the broken file. Thus, one risk management recommendation (ie, keeping complete and accurate patient records) was followed, but compromised by the failure to follow another (ie, never making any changes or additions to a patient's record once you are aware that the patient intends to bring a suit against you, or that a suit has been filed).This is a clear case of *loss without fault* (see section 17.5). Sadly, this set of facts is not uncommon; the author has seen them many times in lost malpractice cases.

Levels of Legal Risk: Informed Decision Making

17.4   *Levels of legal risk* is an artificial legal concept that applies directly to risk management. It is the degree to which a dentist is willing to bear risk in the performance of a professional service. Before deciding what to do in a given situation, dentists make an informed decision about how much risk they will accept. They may even choose to ignore procedures mandated by law if they are willing to risk being caught. A firm risk management rule, however, is that no matter how slight the risk of being found in violation of the law, never do it. One should apply the levels of legal risk concept only to matters not mandated by law. For example, a dentist may decide to treat a patient without first taking radiographs because there is no black letter law that requires a dentist to take radiographs; but a dentist may be found guilty of malpractice should an injury to the patient result that could have been prevented by radiographs.

Accusations of negligence or malpractice are relatively rare, given the numbers of patients a dentist treats within a year and the number of treatment episodes performed on each patient. However, before you decide on a course of action in your practice, you should take into account the risk. You should ask yourself, "How much risk will this involve?" Make an informed decision in view of all the risks and benefits of taking an action.

Refusing to treat patients who do not follow your advice exposes you to little legal risk, while agreeing to treat patients despite their refusal to follow your advice exposes you to great legal risk. A good example of the concept relates to a dentist's advice that a patient seek consultation and or treatment by a periodontist. If the patient refuses and the dentist proceeds with the care (eg, a fixed partial denture) the legal risk to the dentist may be great because if it is shown that the dentist should not have fabricated a fixed partial denture before the patient's periodontal needs were met by a specialist, the dentist may be found guilty of malpractice. If the dentists refuses care, the risk is small. Under some circumstances, you may be willing to take the greater risk after assessing the benefits of continuing to treat the patient, but you must consider the risks before deciding what to do.

Loss Without Fault

17.5   Another artificial legal concept is *loss without fault.* It evolved from a study conducted by the author in the 1980s during the crisis in dental malpractice litigation. The results of this study were both disturbing and enlightening. Four hundred cases of alleged dental malpractice in a metropolitan county in New York were examined, from the initial service of papers to the closing of the case, by a panel of experts who were to advise the dentists' insurance company whether the suit should be defended or, if possible, settled. If the panel recommended a trial, the insurance company was bound by the recommendation of the panel. The panel was made up of specialists in oral and maxillofacial surgery, periodontics, orthodontics, general dentistry, and dental law. The panel had access to the dentist's records, radiographs, professional experience, education, and training; all reports related to the case, including those of any dentist who examined the patient; hospital records if the patient had been hospitalized; the bill of particulars prepared by the patient's attorney; and, in most cases, the transcripts of the examinations before trial of the dentist and the complaining patient. The defendant-dentist always was present to be examined, questioned, and evaluated as a witness by the panel, and the dentist's assigned attorney was often present. The patient was never present. The discussions of the panel, and its results, were confidential and not subject to subpoena; they were the legal work-effort in preparation for trial and so protected by law (see chapter 13).

Of the 400 cases reviewed by the panel that were included in this study, the panel recommended settlement in 160 because it was of the opinion that the dentist had been guilty of malpractice. However, of the remaining 240 cases where no malpractice was evident, 120 were recommended for settlement because the panel was of the opinion that the suit could not be successfully defended. These were cases of loss without fault. The major contributing factors leading to the decision to seek settlement were:

1. Poor or lacking treatment records, including but not limited to omissions, illegible entries, and generally poor documentation
2. The professional arrogance of the dentist during questioning
3. The dentist's lack of sufficient training or experience in the subject of the suit
4. The dentist's inability to answer questions intelligently
5. The dentist's poor demeanor and appearance
6. A host of other reasons why the dentist would make a poor witness

Data on Malpractice Suits Brought Against Dentists

17.6   Only suits decided at the appellate level are available to be counted. However, few suits are taken to appeal, and most of those are appealed on procedural grounds. The number of suits that find their way into the lower courts is a more useful statistic, but that does not tell us how many claims are made against dentists, because many are either settled or withdrawn before trial. Jury and bench trials are seldom reported; however, they are *recorded* in the court records of the jurisdiction in which the trial was held. To count them would require going to the court and reading the transcript, the papers submitted by both parties, and the decision of the judge or jury; a difficult and time-consuming task. Insurance companies have the data, but only from their own records. There is no national central reporting agency to which the insurance companies are required to report data on the number of malpractice cases filed or their outcome. Obtaining reliable information from dentists about their experiences with claims of malpractice is impossible for obvious reasons: Who wants to admit to having been sued?

One can, however, find reliable information in the several states where data on jury trials are published, including New York, California, and Florida. The data reported here is from the *New York Jury Verdict Reporter*. It includes approximately 90% of all jury trials held in the state. One of its publications is limited to medical and dental malpractice cases and appears monthly: the *New York Medical Malpractice: Verdicts, Settlements, and Appeals* (see chapter 1, section 1.8 for details about this publication). Between 1981 and 1999, 310 dental cases were reported in these publications. According to an informal estimate supplied by a number of insurance company attorneys assigned to the defense of dental claims, only about 10% of claims mature to jury trials. Applying the estimate to the number of jury trials reported by the publishing company, which represents 90% of all cases, the total number of claims for the period is approximately 3,200.

The largest number of trials was the 31 reported in 1998; there was a steady increase since 1981 and 1982, when 8 and 6 cases were reported, respectively. In 1982 and 1986, over 80% of the cases were won by plaintiffs. However, from January 1996 until December 2001, the cases won by the plaintiff dropped to 36%, while those in which the dentist prevailed rose to 64%. Medical cases showed a similar decline in plaintiff verdicts.[1]

Risk management educational programs are given credit for the steady decline in plaintiff verdicts, notwithstanding that jury awards to patients have increased. The average jury award between the years 1981 and 1999 was $54,368: $5,513 in 1981 and $211,606 in 1997. The largest jury award during that period was over $1,000,000, and there were two of these. The amount of the awards is not to be taken at face value, because the parties may settle on a lower amount following the decision of the jury, particularly if the defendant's attorney has requested an appeal, in which case the winning party may be willing to settle for a lower amount if the defendant abandons the appeal. Appellate courts may also reduce the jury's award. In the end, the patient does not receive the total amount of the award or settlement; costs and the attorney's fee reduce the money the patient receives.

[1] New York Medical Malpractice 2001;15(4):1.

Dentists' Legal Risk Exposure

17.7 During the course of dental practice, the dentist is exposed to various legal risks. They may be associated with violations of public laws, which are those enacted by a legislative body (eg, Congress), a state legislature, or a local elected body, or the rules and regulations of an administrative agency (eg, the state dental board or the federal, state, or local human rights commission). Another set of risks is associated with private laws (eg, violation of a patient's civil rights by the commission of a tort, such as negligence, malpractice, or any of the intentional torts, or breach of contract). Below is a list of risks.

Violation of Public Laws

17.7.1 Public laws are those that are adopted by elected representatives of the people, or their appointees.

1. The Dental Practice Act (state statutes)—penalties include fines, loss or suspension of license, continuing dental education, drug counseling, and jail time.
2. The rules and regulations of administrative agencies (eg, state dental boards, public health agencies, and human rights commissions).
3. Other statutes and administrative laws that impact health practice.
   a. OSHA—penalties include possible injunctions and fines (but not action against the license to practice).
   b. Other local laws regulating the disposal of hazardous wastes.
4. The Americans with Disabilities Act of 1990—penalties include injunctions and fines (no action against the license to practice).

5. Criminal laws: In all states the dental licensing agency may take an action against the license to practice if the dentist has been convicted of a crime, or is impaired or incompetent.

Violation of Private Laws

17.7.2   Private laws are civil actions in torts and contract law. These result only in money damages because it would be foolish to force health providers to perform services they did not wish to perform even though they have previously agreed to them.

1. Unintentional torts
   a. Negligence
   b. Professional negligence (malpractice)
2. Intentional torts
   a. Assault and battery
   b. Misrepresentation
   c. Deceit
   d. Fraud
   e. Invasion of privacy
   f. Breach of confidentiality
   g. Others as defined by the jurisdiction
3. Breach of contract
4. Violation of special civil rights laws (discrimination)

Stages in Risk Management

17.8   1. Problem prevention
   a. Quality assurance
   b. Caring (interpersonal relations)
   c. Regulatory rule compliance
   d. Procedure risk assessment
   e. Discussion of informed consent with the patient
   f. Communicating progress of care
   g. Monitoring employees and associates
   h. Carefully selecting patients
   i. Not unthinkingly suing to collect a fee
   j. Avoiding abandonment
      — Faulty termination of care
      — Failure to recall
      — Failure to follow-up
2. Between Anger and Claim
   a. Being accessible to patients; communication
   b. Mediation
   c. Return of fee (requiring the patient to sign a release of all claims form)
3. Point of No Return—The Suit
   a. Credibility
      — Personal

— Professional
— Records
— Testimony
b. Cooperation with insurance company and the assigned attorney
c. Strict compliance with the legal process

Legal Claims

17.9   This list represents allegations of malpractice filed against dentists. It does not represent all areas of exposure to suit, eg, undue familiarity, breach of contract, defamation, misrepresentation, assault and battery, or invasion of privacy. Although these and other allegations are possible, they have not surfaced as a major threat that dentists should consider as a continuing risk of practice.

1. Traditional claims
    a. Dentures that are "unsatisfactory"
    b. Faulty fixed partial denture or crown
    c. Fractured root tip remaining in bone (fraudulent concealment)
    d. Missed diagnosis
    e. Posttreatment infection
    f. Fractured jaw
    g. Failure to prescribe
    h. Extraction of wrong tooth
    i. Chemical burn
    j. Laceration
2. Newer claims (since the crisis in dental malpractice in the late 1970s)
    a. TMJ problems
        — Failure to diagnose and monitor
        — Failure to treat
        — Failure to refer
    b. Periodontics
        — Failure to diagnose
        — Failure to treat
        — Failure to refer
        — Paresthesia due to surgery in the region of the mental foramen
    c. Implants
        — Broken fixture
        — General failure
        — Expectations or promises not met
    d. Errors in prescribing
        — Wrong drug
        — Wrong dose
        — History of allergic reactions
    e. Endodontics
        — Broken instrument tip (fraudulent concealment)
        — Faulty consent
        — TMD—long procedure with use of rubber dam

      — Perforation
      — Injury due to failure to use rubber dam
  f. Orthodontics
      — Failure to diagnose caries
      — Failure to diagnose periodontal disease
      — Root resorption
      — Failure to achieve expected results
      — Failure to timely remove fixed appliance for diagnostic purposes
      — TMD
  g. Minor oral surgery
      — Extraction of impacted lower third molars
        • Faulty consent—paresthesia
        • Root tips left in the bone following an extraction
        • Fractured mandible
        • TMD

3. Large awards and settlements
  a. Use of general anesthetics
  b. Use of intravenous sedation
  c. Aspirations
4. Risks related to medical history
  a. Allergies
  b. Drug incompatibilities
  c. Rheumatic fever and other cardiac conditions
  d. Failure to employ pretreatment antibiotic coverage
5. Pretreatment drug use (eg, chloral hydrate)

General Problems

17.10   1. Consent
2. Documentation (record keeping)
3. Professional misconduct
4. Delegation of illegal duties
5. Practicing beyond the scope permitted by experience or law
6. Prescribing controlled substances
7. Refusal to treat (unlawful discrimination)
8. Third-party fraud
9. Failure to refer for treatment and/or consultation
10. Practicing while impaired
11. OSHA violations
12. EPA violations
13. Employing nontraditional techniques
14. Use of experimental procedures that have not been approved by an appropriate agency.
15. Use of Sargenti paste (N2)
16. Abandonment and faulty termination of care
17. Failure to recall
18. Failure to follow-up

19. Employee problems
   a. Sexual harassment, wrongful termination, or discrimination
   b. Employees, past or present, reporting the dentist to a licensing or other government agency
20. Patients reporting a dentist for possible violation of the Dental Practice Act or other laws regulating dental practice

Why Dentists Get Sued When There Is No Fault

17.11

1. Suing to collect a fee. If you sue a patient, or threaten to sue, you will likely be either sued in malpractice or, if you do enter suit, countersued in malpractice.
2. Refusing to negotiate the return of a fee. There is a good chance you will be sued.
3. Guaranteeing a result, or promising a result that you may be unlikely to achieve. You may be sued in breach of contract or malpractice, whichever the patient's attorney advises, depending upon the facts of the case, the statute of limitations, and the amount demanded by the patient.
4. Inaccessibility to patients with complaints. Make certain your employees do not shield you from complaining patients.

All of the above make patients angry with their dentist and may lead them to express their anger in a lawsuit. Each can result in loss without fault.

Consent

17.12

Keep in mind two suggestions about consent: *(1)* Always consider the level of legal risk and *(2)* always have the patient sign a consent that includes all necessary requirements for all procedures. It is not the easiest thing to do; but if you do it you will never make a mistake.

A signed written treatment plan that includes the fee will not substitute for a signed consent if it does not include the risks, benefits, etc. The consent to treat a minor, unless emancipated, must be signed by one of the parents or a legal guardian. Oral consents may be satisfactory provided you can show that they are a *business habit,* ie, that you follow the procedure for all patients undergoing the same treatment.

But, again, written consents are safest. You do not need them for procedures you expect the patient to know about, both as to the process and the risks, eg, a simple dental examination. The general rule is to require them for all treatment procedures that are invasive or present a high risk (see chapter 9).

Office Records

17.13

Office records are of major importance in the trial of a suit brought against a dentist. If properly kept they can do much to assist in the defense of a claim of malpractice. A poor record may contribute to a loss without fault. The credibility of a dentist being sued for malpractice is initially judged by the attorney for both the patient and the dentist on the basis of the patient's treatment record. The record should be complete and accurate, with no abbreviations unique to the office. All entries should be made in ink at regular spacing on the form, no entries in the margins or following the last line on the form.

Financial information, eg, payment arrangements, fees, payments, and balances, should be kept on a separate record.

The appointment log should be maintained with the same degree of care as the treatment record. It is an official record of the office. The evidence it may present of patient cancellations, late arrivals, and no-shows may lead the jury to find contributory negligence in the patient.The treatment record, appointment log, and all other records related to the care of the patient should be kept for as long as possible, not just for the limited period prescribed by the black letter law of the state.

Never, under any circumstances, surrender the original records or radiographs to anyone, unless ordered by a court or an agency having subpoena powers. If the state in which you practice requires you to deliver a copy of the patient's record to the patient or to whomever the patient wishes, give or send copies. However, before complying, require the patient to make the request in writing.

Errors on the record should never be blocked out so that they cannot be read. Draw a single line through the error and write the correction in the next space on the record. Once you hear that you are being sued or may be sued, do not make any changes on the patient's treatment record.

If you are an employee of a dentist, make certain by agreement, preferably in writing, that should you leave the employment, the original records of the patients you treated will be made available to you should you need them for any judicial proceeding. The same is true if you sell your practice, and, in addition, you should require the purchaser to retain the records for at least 10 years after the date of the sale (see chapter 12).

Employees

17.14   Employees are your agents. You are bound by what they say to your patients. Monitor their conversations with patients carefully and do not permit them to make statements that bind you to conditions, or to results of treatment, that you may not be able to meet or achieve. Do not permit them to shield you from complaining patients.

Make certain you are familiar with all laws that affect dental practice, including those that define the scope of practice of your employees. Hire and supervise them carefully. If they provide services to patients, make certain that they act within the scope permitted by law, and never ask them to provide a service that is unlawful. Before hiring employees permitted to treat patients, make certain they are healthy. Check their malpractice history and whether they have ever been accused of any violation of the law, including the Dental Practice Act (see chapter /).

Associates

17.15   Do not hire dentists as independent contractors unless they clearly fall within the definition of an independent contractor as described by the Internal Revenue Service. If there is any doubt, hire them as employees. If you hire a dentist, include a hold harmless clause in the employment agreement.

Avoid partnerships. Professional limited liability (PLL) arrangements are better than professional associations (PA) or professional corporations (PC). It is best to have all members of the PLL, PA, or PC insured by the same professional liability insurance company (see chapter 7).

Insurance

17.16   Make certain you have adequate insurance coverage. Buy as much as you can afford. In the litigious environment in which dentistry is practiced, jury awards over $1,000,000 are rare, but they have occurred. The difference between a suit for $50,000 and $500,000 is a zero added on an attorney's computer. Make certain those of your employees that are permitted to treat patients have professional liability insurance coverage (see chapter 19).

Referrals

17.17   Never accept a referral fee, or a split fee, from a dentist or physician to whom you referred a patient. Never refer a patient to a practitioner you know, or have reason to suspect, is impaired or incompetent. Never send the original records or radiographs to the doctor to whom you have referred the patient. If necessary, send copies (see chapter 7).

Patients

17.18   There are patients who have a history of suing health practitioners. At times this characteristic may be recognized by the dentist. Too often, dentists who are sued have said, "I should have known." When you have reason to believe that the patient you are considering for treatment might be inclined to sue, you should consider not undertaking that treatment. When patients speak about their experiences with other dentists, their negative attitude may provide you with a clue. Unless the patient falls into the class of those protected by antidiscrimination laws, you may choose not to accept a patient for any reason.

During the treatment of a patient, you are free to discontinue care provided you do not do it at a time when it would compromise the patient's health. You must complete the procedure you have begun before discontinuing care. To avoid a finding of abandonment, you must notify the patient, orally and then by certified letter with signed receipt requested, that it is in his best interest to seek treatment elsewhere, that you will provide emergency care for a reasonable time until a new dentist is engaged, and that you will cooperate with the new dentist by providing him with copies of the patient's records, radiographs, etc, but only on the written request of the patient, and only copies.

If a patient fails to comply with any of your recommendations, including referral to a specialist or home-care instructions, make a careful decision about whether to continue to treat the patient. If you decide to continue to do so, make appropriate notes on the patient's treatment record, and, if possible, have the patient sign an "Against Dental Advice" form, listing the possible results of noncompliance.

Patients who do not respond to recall notices, despite reminders, should be notified by certified letter, with signed receipt requested, that they must either respond to your recall notices or seek the services of another dentist.

Do not return a fee, or part of a fee, to a patient unless the patient signs a release of claims. Think carefully before entering suit against a patient to collect a fee. If you use a collection agency, review all letters the agency sends to your delinquent patients.

Inform the patient, and make appropriate notes on the patient's record, of any untoward results of your treatment, eg, a broken instrument tip lodged in the canal, fractured roots remaining in the bone following an extraction, etc. Ask the patient to sign the entry on the record. Do not admit that you were at fault.

Be available, or have a competent substitute available, to your patients 24 hours each day, 7 days a week, 52 weeks of the year. Inform your patients who they are to call if they need immediate care and you are not available. Arrangements may be made with a local hospital that has a dental department.

Health History

17.19 All patients must complete a health history before treatment is begun. It must be reviewed by the treating practitioner, dentist, or hygienist, and evidence that it was reviewed must be documented on the form or in the patient's record.

The patient's physician should be consulted if the history might present a problem in the provision of care to the patient, or if the dental care may affect the patient's general health. Make an effort to get any recommendation of the physician in writing; at the very least, make a note of the physician's statements on the patient's record.

Anyone who refuses to inform you of any medical problem, or who has not answered any of the health questions honestly, should not be accepted as a patient (see chapter 11).

Miscellaneous

17.20 If you suffer from AIDS, or are HIV-positive, although the local law may not require you to inform your patients, common law may require this in order for any consent to care to be valid. Your health status may constitute one of the risks you are required to inform patients about before treatment is begun. It you do suffer from AIDS, or are HIV-positive, it may be advisable to retire from practice after consultation with the local health department and a physician.

Never treat a patient while under the influence of alcohol or drugs.

If you are notified by the licensing agency that you are the target of an investigation, do not meet with any of their agents without your attorney present. If an agent shows up in your office unannounced, inform him that he should return when it is convenient for you to meet with him and your attorney. The same rules apply if a representative of Medicaid, OSHA, or the human rights commission comes to your office. You can do without a lawyer only if the licensing agency assures you that another practitioner is under investigation and it wants to examine your records for information about the patient's prior care. Licensing agencies usually have subpoena powers. You should consult an attorney before surrendering any of your records.

Final Advice

17.21   Keep up with the advances in the profession; do not exceed your level of ability based upon your experience and training, and document all continuing dental education programs you attend.

And finally, the best advice to avoid an allegation of malpractice is to treat your patients as you would want to be treated, and above all, to be careful and caring.

CHAPTER EIGHTEEN

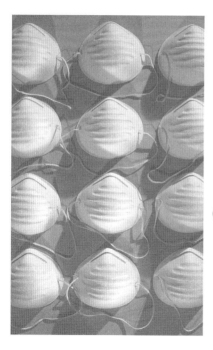

Office Audit Risk Assessment for the General Dentist

The audit is designed to provide the general practitioner with a detailed review of office procedures and policies for the purpose of ensuring that the office meets with standards that will lessen the risk of a suit, or lessen the resulting losses.

The audit is prepared in the form of questions. Following each is a discussion. In reading the answers to the questions you should keep three things in mind:

1. Not all possible situations that may lead to difficulties in office practice, especially specialty practice, are included.
2. Where legal answers are presented, the answers represent the author's opinion about how these matters are best handled based upon a review of several hundred dental malpractice suits; attorneys, however, do not always agree.
3. Each state has its own set of laws regulating dental practice, and it is not possible to include them all. If you have any specific questions about any topic in the audit, you are advised to consult a local attorney.

Some questions and discussions are repeated in more than one section. This is by design, not error. The purpose is to make each section complete and avoid the need for cross-references.

18.1   Office Equipment

Do you have a paper copier in the office?

In today's environment, where copies of records must be sent to third-party payers and to patients upon their request, a paper copier is essential office equipment. Originals of office records should never leave your possession, unless ordered by a court or used in judicial proceedings.

If yes, does the copier reproduce all the colors you use to make entries in all office records?

On occasion, you may have made entries in old records in colored ink or using a ballpoint pen, which all copiers will not accurately reproduce. To avoid the problem, purchase a copier that will reproduce all colors represented in your records.

Do you have the capability to reproduce radiographs?

As with patient paper records, radiographs may have to be delivered to persons outside your office. Like paper records, you should never part with the originals. You should therefore have a high-quality radiograph reproducer; if you don't, you should always use two-film X-ray packets.

Are you and members of your staff provided with radiation tags to determine your exposure to stray radiation?

Stray radiation may reach office personnel. All of them should therefore wear radiation exposure tags, which are available from companies specializing in this service. If they don't, you may be sued if any of them becomes ill and suspects excessive X-ray exposure as the cause. Take special care with pregnant employees.

If you use a nitrous oxide/oxygen machine in the treatment of patients, does it have adequate fail-safe devices?

Older nitrous oxide/oxygen equipment was made without fail-safe devices. Modern machines are equipped with double ones. If your equipment is old, you should have it either upgraded or replaced. You and your patients have too much at stake to rely upon anything less than the best and safest equipment.

If you use a nitrous oxide/oxygen machine, do you inspect it regularly to determine if it is functioning properly?

You must inspect your nitrous oxide equipment regularly. Print a schedule and adhere to it. Your schedule should include columns documenting the date the equipment was inspected, who inspected it, and the results. Store the schedule in a safe place and keep it for as long as possible. If the equipment fails to meet a rigid standard, correct the fault as soon as possible and document the results on the form.

Do you regularly test the efficacy of your sterilizing equipment?

Sterilizing equipment may lose its effectiveness; you need to make sure it does not. Commercial biologic laboratories can evaluate your sterilizing equipment. The results they provide should be documented. Current laws in all states require that sterilizing equipment be tested at regular intervals.

Do you sterilize your handpiece before using it on another patient?

You must; the law requires it, and it has become the standard of care. If a patient becomes ill following treatment, and you are shown not to have sterilized your handpiece or to have violated any other rule on the use of infection control protocols and barrier techniques, you will be found guilty of malpractice.

Is your office equipped with eye-wash devices to wash away chemicals that may enter the eyes of patients or staff?

The Occupational Safety and Health Administration (OSHA) requires that eye-wash devices be located in each room of the office in which chemicals are used. They should be inspected regularly and restocked as needed. The inspection should be documented. Failure to provide an eye-wash device may expose you to suit by OSHA or by an injured patient or staff member.

Do you inspect all office equipment regularly for safety problems?

The modern dental office has many pieces of office equipment, some directly related to the provision of dental services and others related to the general conduct of business. Problems with either may result in an injury to a patient. Document regular inspection of all equipment

18.2   Emergency Preparedness

Are you trained in CPR?

All health workers are expected to be proficient in CPR. In some jurisdictions statute or administrative law mandates it. And in all jurisdictions, if you are faced with an emergency in which a patient requires CPR and you do not administer it, the courts may find you guilty of negligence.

Are all members of your office staff trained in CPR?

The prudent dentist insists that all office personnel have training in CPR. Some states require that all health care providers be trained in CPR. Check with your local health agency.

Do you have emergency equipment and supplies readily available to manage medical emergencies in the office?

The same duty that requires you to be trained in CPR requires you also to maintain equipment and supplies to deal with medical emergencies. It is essential that you inspect this equipment regularly. Print a schedule and adhere to it. Your schedule should include columns documenting the date the equipment was inspected, who inspected it, and the results. Store the schedule in a safe place and keep it for as long as possible. If the equipment fails to meet a rigid standard, correct the fault as soon as possible and document the results on the form.

Do you have a written protocol to deal with emergency situations?

OSHA requires that employers prepare a written protocol describing what office personnel are to do in emergency situations. Moreover, you are responsible for the general health and safety of patients while they are in your office; therefore, you and all members of your staff should be prepared to deal effectively with an emergency that threatens patients. A written protocol describing what should be done in an emergency is the most effective means to this. All employees should become familiar with the protocol.

Do you conduct test drills of emergency situations?

Merely having a written protocol for emergencies, or discussing with your staff how to handle them, does not satisfy either OSHA regulations or prudence. You should conduct drills at regular intervals to make certain each member of your staff knows exactly what to do when an emergency arises. Drills should be documented in a permanent record.

Does your office staff know the telephone number to call in an emergency?

This number should be prominently displayed in all rooms of the office. Consult the local rescue squad as to the proper number to call. In most areas, 911 may serve the purpose, but in some another number may be better equipped to respond quickly to health-related emergencies.

Have you instructed all members of your staff in their exact duties in an emergency?

Each member of your office staff should have assigned duties in an emergency. Explicitly describe these duties to each staff member. Distribute them in writing and conduct drills regularly; document all drills.

18.3   Infection Control and Use of Barrier Techniques

Do you have a copy of your state's enacted laws (statutes, regulations, and/or rules) that prescribe the infection control protocols and barrier techniques to be used in your office?

> Each state was required by federal legislation to adopt the recommendations of the Centers for Disease Control and Prevention as they relate to infection control procedures in the dental office. These may be obtained from either the dental board or the health department in your state.

Do you and all your office personnel always wear face masks, surgical gloves, approved surgical gowns, and eye shields when examining and treating patients?

> All are required by law to be used when examining or treating patients in the office. In addition, it is likely that courts will declare their use part of the standard of care to which every patient is entitled. Therefore, not complying with the law may lead to penalties imposed by government agencies and damages imposed by a patient in a civil suit should a patient allege illness as a result of your not complying with infection-control protocols.

After examining or treating each patient do you and your assisting staff discard the gloves?

> New gloves are to be worn when treating or examining each patient. Once used, gloves are to be discarded, not washed and reused.

Do you remain current on local laws on infection control and barrier techniques?

> It is one of your professional responsibilities to remain current on the laws regulating your profession. Make an annual phone call to the licensing agency in your state and ask for a copy of the latest laws. Remember the adage, "Ignorance of the law is no excuse."

Do you dispose of your sharps in a manner consistent with OSHA regulations and other laws that relate to the management of sharps?

> OSHA, and other agencies, both local, state, and national have adopted standards for the disposal of sharps. These standards have the effect of law, and unless you comply with them, you may be subjected to a heavy fine. You should contact the local OSHA office to determine the standards. In addition, there may be local laws relating to the disposal of sharps. If you are unaware of them, call the local health authority.

Do you dispose of the medical wastes of your office in compliance with the Environmental Protective Agency (EPA) regulations?

The disposal of medical wastes is carefully regulated by a government agency. You should contact the local EPA to determine the local regulations, and comply with them strictly.

18.4   Treatment Procedures

When discussing with the patient the need for endodontic therapy, do you inform the patient of the alternatives, including those you do not provide?

In obtaining the informed consent of a patient you must inform the patient of the alternatives to the care you recommend. Before endodontic therapy is begun, the patient should be told that extracting and replacing the tooth is an alternative to your recommendation, even though you do not provide this service.

When discussing with the patient the need for endodontic therapy, do you inform the patient of the possibility of failure and its consequences?

When discussing with the patient the need for endodontic therapy you must inform the patient of the possibility of failure and its consequences, including surgery, extraction and replacement, and redoing the procedure.

Before beginning endodontic therapy, is the patient required to execute a written consent?

A written consent to care, especially when the care involves an invasive procedure such as endodontic therapy, is essential, lest the patient deny consenting.

When performing endodontic therapy, do you apply rubber dam whenever possible?

One of the risks to which the patient is exposed during endodontic therapy is that of swallowing or aspirating a foreign object. To prevent this, you should apply rubber dam whenever possible.

Do you record the number of times you use a reamer and file in endodontic treatment or discard the instrument after the first use?

All metal instruments are subject to metal fatigue and so to breakage. You should always keep track of how many times you use a file and reamer, eg, by scoring their handles after each use, and discard them after a limited number of uses. An even safer practice is to discard the instrument once it has been used.

Do you record the manufacturer of the files and reamers you use during an endodontic procedure?

You should keep an accurate record of the manufacturer of all endodontic instruments. Should a reamer or file fracture during treatment, causing you to be sued, the defense counsel may feel that the manufacturer of the instrument should be impleaded as a codefendant under the theory of product liability. You should also retain the broken portions of the instrument.

During endodontic therapy, if the tip of a file or reamer breaks and becomes permanently lodged in the end of the canal, do you inform the patient?

Notify the patient once you decide you cannot remove the tip, and tell the patient what should be done as a result. Make a note of the occurrence in the treatment record and have the patient initial or sign it.

Before removing a mandibular third molar do you inform the patient of the possibility of paresthesia?

One of the most frequent allegations of malpractice relates to the dentist's failure to inform the patient of the risks of treatment. You should explain to a patient that paresthesia is one of the risks of such an extraction.

Before removing a mandibular third molar, do you have the patient sign a consent form listing paresthesia as one of the complications?

A signed consent including all the essentials for consent to be valid is far better than an oral consent. It avoids the possibility of later disagreement.

If during an extraction you fracture a root, the tip remains in the bone, and you decide it best to allow it to remain in the bone, do you inform the patient?

You should inform the patient if anything untoward occurs during treatment, including this. Make appropriate notes in the patient's treatment record.

If, when performing a surgical procedure, you encounter a problem that you cannot solve, such as fracturing a root during an extraction, at what point do you recommend that the patient go to the office of an oral and maxillofacial surgeon?

If you are unable to complete the procedure successfully within 10 minutes, stop and have the patient seek the services of the specialist. The same general rule applies to other services you perform that are performed by specialists, eg, endodontists.

During the initial series of visits of a new patient entering your practice for general care, do you conduct a thorough periodontal examination and record the findings?

As a part of your routine examination of a new patient, complete a periodontal examination. This should be as routine as the health history, the examination for caries, and the soft tissue examination. The details of your findings should be entered in the patient's record. This will defuse any future conflict as to whether a periodontal examination was completed.

Do you monitor the patient's periodontal status by recording pocket depths, bleeding points and mobility at regular intervals consistent with the patient's overall oral health?

Current standards of care require that you monitor the patient's periodontal status during the entire course of care and treatment. The frequency depends upon many factors, including the patient's general oral health, compliance with home-care instructions, periodontal health, and diet. A minimum examination consists of recording pocket depths, bleeding points, and tooth mobility.

On each recall visit, do you complete a periodontal examination by recording pocket depths, bleeding points, and mobility on teeth to indicate the patient's periodontal status?

You should record a periodontal examination and evaluation of each patient during each recall visit. As stated above the examination should include pocket depths, bleeding points, and mobility.

During the initial series of visits of a new patient entering your practice for general care, do you evaluate the status of the temporomandibular joint (TMJ)?

During a patient's initial series of visits you must examine the TMJ. Failure to record the results may support an allegation that you failed to advise the patient of a TMJ problem.

If the treatment of the patient affects the occlusion, do you monitor the TMJ for any objective or subjective changes?

Changes in the occlusion have been known to affect the functioning of the TMJ; therefore, you should note and attend to any subjective or objective changes. Even if you find no changes, and the patient has no complaints, it is important to enter your findings on the patient's record.

Except in responding to a patient's immediate need for care, eg, pain or infection, do you present a treatment plan to the patient before beginning treatment?

To adhere to the general standard of care you must have the patient agree to a treatment plan before treatment. The rule applies to single treatment episodes as well as long-range care.

Is the taking of radiographs part of your regular diagnostic procedure?

The current standard of care requires you to have a complete set of radiographs, including bitewings, before you begin treatment, whether you take them yourself or get them from other sources.

Do you take radiographs at regular intervals during the course of your treatment of your patients?

You should take radiographs at intervals necessary to monitor the oral health of the patient properly.

Do you check the quality of each radiograph you or your staff takes for proper developing and placement?

You should inspect all radiographs taken by your office staff as to their placement, developing, and fixing. Radiographs that do not meet general standards of readability should be retaken. Pay special attention to cone cuts.

How do you orient a new patient to the procedures and policies of your office?

The best and most efficient way to orient new patients to your office is to give them a written description of how your office is run and what is expected of them. Included should be instructions regarding changing or canceling an appointment and exhortations about issues such as the need to be prompt in keeping appointments, the need to follow home-care instructions, and the need to keep the office informed about any change in health. Each new patient should be given a copy of the office policy and a note of this should be entered on the patient's record.

If you recommend that your patient be treated by a specialist (orthodontist, surgeon, periodontist, or endodontist), and the patient refuses but asks you to provide the service, do you understand the risks associated with agreeing to perform the treatment?

Under these circumstances you may be held to the standards of the specialist. Ordinarily, a generalist is held to the standards of other generalists, but if you undertake to provide care that other generalists would have referred to a specialist you may be held to the standards of a specialist, especially if you have recommended that the patient be treated by a specialist.

As part of your routine examination of the patient, do you, or does one of your office staff, record the patient's blood pressure?

This procedure is strongly advised. It should be repeated at each recall visit, especially if the patient reports a change in health. Anyone who is trained in the procedure is permitted to take blood pressure, but not necessarily permitted to advise the patient if the reading is not within normal limits.

Are you consistent in the criteria you use in the referral of patients to a specialist?

When you refer a patient to a specialist, make certain that the referral is based upon consistent criteria. Making exceptions not based upon sound dental judgment can lead to difficulties.

Do you refer all patients who are in need of care that would best be provided by a specialist?

A major cause of a patient suing a dentist is the dentist's failure to make a timely referral for specialty care. Do not undertake treatment of a patient that would best be provided by a specialist. Most failure-to-refer cases fall in the field of periodontics.

Is someone always present in the room while you are treating a patient?

When you or a provider employee are treating a patient of the opposite sex, another member of the health care team should be present. This is especially true if the patient is sedated or under general anesthesia.

If you respond to a telephone call from a patient during office hours, and the patient's record is not at the telephone location, do you have a procedure to enter the nature of the call and your response into the patient's record?

You should keep a written record of all calls you receive from a patient no matter where you are. Telephone note pads should be placed around the office where you are likely to receive patient calls. The record should include the time the call is received, the patient's statement or complaint, and your response or advice. The note should be placed in the patient's record folder, and its information entered on the patient's treatment record.

Have you instructed your staff on how to respond to calls made by patients?

Your staff should make written notes of the substance of all calls they receive from patients about their care, but before transferring these notes to the patient's record, you should review them.

Have you instructed your staff on how to manage telephone calls from patients who demand to speak with you?

Each office has some patients who demand to speak with the dentist when speaking with a receptionist will adequately meet their needs. Except in rare instances, the staff should not shield the dentist from these demanding patients.

Have you instructed your staff on how to manage telephone calls from patients who wish to complain to you?

Many staff members become protective of their employer and try to shield her from complaining patients. This policy leads to difficulties and disgruntled patients. It serves no good purpose. Whoever answers the phone should inform the dentist who is calling and why, and allow the dentist to decide what to do.

If you call in a patient's prescription to a pharmacy from your home, do you make a note of it at the time and, when you return to the office, enter it on the patient's record and in the patient's medication log?

When you prescribe drugs away from the office it is easy to forget what has taken place. To prevent this problem, make a note of what you prescribed and as soon as possible enter the information on the patient's record and in the patient's medication log.

18.5 Treatment of Minors

Are you aware of the age at which a minor is able to grant a valid consent to dental care in the jurisdiction in which you conduct your dental practice?

The age at which a minor reaches maturity for the purpose of consenting to health care without the consent of the parent or guardian is determined by the local jurisdiction (state). Generally it is 18 years of age. Because of the disparity among the jurisdictions, you should check with your state health department.

Do you know the criteria that must be met for a minor to become emancipated?

Each jurisdiction (state) has set out the special conditions which allow a minor to grant a valid consent. Minors falling in this category are called *emancipated minors*. Some states have done this by statutes, others by administrative rules or regulations, and some others by case law. Because of the disparity among the jurisdictions, you should check with the state health department. Traditionally, an emancipated minor is one who is no longer dependent upon a parent or guardian for support.

In your treatment of a minor of divorced parents, do you know which parent has the right to consent to dental care and must pay for the services?

> If you are aware that the parents of a minor patient are divorced, you should ask one of the parents who is responsible for making decisions about and paying for dental care before beginning treatment.

If a minor, a patient of record, is brought by a friend of the minor's family, or the minor's teacher, to your office and the minor is in need of immediate care, are you familiar with the proper procedure to follow for obtaining consent for treatment?

> In this situation, you should try to contact either parent by phone. Inform the parent of the child's condition and the appropriate treatment. All elements needed to obtain a valid consent must be communicated to the parent. An additional party located in the office, eg, a dental assistant, hygienist, or receptionist, should listen to the conversation between you and the parent.

In the previous situation, are you aware of the best method to document that you received the consent of the parent to treat the minor?

> The most reliable method is to make an entry on the minor's record, sign the entry, and have the third party who listened to the telephone conversation between you and the parent countersign the entry.

18.6   Following up on Treatment

When a difficult procedure is completed, is the patient later contacted to determine the patient's condition before the next visit?

> Maintaining contact with a patient who has undergone a difficult procedure, or experienced difficulty during a procedure, will do much to reassure the patient and keep you informed of any untoward reaction after the patient left your office.

Is the follow-up contact recorded in the patient's treatment record?

> You should document on the patient's record that you made the follow-up contact. Include the details of the conversation.

If the patient reports a problem, is it managed before the patient's next scheduled visit?

> If you determine that the patient experienced an unanticipated problem following treatment in your office, you should make every effort to deal with the problem before the patient's next scheduled visit.

Do you inform patients whose care has been completed that you will place them on a scheduled recall visit list?

> Such patients should be informed of scheduled recalls. Make clear to them that maintaining the list and notifying the patient to return to the office is in their best interest.

Do you have a procedure to follow if a patient does not comply with the notice to return to the office for a recall visit?

> Your office should have a policy for dealing with such patients, eg, a patient who does not comply after two reminders should be sent a reminder of the need to comply and the consequences of neglect.

18.7   Availability

Can patients reach your office, you, or a substitute dentist in your absence at all times?

> Once you accept a patient for care, one of your contractual responsibilities is to be available to the patient during your absence. The responsibility may be satisfied during your absence by arrangement with another dentist. There was a time when dentists made special arrangements not to be bothered by patients during "off times." This policy is no longer acceptable, and may result in an allegation of abandonment by the patient and an action by a licensing agency. It also violates the code of ethics of the profession.

Are patients under active treatment notified in advance when you plan to take an extensive (more than 2 weeks) leave from the office?

> You should notify all patients under active care if you plan to leave the practice for an extended period of time. In your absence you should make arrangements with a colleague to cover your practice, and make the substitute known to your patients. A message should be left on your office telephone informing the caller whom to contact in your absence.

Are patients informed what action to take in the event of the need for emergency care?

> As soon as you accept patients for care by your office, tell them exactly what procedure to follow if emergency care becomes necessary. The instructions should be included in any written office policy given to the patient.

If you respond to a patient's telephone call when at home, or at a place other than in your office, do you have a procedure to enter the call into the patient's record?

You should keep a written record of all calls you receive from patients no matter where you receive them. The record should include the time of the call, the patient's statement or complaint, and your response or advice. When you return to the office you should place the written record in the patient record folder and enter the information in the patient's treatment record.

Except when you are away for an extended period of time and have notified patients in advance of your absence, are you or a substitute easily accessible to your patients, in person or by telephone, 24 hours each day, 7 days of the week, and 52 weeks of the year?

This is the prevailing rule. Once you accept a patient for care, the patient reasonably expects and the courts demand it.

18.8   Patient Complaints

Are patient complaints documented and filed?

For all patient complaints, record the nature of the complaint, when and by whom it was received, and what action was taken. Review the complaints regularly to determine what action you should take to reduce or eliminate them.

Are the complaints resolved?

All complaints should be resolved. A record should be kept of how the matter was managed and the outcome.

If a complaint relates to the actions of an employee, do you counsel the employee?

When the complaint involves an employee, the employee should be counseled, and a record kept of the counseling session and the response of the employee.

Have you instructed your office staff to report all patient complaints to you?

Office employees should be advised that all complaints are to be recorded and reported to you. Some may require immediate resolution. The decision should not be left to anyone other than you.

18.9   Noncompliant Patients

When you recommend that a patient obtain a consultation from another practitioner, do you describe to the patient the purpose of the referral and the risks of not following your recommendation?

> When referring one of your patients to another practitioner, always explain the need for the consultation and the consequences of proceeding without it.

Do you have a form for the patient to sign acknowledging the above?

> There are such forms, known as "Against Dental Advice" forms. They describe the recommendation made, the purpose of the recommendation, and the consequences of noncompliance, and should be signed by the patient. If such a form is not available, it can be designed in the office as the need arises.

Do you know what to do if the patient does not follow your recommendation to consult a specialist?

> Your course of action will depend upon the severity of the patient's need for specialist consultation and care. If you feel that the patient's noncompliance will compromise your care, dismiss the patient.

For patients to whom you have prescribed a home-care oral hygiene regimen, do you describe the purpose of the regimen and the consequences of noncompliance?

> All dental patients require some home-care instructions. However, to encourage compliance you should inform your patients why this is essential and the consequences of noncompliance.

For patients for whom you have prescribed medication to be taken at home, do you describe the purpose of the medication and the consequences of noncompliance?

> To prescribe medication for the patient without describing why it should be taken, the dose, and the consequences of the patient's failure to adhere to the medication schedule invites the patient's noncompliance. It is your professional responsibility to explain fully all that the patient needs to know to ensure compliance.

Do you know how to properly manage patients who do not keep appointments or who are habitually tardy for them?

> One of the patient's important responsibilities is to keep appointments and arrive for them on time. If you feel that the outcome of your care will be compromised by a patient's failure to keep appointments or chronic lateness, drop that patient from your practice, but not at a time that would jeopardize the patient's health.

Such a patient's noncompliance must be documented in the medical record and in the appointment log (see sections 18.10 and 18.11).

18.10   Dropping Patients from the Practice

When you decide that a patient's behavior or attitude presents difficulties for you or your staff, do you discuss the situation with the patient before dismissing the patient from the practice?

Dropping a patient from the practice is a very serious step. You could be accused of abandonment, breach of contract, or malpractice. However, you are free to discontinue the care of a noncompliant patient. To avoid inviting a lawsuit, you should first discuss the matter with the patient. Always inform such patients that is in their best interest to seek services elsewhere.

In addition to informing patients that they would best be served by seeking the services of another dentist, do you know what other information to provide?

The law is clear on what you need to tell such patients: *(1)* that until a substitute dentist is engaged, you will provide emergency care; and *(2)* that you will cooperate by providing copies of your patient records and radiographs upon written request.

Do you follow the discussion by sending the patient a certified letter, with return receipt requested, informing the patient of your decision?

This final step will protect you should you later be accused of abandonment. Reiterate that you are available for emergency care until the patient engages a new dentist and that you will forward copies of all relevant records held in your office upon written request.

Do you refrain from recommending a replacement dentist to the patient you have dismissed?

It is best not to recommend a replacement dentist to a patient that has been dismissed from your practice.

Are you aware of the rules regarding your right to terminate the care of a patient at any time if the patient has not kept up with the payment of fee agreement?

Generally you may dismiss a patient who has not complied with the terms under which you accepted that patient for care. If the payment agreement is one of those terms and the patient defaults, you are not held by the agreement to provide care for the patient. However, the rules of contract law are not strictly applied in health care. Although you may discontinue care, you are advised not to do it at a time that the patient's health may be compromised, eg, during the fabrication of a crown after the tooth has been prepared but before the impression is taken. Complete the crown and then stop the treatment.

Do you provide the patient with a copy of your records and radiographs upon the patient's written request?

In many jurisdictions you are required, on the patient's written request, to deliver to the patient, or to whom they designate, copies of all the patient's records, radiographs, and reports in your possession. You may charge a reasonable fee for their duplication. In jurisdictions that do not have such a law, it is prudent to follow the same procedure. In some jurisdictions, you may not withhold records from a patient that owes you money. Some jurisdictions require the dentist to supply to the patient only a summary of the treatment.

18.11   Financial Issues

If a patient demands the return of a fee, do you comply?

Before you decide whether to return a fee for services you have performed, consider the following: A patient who makes such a demand is not satisfied with the service. Refusing such a patient will probably result in a suit against you alleging malpractice. Only if you are willing to take that risk should you refuse to return the fee.

If the occasion arises that you return a fee, do you have the patient sign a "Release of Claims" (or "Waiver of Claims") form?

Again, you should consider that a patient who demands the return of a fee is not satisfied with the service and may sue. Thus, should you decide to return the fee, or any part thereof, you must have the patient sign a "Release of Claims" form, which is designed to relieve you of any responsibility for acts you performed before the date upon which the form was executed. In most situations, the release will be effective.

Do you record financial information on a form separate from the patient's treatment record?

You should never enter financial information in the treatment record. It should instead be recorded on a form specially designed for that purpose. The treatment record should only contain information about the patient's treatment and other notes limited to the patient's care. If the record is entered into evidence during a trial, it may not be in your best interest for the jury to know how much you charge for your services.

Are you thoroughly familiar with all rules of reporting and billing of the third-party payers that insure your patients?

To ensure payment to you from third-party payers, you must comply with the rules for submitting fees and reporting services you intend to provide. You should become familiar with these rules before beginning treatment and before you submit your bills. Keep in mind that the rules are not the same for all third-party payers.

Do you refuse demands from third-party payers that you submit original radiographs as a condition for payment?

You should never submit any original radiographs to a third-party payer; only send copies!

Do you refuse demands from a third-party payer that you submit a radiograph of a completed procedure that is not essential to the care of the patient as a condition for payment?

The only X rays that a patient should be exposed to are those that are essential to care. Radiographs should never be taken for administrative purposes, including demands to approve payment. In some jurisdictions, eg, New York, such procedures are in violation of the law.

Do you know the steps to take if you receive a request from a third-party payer for the records of a patient insured by the payer?

If you receive such a request, you should first determine if the third-party payer has your patient's permission to obtain copies of these records. If such agreement exists, ask for a copy of the agreement before you send the copies. If not, have the payer include with its request for the records a copy of an authorization signed by the patient to release the records.

18.12   Records

Are entries on the patient's records you keep made in black ink or using a black ballpoint pen?

You should make certain that all entries made on all records related to the patient are completed in black ink or using a black ballpoint pen. Other colored entries may not accurately reproduce on a paper copier, and copies would not show your intent in using differently colored entries.

Do you know how long to retain your patient records?

Periods of retention of patient records are often set by local law. However, this is a minimum requirement. For protection in a civil suit, you should retain all office records for as long as you can. The shortest retention time is 10 years after the last visit for adults, and for minors, 5 years after the minor reaches majority.

Are all entries in the record legible?

Recent court rulings have stated that health records, to be accurate, must be legible. They should be easily understood by health practitioners in the same school of practice as the practitioner making the entries. To ensure legibility you may print or type record entries. Computer-generated hard copies are satisfactory, provided they are dated and signed by the person who generated the data at the time the hard copy was produced.

Do you use only standard abbreviations in recording treatment or observations in the patient's record?

If you use your own unique abbreviations in recording treatment or observations in the patient's record, you should stop. They may not be understood by other dentists. Only universal abbreviations should be used. If you do use your own abbreviations you should keep a list of exactly what these abbreviations mean, and if called upon to explain them, you should make the list available.

Do all people in your office who enter information in the patient's record sign or initial the entry?

All people in your office whom you authorize to enter information on the patient's record should sign opposite the entry. Long into the future you may be asked who made the entry, or the person who entered the information may be asked to provide information at some form of judicial proceeding. You may be expected to identify each person who recorded information in your patient's record. Keep a typed written record of all employee and associate names, along with a specimen of their initials and signature for future reference.

If you receive a request from a dentist for the records and radiographs of a former patient of yours, do you comply?

You should not. Instead you should inform the dentist that you will forward a copy of the patient's records and radiographs if the patient sends you a letter asking you to do so, or if the dentist includes in the request an authorization signed by the patient permitting you to release the records.

You refer your patient for consultation to a periodontist who then asks you to forward a copy of the patient's records and radiographs. Do you comply?

Yes. If the patient agrees to seek the services of another practitioner to whom you referred the patient, the patient has waived confidentiality.

You receive a letter from an attorney asking you to forward to his office copies of a patient's records. He further states that he represents your patient in a lawsuit unrelated to the care you provided. Do you comply?

No, unless his request is accompanied by a release signed by the patient.

In the previous situation, the lawyer states that he intends to bring suit against you, asks for a copy of the records and radiographs, and includes a written statement by the patient giving you permission to comply with the lawyer's request. Do you comply?

Yes, but remember, only copies! If the lawyer does not include the patient's permission, do not send the records. In any event, your insurance carrier should be notified by phone and by a certified letter of the lawyer's request. A copy of the lawyer's letter should be included in your letter to the insurance carrier.

If you wish to enter a reminder for the patient's next visit, do you have a procedure to accomplish this without entering it on the patient's record?

Reminders related to the patient's next visit are very helpful in carrying out treatment plans. However, you should write the reminders not directly on the patient's treatment record, but instead on a separate sheet, placed in the patient's folder and reviewed before treatment at the patient's next visit. Reminder notes on the treatment record clutter up the record, and may confuse readers as to what actually was done.

Do you ever enter pencil notes in the patient's record, intending them either to remain permanently, or to be erased at a later date?

You should never make entries in the record in pencil. Notes in pencil raise a suspicion that the record was altered, or subjected to *spoliation*. Entries should be made in ink or using a ballpoint pen, preferably black.

Do you maintain a separate X-ray exposure log in each patient's record?

An X-ray exposure log is a record of all the radiation to which the patient has been exposed in your office. It notes the date the radiograph was taken as well as the area in the oral cavity that was exposed. It allows you to review what films were taken, when, and where. It should prevent you from taking films you shouldn't, or not taking films you should. However, an X-ray log should not be a substitute for appropriate entries in the chronologic daily treatment record.

Do you maintain a separate medication log in each patient's record?

A medication log records all medications the patient has taken and is currently taking. It notes the date the medication was prescribed, the dosage, and the condition for which it was prescribed. It will allow you to see at a glance the patient's medication history. However, a medication log should not be a substitute for appropriate entries in the chronologic daily treatment record.

Do you have a method of keeping track of referrals and consultant reports for each patient?

A referral log will help you keep track of all referrals and requests for information related to a patient. You should enter information about the referral or request and the date you received it. This log will prevent the misplacement of reports from outside sources.

18.13 Health Histories

Are health histories taken on each patient?

Before making a diagnosis, or beginning treatment of any patient under any circumstances, you must first take a health history and make a record that you did so. You should apply this rule to every patient you see without exception. Only in a true emergency, in which you are called upon to provide assistance without being able to get a history first, may you proceed without one. This exception is rare.

Are patients informed about the importance of the health history?

To ensure that patients supply honest answers, you should inform them that you cannot make a diagnosis or begin treatment without properly evaluating their health status. Inform them of this both orally and in writing on the form.

Do you personally review the health history with the patient?

Rarely can you learn the entire health history of a patient through answers to questions on a generic form. This should never be the sole source of information. Rather, it should serve only to direct your attention to certain aspects of the health history, which you should then discuss with the patient.

Do you make certain that all questions are answered?

You should tell the patient, preferably in writing on the form, to answer all questions, and when reviewing the form with the patient you should make sure that this has been done. There should be no blank spaces on the form when it is completed.

Do you make a note in the patient's treatment record that the history was reviewed with the patient?

Make some record that you reviewed the health history with the patient, both on the form if space is provided, and on the patient's treatment record.

Do you make certain that the history form was signed and dated?

Have the form signed by the person who completes it, and make sure it is dated.

If someone other than the patient completes the history form, do you make certain the form shows who completed it?

Note who completed the form, and, if it is not the patient, that person's relationship with the patient.

Does your form inquire about the patient's history of infection with AIDS, HIV, or any other communicable disease?

Dentists must know the complete health status of their patients, including infection with AIDS and other communicable diseases. To avoid charges of discrimination, however, you must be able to show that you asked all patients the same questions. Therefore, include these questions on the form you give all patients.

What do you do if a patient refuses to answer any question on the health history?

First, you should explain to patients why the information is important in the provision of dental care, both to their general health and to their dental treatment. If they still refuse to answer, you should refuse to treat them. Enter suitable notes in the patient's record.

When patients mention a health problem, do you follow up with consultation with the appropriate health practitioner or institution?

Whenever patients mention any health problems, you must follow up to determine if the problem will affect your treatment, or if your treatment will affect their health. Health histories are useless unless you can show that you reviewed the information the patient supplied, and, if it could possibly affect the patient's dental treatment, that you made an effort to accommodate or correct any problems.

Is the follow-up response made in writing?

Any response to your request for information from another practitioner or health facility should be made in writing if at all possible.

Is the follow-up report entered in the patient's record?

If you receive a report from a consultant, a laboratory, another health provider, or a health facility in response to your request, note receipt of the report in the patient's treatment record and file it in the patient's record folder.

Do you know what to do if a physician does not respond to your request for written information about the patient?

If you receive no written report, note in the patient's record that you called the physician and requested the report, and note the physician's response (or lack thereof).

Is the need for consultations explained to the patient?

If you feel that another practitioner's consultation is essential to proper care of your patient, you should tell the patient this. It is not enough simply to tell the patient that a consultation is necessary. If you don't explain why, the patient may refuse.

Are consultations requested in writing?

You should request all consultations in writing. If the request is made by phone, or directly by the patient, follow it up with the written request.

Are consultant's reports discussed with the patient?

Once you receive a consultant's report, you should discuss it with the patient, and its effect upon the care you intend to provide. Enter notes in the patient's record regarding the discussion and the patient's response.

Is the health history form you use arranged in "yes/no" columns that call for a check mark, underline, or circle?

Health history forms on which the patient can only make check marks, circles, or underlines indicating yes or no answers can raise doubts as to who entered the responses if the health history is reviewed in a judicial proceeding. Your history forms should be designed so that patients write their responses to open-ended questions.

Does the health history form ask the name of the patient's physician, the date of the last medical visit, and the reason for the visit?

The questionnaire used in your office, whether it is a registration demographic form or a health history form, should ask patients the name, address, and telephone numbers of their physician, the date of the last visit, and the reason for the visit.

Is the patient's physician contacted if the patient notes a history of any cardiac or cardiac-related problem?

If, in taking or reviewing the patient's health history, you discover that the patient presents a cardiac-related health problem that may affect dental care, or that the dental care you plan may affect the general health of the patient, you should contact the patient's physician before you begin any dental care or prescribe any medication for the patient.

Does the health history ask about drug allergies?

Dental care often includes the administration and prescription of drugs and medications. Many patients take a variety of drugs not related to dental care. Before you administer or prescribe any drugs, you should determine what drugs the patient is taking and if the patient has had any allergic reaction to the drugs you intend to prescribe or administer.

Does the health history ask about problems with the TMJ?

Include in your overall examination of a patient an evaluation of the patient's TMJ and surrounding structures. It is a good idea to include questions related to TMJ difficulties, such as pain in the area, clicking, and dislocations, in the health history form. If you do not, you should ask the patient about any problems in the joint area and record the patient's responses on the patient's record.

If the dental treatment provided to the patient affects the occlusion, do you monitor any changes in the TMJ?

There are those who believe that a change in the occlusion may adversely effect the TMJ. You should therefore monitor the joint when your treatment changes the occlusion.

Is someone experienced in supervising completion of health histories available to assist the patient?

Before, during, and immediately after the patient completes the history form, you should ensure that someone in your office, trained in the procedure, is available to discuss the completed form with the patient.

At the top of the history form, is the patient's name either typed, printed, or otherwise imprinted along with some other readily identifying entry to clearly indicate whose health history it is?

You should be able to identify the patient whose history the form represents because papers sometimes stray from the proper folder.

Are patients told to request help if they don't understand any of the questions?

Patients do not always understand questions on a medical history form. They should be instructed that if they don't understand a question they should be discuss it with you or a member of your office staff assigned to work with them.

Are patients told that if there is a change in their health they are to inform you at the start of their next visit?

This instruction is important because such changes may affect the continued provision of care. Don't leave it to the patient to decide if the change is significant.

18.14   History Updates

At each recall visit do you update the patient's medical history?

You should update the patient's history at intervals appropriate to the patient's health status, but at least at every recall visit. Unless the patient reports a change of health, a short form may suffice.

Do you update the patient's medical history when continuous treatment extends over 6 months?

Updating a medical history is not difficult. When you treat patients over an extended period of time, you may ask them, at regular intervals, "Have you recently had any health-related problems?" If they answer in the affirmative, you should discuss the problem. Based upon what you learn during the discussion you might have the patient complete a new history form. However, at the very least, make an entry in the patient's chart indicating that the question was asked and the answer given.

If and when medical updates are taken, are the results recorded in the patient's treatment record?

You should always record in the patient's treatment record the fact that a medical update was completed, whether the history form was completed by you, your staff, or the patient.

Do you have a form upon which the patient records the results of the medical update?

If you feel that the patient should complete a medical update, it is best to have the patient indicate on a form designed especially for that purpose that the health history was updated, and to include the results of the update.

If the patient indicates during the medical update that there is a new medical problem, do you follow up on it?

If you learn that the patient has a new medical problem since an old history form or update was completed, you should always follow up, and have the patient complete a new form.

Are the results of the follow-up recorded in the patient's treatment record?

Results of all follow-ups resulting from health history information should be recorded in the patient's treatment record. If these results are in the form of a report, it also should be placed in the patient's record folder.

18.15   Consent

Do you obtain the consent of the patient for every service you provide?

It is essential that you obtain the consent of the patient before providing any treatment or diagnostic service.

Does the office have consent forms?

All treatment and diagnostic procedures carried out in your office require the patient's consent. Some consents may be implied by the patient's willingness that you proceed. However, should the procedure be invasive, eg, surgery, endodontic treatment, or injections, written documentation of informed consent becomes important. To facilitate the process you should have written consent forms available for the patient to execute before initiating treatment. In the absence of consent forms, you should make notes in the patient's record of the patient's consent to the treatment, and have the patient initial or sign the entry.

When you obtain the consent of the patient, what information do you provide?

Before beginning any procedure, you must inform the patient about its nature, purpose, risks, prognosis, and any reasonable alternatives to the procedure. Pay careful attention to the risks of an invasive procedure and of any alternatives to the procedure you recommend. You must provide this information in language the patient understands, invite the patient to ask any questions, and answer those questions.

Does the patient sign the consent to the treatment plan?

For the consent to be effective it must be signed by the patient and dated. The rule applies whether the consent is recorded in the record or on a specially designed form.

If you do not have consent forms, what process do you use to obtain consent for invasive procedures?

By accepted definition any surgical procedure is invasive. A written, signed, and dated consent should be completed for all invasive procedures. By an appellate court decision in one jurisdiction (Pennsylvania), endodontic therapy is considered surgical.

In situations in which an invasive procedure can be postponed, do you permit the patient to take the consent form home before asking the patient to agree with the procedure?

Whenever possible, you should insist that the patient take the consent form home along with any written material describing the procedure before signing the form. Depart from this policy only when you feel that the procedure should be carried out during the same office visit as when the consent form is given.

On your written consent form, is there a place for it to be witnessed?

Completed consent forms should be witnessed, but not by the practitioner. Any other person in the office, including an employee, may witness the patient's signature.

Is the patient given a copy of the signed consent form?

Consent-to-treatment forms should be signed in duplicate, or a copy made of the original. The original should be placed in the patient's record folder, and the copy given to the patient.

Are the consents reviewed by each provider in your office before treatment is begun?

Each provider in your office, including associates, dentist/employees, dental hygienists, and dental assistants in states where they are permitted to provide care, should review the consent form for the purpose of ensuring that the procedure they are to carry out has the consent of the patient.

May anyone other than the provider of care obtain the consent of the patient?

The courts in two states, New York and Pennsylvania, have ruled that any employee of the dentist may supervise the obtaining of the patient's consent. Courts in other states would likely rule the same. However, the employee must be trained in supervising the consent, and the provider of care should be available to answer the patient's questions.

In addition to the patient's signed consent form, is a note made in the patient's record that the treatment was discussed with the patient?

> After obtaining the informed consent of the patient, you should make appropriate entries in the patient's record.

If you take photographs or make videos of your patients, do you have them sign a release?

> If you intend to take photos or video recordings of a patient, you should execute a form describing what you intend to do, and your reasons for doing it. If the patient agrees, you should have an appropriate form available for the patient to sign. Personal identification on the photo or video should be avoided whenever possible.

Do you provide any of your patients with general anesthetic agents?

> The use of general anesthetic agents to complete the care of a patient may cause serious and permanent injury. These cases bring the largest awards and settlements in dental malpractice cases should a court find the dentist negligent.

If the answer to the above is yes, do you have the patient sign a consent form specifically designed for this purpose?

> Having the patient execute a properly prepared consent form may avoid many problems. The form should list all foreseeable risks, and you should discuss these with the patient before treatment. If possible, allow the patient to take the form home and return with it at the appointment during which the treatment is to be carried out. At that time the patient should be invited to ask any questions about the procedure and sign the form.

18.16   Waivers and Authorizations

Do you routinely have patients sign a form giving your office permission to obtain information from past dentists?

> At times your treatment of a patient might benefit from your review of the records of the patient's past dentist. However, a dentist should not release the records, radiographs, or any other information relating to the patient without written permission from the patient. Therefore, you should accompany your request with a signed release from the patient.

Before releasing any information to a third- or fourth-party payer, do you make certain that the patient has executed a permission-to-release form?

Dentists should never release copies of the records, radiographs, or any other information about their patient or their treatment of the patient to anyone, including another health practitioner, without written permission from the patient. Therefore, before making such a request you should obtain written permission, properly signed and dated, from the patient.

If you refer the patient to another health provider, and the patient agrees to follow your recommendation, is a release of information needed?

No. By following your recommendation, the patient has waived the right to confidentiality of information.

In the above situation does the same rule apply if the information relates to the patient having AIDS or HIV?

Yes, provided you feel the information is important to the recipient practitioner's care. However, it is best to discuss the matter with the patient before sending the information.

Do you give information about your treatment of a patient to an attorney for the patient or an insurance company without the patient's written permission?

You should never provide any information about any of your patients without written permission. This includes information requested by an attorney or insurance company for the patient. Some third-party payers have the patient agree to the release of information by a health practitioner to the company as a condition of benefits. You should determine if this condition exists before releasing any information.

Do you report any information about a patient to the health department or any other administrative agency?

In certain jurisdictions a dentist is required to report patients with some communicable diseases and minors who have been the subject of child abuse or neglect. A release by the patient or parent under these circumstances is not required.

18.17 Appointment Logs

Are all entries in the appointment log legible?

The appointment log in your office is part of your record keeping. Like all other records, entries should be legible.

Do you write scheduled appointments in the appointment log in ink?

Entries often are made in pencil to enable erasures when the patient cancels, but entries should be made in ink, and if a patient cancels a single line should be drawn through the appointment note and "canceled" should be written next to the appointment. The log may be important in the defense of a suit to show that the patient did not cooperate.

Are late patient arrivals noted?

You should document in the appointment log and in the patient's treatment record all late arrivals. They may serve to demonstrate at some future date that the patient contributed to an injury by failing to keep appointments on time.

Are patient no-shows recorded?

You should document in the appointment log and in the patient's treatment record all appointments the patient failed to keep. They may serve to demonstrate at some future date that the patient contributed to his injury by failing to keep regular appointments.

If you examine the appointment log can you identify the person who made a specific entry?

The appointment log may serve your purposes in a judicial proceeding. You may be asked to identify who made specific entries in the log. If you cannot, your credibility may be compromised. In addition, you may have to have the person testify as to the authenticity of the entries made in the log.

Is the appointment log placed in a fireproof cabinet at the end of each day?

Your office should have a fireproof cabinet in which to deposit important documents such as the appointment log.

Do you keep old appointment logs?

Like all patient records, appointment logs should be retained in a safe place as long as possible, 10 years at the least.

18.18   Recalls

Are patients whose treatment is completed placed on recall?

Except in unusual situations, all patients whose care is completed should be placed on a regular recall schedule.

Are these patients informed of the recall policy of the office?

You, or a responsible member of your staff, should explain the recall policy of the office.

Is the recall policy of the office included in any written document describing the policies of the office?

Your office should prepare a written recall office policy.

If the recalled patient does not keep the appointment, is a written reminder sent?

All patients who miss appointments should be sent a written reminder that includes the policy of the office if a patient does not keep a scheduled appointment. Chronic offenders should be considered for dismissal from the practice.

If the recalled patient continues to ignore recall notices, is an attempt made to contact the patient by telephone?

Your office should attempt to contact by telephone a patient who ignores a recall notice, and a note should be entered in the patient's record of the call and the patient's response.

If all attempts to recall the patient fail, is a letter sent to the patient concerning the risks of not being regularly examined?

If all your efforts to have a patient comply with recall notices fail, you should send the patient a letter concerning the possible consequences of failure to adhere to regular oral examinations, or the failure to appear for an examination of the specific care you have provided, eg, follow-up on a surgical procedure. Send the letter by certified mail, signed receipt requested.

Is a written record kept of patients who do not respond to recall notices?

Your office should be meticulous in keeping records relating to failure of a patient to comply with a recall notice. This record may play an important role should the patient later claim that the services you rendered were substandard.

Are patients who continue to ignore recall notices dropped from the practice?

Continuing to treat patients who ignore recall notices not only wastes your time, but exposes you to additional legal risk. Such patients should be dropped from your practice following appropriate notice.

Are dropped patients informed by certified mail, signed receipt requested, of the consequences of discontinuing regular care?

Your office should notify all patients dropped from your active list of patients of the consequences of their failure to seek regular dental examinations and care. The notice should be carefully written and sent by certified mail, signed receipt requested.

18.19   Medications and Prescriptions

Do you prescribe controlled substances?

If you write prescriptions for controlled substances, you are held to strict compliance with federal and state laws. It is difficult to conduct a modern dental practice without prescribing controlled substances. You should never sign blank prescription forms or leave a stamp of your signature accessible to anyone.

Is your DEA registration current?

You should make certain that your DEA registration is current. Although the agency sends out application renewal notices, the burden to renew on time is on the holder of the registration. It is no defense that the agency did not notify you at the time of renewal if you write on an expired registration.

Do you write prescriptions for members of your family or friends who are not documented patients of record?

At times it is difficult to avoid writing such prescriptions, but it is a dangerous practice. Never do it. Writing such prescriptions and taking the drugs yourself will, if discovered, have serious consequences for your personal and professional life.

Do you comply with the laws regulating the prescription of controlled substances?

You should become thoroughly familiar with the laws, both federal and state, that apply to prescribing controlled substances, and adhere to them meticulously. Also make certain the laws you follow are current.

Do you retain copies of your prescriptions for controlled substances the length of time required by law?

The laws that regulate prescriptions for controlled substances mandate that the doctor retain copies of the prescription for a specific period of time. Make certain you are aware of the mandated time, and that you comply with the law.

Do you keep controlled substances in your office?

If you keep controlled substances in your office, you must abide by laws that apply to the inventory and the manner in which they are dispensed.

Do you keep a record of the controlled substances dispensed to patients in your office?

If you dispense controlled substances to your patients, you should note on the patient's record what you have prescribed and the dose. You should also record the activity as required by the controlled substances law.

Do you write prescriptions for medications that are not on the controlled substances list?

Writing prescriptions for medications is common in the practice of dentistry. Although the laws that apply to drugs not on the controlled substances list are less restrictive, they must be followed.

When you write a prescription for a drug that is not on the controlled substances list, do you note it in the patient's treatment record?

You should note on the patient's treatment record any medication dispensed to the patient or prescribed.

Do you maintain a separate medication log in the patient's record folder?

In each patient's folder for whom you prescribe or administer a drug other than those used in the usual course of dental treatment, you should maintain a separate log, and before prescribing or administering a drug, you should review the log.

Do you prescribe drugs for patients over the telephone?

It is an accepted procedure for dentists to prescribe medication over the telephone. However, this should only be done for patients of record. If the prescription is for a controlled substance, special laws apply concerning the submission of a follow-up written prescription. Know these laws.

If you prescribe drugs for patients over the telephone, do you make a note of it in the patient's treatment record?

Keep a record of all prescriptions, whether they are written in the office or delivered by phone. When you prescribe by phone you should note what you have done, and at the earliest possible time enter the information in the patient's record.

If a patient reports an untoward reaction to a prescribed drug, is it noted in the patient's treatment record?

If the patient reports any untoward reaction to what you have prescribed, you should describe it in detail in the patient's record.

During the taking of the patient's medical history, is the patient asked about adverse drug reactions and allergies?

Adverse drug reactions, allergies, and drug incompatibilities are a major risk to patient health and to the dentist who prescribes the drug or administers the medication. Your history taking should be designed to determine if patients ever experienced an untoward reaction to any drug or medication. If they have, you should carefully avoid prescribing or administering that drug, and the information should be entered in the their drug and medication logs.

If the patient reports an adverse reaction to a drug or medication, do you follow up on the information?

If a patient reports an adverse reaction to a drug or medication you either prescribed or administered, you should employ appropriate follow-up care by either performing the care yourself or by referral to a physician or hospital, depending on the nature of the patient's reaction.

If the patient reports an adverse reaction to a drug or medication, is an alert sticker placed in an appropriate location on the patient's chart?

You should place medical alert stickers noting that the patient is allergic to a specific drug or medication in all appropriate places on the patient's record, but not on the outside of the patient's record folder.

Before you prescribe a drug, do you ask the patient about any adverse reaction if the drug was previously taken?

Before prescribing or administering any drug or medication, you should review the medication log, if your record system includes one; review the history form, including notes attached or entered on the form; and ask the patient if he or she ever experienced any reaction to the drug or medication you intend to administer or prescribe.

After the patient takes a drug you prescribed, do you ask the patient if there was any untoward reaction?

Often patients are unaware of untoward reaction to drugs. Therefore they should be asked about them explicitly.

tion
Office Audit Risk Assessment for the General Dentist • 18

If the patient reports an adverse reaction to a drug you prescribed, do you advise the patient to report the fact to all subsequent health practitioners?

You should advise a patient who exhibited an untoward reaction to any drug or medication you administered or prescribed to inform any subsequent practitioner of the fact. You should note in the patient's record what you have told the patient.

Is the advice about the patient's adverse drug reactions or allergies given to the patient in writing?

A good policy is to give patients a written note about any untoward reaction they experienced to any drug or medication you prescribed or administered. A copy of the note should be placed in the patient's record folder.

Before prescribing or administering a drug or medication do you consult the latest issue of the *Physician's Desk Reference (PDR)*?

Some courts have admitted the write-up of drugs and medications in the *PDR*, and health practitioners have been held responsible for the information contained in it.

18.20 Employees

Have you advised those employees who provide patient care or assist in the provision of patient care about laws regulating their activities?

You should become thoroughly familiar with all laws and regulations that apply to employees involved in patient care. This information should be given to the employees as well. Copies of the laws regulating dental practice and medical employees may be obtained from your state licensing agency.

Have you advised employees of the penalties for violating the regulatory laws?

Administrative health agencies, including dental ones, have increased their surveillance of the profession, particularly as it applies to the performance of illegal acts. Penalties have been severe, and employees should be advised of these penalties.

Have you told your employees that you are held to statements made by them to patients, such as, "You will be satisfied with the dentures made by Dr X"?

All your employees should be informed that what they tell patients binds you. Offhand remarks, made by an employee with the best intentions, may commit you to what you wish to avoid, such as guarantees about the results of care.

Do you periodically review what your employees tell your patients?

Because patients may rely on what one of your employees tells them about the care you provide, you should periodically review what employees tell patients, particularly complaining patients.

Do you conduct regular office management meetings with your employees?

You should conduct regular office meetings with you entire staff. It builds morale and allows you to caution them about inappropriate behavior and statements made to patients that you deem inadvisable.

Before instituting a new office management procedure, do you discuss the proposed change with your employees?

You should discuss all proposed changes in office procedures with your employees. Their response may affect your decisions, and they should all be made aware of current procedures. Lack of uniformity may lead to patient confusion and dissatisfaction.

Do you advise your employees on how to deal with a patient whose behavior or attitude presents a problem?

Your employees should report immediately to you when they find that the behavior or attitude of a patient presents a problem. If you become aware of such a problem, you should instruct your employees regarding how to deal with it. Their failure to deal appropriately with the problem may result in a patient taking steps against you that are not in your best interest.

Have you told your employees that you are to be told of all patient complaints at the earliest possible time?

Too often employees attempt to protect the dentist from complaining patients. This may lead to a suit against you. Your employees must be told to allow you to deal directly with such patients.

If you discover that one of your employees is the target of patient complaints, do you know the best course of action to take?

In a private meeting, counsel the employee and suggest changes in the employee's behavior. If you feel that this is futile, let the employee go. However, document the entire process as it takes place.

Do you ever ask an employee dental hygienist or dental assistant to perform a service that is not authorized under the law?

Don't ever do it!

18.21   Hiring Policies and Associate Practice

Before hiring an employee (associate, hygienist, or assistant), do you inquire if a government agency ever took action against the person's license or right to practice?

> Prudence demands that you make an effort to determine the past professional experiences of your employees. You owe this duty to your patients. One of the essentials is to determine if the prospective employee or associate has ever been charged with unprofessional or illegal professional conduct by a government agency. If the applicant reveals the fact that charges have been brought, you should further investigate before making a hiring decision.

Before hiring a dentist, do you inquire about past malpractice suits or investigations by government agencies, including the professional licensing agency?

> Prudence demands that you make an effort to determine the past professional experiences of a dentist you intend to employ. You owe this duty to your patients as well as yourself. One of the essentials is to determine if the prospective employee or associate has ever been formally accused of malpractice. If the applicant reveals that this is the case, you should investigate. A similar inquiry should be made of the professional licensing agency.

Before hiring any office staff, do you ask for the names of past employers and contact them to determine the work record of the applicant?

> Former employers of applicants for employment in your office should be contacted regarding their experiences with the applicants. This information should contribute to your decision.

Do you provide all employees with information regarding the laws of confidentiality concerning patient records and information?

> Patients and the law are adamant that information obtained from a patient in the course of treatment be held in confidence. A breach of this duty, by you or any of your employees, may result in a civil suit against you, and an action by the licensing agency against your license to practice. Breach of a professional confidence in a civil suit brought by a patient may not be covered by your professional liability insurance policy. An action brought against your license is never covered by an insurance policy.

Do you have a written contract with your professional associates?

> If at all possible, you should enter into a legally binding contract with your professional associates. Failure to do so may lead to future serious misunderstanding, legal problems, and the breakup of a friendship.

If you are an employee in a practice, do you have a written agreement with your employer?

As a general rule, employer dentists appear reluctant to enter into written contracts with employees. If you can, you should make an attempt to enter into such a contract. There are too many intricacies in joint dental practice to trust to memory. Disagreements may interfere with an otherwise profitable relationship.

If you are an employee in a practice, have you made an agreement with your employer to have access to the original records of the patients you have treated should you need them in a judicial proceeding after you leave the practice?

Without any agreement to the contrary, the records of all patients treated in a practice belong to the employer. An employee may be sued for malpractice long after leaving an office for treatment rendered while employed in that office. The treatment records may become important in the suit, which may be lost without them. If the employer dentist has no contractual duty to deliver the the patient's original records to the former employee, they may be difficult if not impossible to obtain. To avoid the problem, the contract of employment should provide that, upon employee's written request, the employer shall deliver to the employee the records of all patients treated by the employee if they are needed in any judicial proceeding. In addition the employer should be required to retain the records of all patients treated by the employee for a period of 10 years following the patient's final visit to the office.

If you have associates in practice, do you have an agreement with them relating to restrictive covenants should they leave the practice?

Restrictive covenants are agreements that prevent one party from competing. In dentistry these restrictions are common in employment and associate contracts. They are designed to prevent an employee or associate from engaging in competitive practice in another location should they leave the practice. The restrictions usually specify time and distance, for example preventing a former employee (associate) from engaging in dental practice within 5 miles of the former office of employment for a period of 3 years. If the time and distance are reasonable, the courts have upheld restrictive covenants. Some covenants prohibit contacting patients treated in the former office. The courts have also upheld these restrictions.

If you use the services of independent contractors in your office, have you executed a hold harmless clause with them?

You should make every effort to separate yourself legally from the acts of an independent contractor in your office. One method is to execute a hold harmless clause with the independent contractor. It is designed to hold you harmless for any negligent act committed by the contractor. In most cases courts will uphold such agreements.

18.22   Professional Liability Insurance and Notice of Suit

Do you carry malpractice insurance?

Going without professional liability insurance ("going bare") invites major financial difficulties. The cost of an attorney, usually paid up front, will far exceed the cost of a policy, and, should you lose, the award may send you into bankruptcy. Becoming judgment-proof by disposing of your assets is a risky business, and not looked on favorably by the courts in matters related to health care. The court is likely to find that you have prevented patients you have injured from being compensated for the injury you caused.

Are you certain that your policy covers you for the negligent acts of your employees?

Case law has held an employer vicariously liable for the negligent acts of employees while carrying out their defined duties. If your employee commits a negligent act and as a result the patient is injured, you will be sued; you have the deepest pockets, and you profited by the services of the employee.

Do your employees, whether dentists, hygienists, or assistants, have their own policies insuring them for their negligent acts?

In all malpractice policies you are covered for the acts of your employees, but the employees may not be covered. If named as defendants they may have to bear all the expenses. In some policies your employees are covered, and if named in a suit will be provided legal assistance and indemnification for losses. If they are not covered by your policy, avoid all problems by having each employee covered by a separate policy.

How much malpractice insurance coverage do you have?

Today, the minimum is $1,000,000/$3,000,000. It means that you are insured up to $1,000,000 for each claim, and a maximum of $3,000,000 for the year. If you are an oral and maxillofacial surgeon, or administer intravenous sedation or general anesthetics in your office, that is hardly enough.

Do you have insurance as an employer?

You should. This is called *Employment Practices Liability Insurance.* It covers you if an employee claims wrongful termination, sexual harassment, or discrimination. The coverage extends to civil suits. If the employee sues you, the policy will provide you with an attorney and pay money damages. However, no coverage is available for criminal suits; it is against public policy and not permitted by law.

Do you have coverage for other risks of practice?

There is another essential form of insurance, known as *Business Owners Policy Insurance* (BOP). This will cover you for office property, business personal property, loss due to criminal acts, loss of valuable papers and records, instruments, furnishings, precious metals, injuries to patients not related to treatment, etc.

Have you secured your professional liability policy in a safe, easily accessible place?

Your professional liability policy is your lifeline to financial security in times of legal stress; guard it carefully. Make certain you know where it is. You may have to read it when you least expect it. Keep it in a safe place at all times.

Do you know exactly whom to contact should you receive a threat of a lawsuit or suit papers?

Once suit papers are filed, the legal clock begins to run. Missing a legal deadline may be fatal to your defense. As soon as possible after you receive suit papers or written threat of a suit, you should read your professional liability policy to determine whom and how to notify.

Are you familiar with what untoward incidents are to be reported to the professional liability insurance carrier?

Professional liability policy terms regarding what is to be reported to the insurance company vary with each policy. The one rule all have in common is that when served with suit papers, or informed by a patient's attorney or by the patient that a suit is contemplated, you must notify the insurance company as soon as possible. More doubtful is whether untoward events should be reported to the company. To decide this you should read your policy. If such an event occurs, and after reading the policy you are still in doubt, call your insurance agent. If you have no direct access to an agent, call the company and ask one of its representatives. Make a written note of the response, including the date, time, and name of the representative, and keep it in your professional liability file.

Have you kept a record of all professional liability insurance carriers that have insured you in the past 10 years?

The period in which you are subject to suit for malpractice may extend over many years. In addition, some acts of negligence may be continuing. If you have changed carriers during the period of vulnerability, several insurance companies may be responsible for your defense and indemnification; all must be notified. You should prepare a chart listing the names, addresses, and dates of coverage for each company that insured you since you entered dental practice. When you change carriers, add the new one to the list. Keep all policies in a safe place.

If you have relocated your office since taking out professional liability insurance, have you notified your insurance carrier?

In all professional liability policies there is a question as to where you conduct your practice. If you should relocate or open an additional office, you should notify the company at the earliest time possible. Rates may vary depending upon where you practice, and you do not want the company to accused you of not complying with the terms of the contract of insurance.

When you employ a new licensed dental health professional, do you notify your professional liability insurance carrier?

You should notify your insurance carrier if you employ a licensed health practitioner. You should also notify the carrier if one leaves. As the employer, you are liable to patients for the negligent acts of your employees, and the professional liability insurance company is responsible to provide you with an attorney to defend you and to indemnify you for any financial loss you may suffer as a result of the claim.

Are you thoroughly familiar with all the terms of your professional liability insurance policy, and with what you are to do if you receive notice of a suit against you for malpractice?

Your insurance policy is your lifeline to financial security if you are accused of a negligent act that resulted in an injury to a patient. You should read and become thoroughly familiar with all its terms. A good practice is to read the policy at least once each year. You should commit to memory facts such as what acts are covered by the policy, when to report a problem, what problems are to be reported, how to report, and the expiration date.

If a patient enters suit against you, should you allow that patient to see you for care?

Once patients enter suit against you, they have voluntarily elected to begin an adversarial relationship. All contacts with such patients or their representative, probably an attorney, should be forwarded to the attorney assigned to the case by the insurance company. To do otherwise may compromise the claim against you and violate the terms of the policy. The insurance company may take a dim view of any contact you have with the patient following the start of a suit against you.

If a patient enters suit against you, should you try to dissuade the individual from continuing the suit?

All contacts between you and the patient should end once the patient has elected to enter suit against you. Once the suit is begun, your representative, by the insurance company contract, is the insurance company or its representative. Acting on your own may jeopardize your relationship with the company.

If a patient enters suit against you, and you discover that another dentist has written a letter criticizing the care you provided the patient, should you discuss the matter with that dentist?

When you learn that another dentist has submitted a report to the patient's attorney that is critical of the care you provided, you may be tempted to call the dentist to discuss the matter and attempt to explain what you had done and why. Do not do it! You may be accused of conspiracy.

If you receive a letter from an attorney threatening a lawsuit, should you call the attorney to discuss the matter?

You should never contact the patient's attorney. Some dentists feel that a call to the attorney will result in the withdrawal of the suit. Others feel that a threat of retaliation against the attorney for bringing the suit will be effective. Neither is ever proper, and either may increase the commitment on the part of the patient and the attorney to pursue the claim. Moreover, your insurance carrier will be upset by what you have done.

If you receive a letter from an attorney demanding the dental records of her client, should you comply?

You should comply with a request by an attorney to submit copies of a patient's records, but only when the request is accompanied by a signed authorization from the patient.

If you recall an event that took place during the treatment of the patient, should you enter it in the patient's record after you have received notice of suit?

If after a suit is begun you recall an incident about the patient's care that took place before the suit, do not enter it in the patient's treatment record. Instead make a note of it on a separate sheet marked *personal note*. Whatever else you do, do not make any changes or additions to the original record once you become aware a suit against you is contemplated or begun.

If you recall an event that took place during the treatment of the patient, should you enter it in the patient's record if you do not anticipate at the time that you may be sued?

You may make any additions to a patient's treatment record before becoming aware that the patient intends to sue you, provided that the entries are made in good faith and are accurate as to fact and date.

After you receive notice of suit, do you inform your office staff?

If you are sued for malpractice, you should immediately notify all members of your office staff. Do not let them hear it for the first time from an outside source. Instruct them never to communicate with anyone about the case or the patient. Inform them that they should refer all inquiries to you. You in turn should report such inquiries to the attorney assigned by the insurance company to defend you.

Do you discuss the fact that you have been sued with any of your colleagues?

Once you receive notice of a suit you should not discuss the matter with anyone other than your staff, your attorney, and your insurance carrier. Your spouse may be an exception.

Do you ever tell a patient that you have malpractice insurance?

The old rule of never discussing politics or religion with patients should be expanded: Never tell a patient that you have malpractice insurance.

18.23   Final Admonition

To conduct your practice in a worry- and stress-free environment, in addition to the above, *never* lie to a third-party payer, either to collect a fee to which you are not entitled, or to enable patients to have their insurance companies indemnify them for their dental care.

CHAPTER NINETEEN

Insuring a Dental Practice

Richard F. Breitweiser, Esq*

Glossary of Terms

19.1   Following is an alphabetized list of terms you may find in an insurance contract.

Ab initio: from the beginning

Ambiguity: doubtfulness, uncertainty of meaning

Claims-Made Policy: a policy of insurance that makes the benefits of the policy conditional on the reporting of a claim during the policy's term

Contribution: a legal action that demands another party to contribute to a loss

Contract of Adhesion: a "take it or leave it" contract that does not afford the consumer a realistic opportunity to bargain

Estoppel: a situation in which a party is prevented by his own conduct from claiming a right to the detriment of another party who was entitled to rely on such conduct and has acted accordingly

Exclusion: a provision that eliminates coverage

Expiration Date: ending date of the policy term

Inception date: beginning date of the policy term

Indemnification: loss shifted from one person to another person

---

*Richard F. Breitweiser, Esq, is the vice president and director of the dental program and a senior claim officer with the Redwoods Group Dentists Insurance Program in Coral Springs, Florida.

Insurance Contract: a contract whereby, for a stipulated consideration, one party undertakes to compensate the other for loss on a specified subject through specified perils

Insuring Agreement: sets forth the basic terms of the insurance contract

Occurrence Policy: a policy of insurance that makes the benefits of the policy conditional on the occurrence during the policy's term of a certain incident or event

Prejudice: the late or lacking notice that has led to the waiving of affirmative defenses that otherwise would have been available

Purchasing Group: insurance buyers who band together to purchase their liability insurance coverage from an insurance carrier, eg, the National Society of Dental Practitioners

Reasonable Expectation: fair and proper expectation suitable under the circumstances

Retroactive Date: used in claims-made policy forms, it is the date as of which the carrier agrees to indemnify an insured for prior acts of negligence

Risk Retention Group: a liability insurance company owned by its members

Subrogation: the carrier takes the place of the insured as the entity with a lawful claim against another

Third-Party Beneficiary: one for whose benefit a promise is made in a contract (in dentist malpractice insurance, the patient)

Vicarious Liability: indirect legal responsibility for the acts of another

Waiver: relinquishment of a known right

Introduction

19.2 This chapter examines the insurance coverage available to dentists. Because of constant changes in the insurance market, it is not practical to examine or survey the various companies that underwrite dentists' professional liability coverage. The American Dental Association periodically reviews such information.

The availability and cost of insurance depends, in part, upon the return that insurance companies can achieve on investments. In the early to mid 1980s, many jurisdictions, such as New York, experienced a diminishing market in which very few underwriters were willing to insure the professional liability of dentists. Alternatives to private insurance were seriously examined and pursued. Some state dental societies implemented risk retention groups and risk purchasing groups that continue to operate today. In the late 1980s, an increase in the rate of return on investments made professional liability insurance more available, and by the 1990s, competition resulted not only in an increase in the number of insurers, but also in a reduction in premium costs and a broadening of the coverage available.

Although there is substantial diversity among insurers in the specific provisions of dentists' professional liability forms, they all take the same basic approach in their insuring agreements and exclusions. These are catalogued and examined in this chapter.

General Rule of Construction

19.3   Although the subject of this chapter is dentists' professional liability insurance, citations include other professional liability insurance and general liability insurance decisions as well because a dentist's professional liability policy is interpreted by the same rules that apply to other professional liability policies. Vast bodies of law and multiple jurisdictions make it impractical to review all decisions and rules. However, there are some rules that are generally followed.

First, in construing a contract of insurance, the court will decide on whether to apply the law of the jurisdiction in which it sits, of that where the contract was made, or of that where the alleged wrongful acts occurred. The choice is important because it may affect the case's outcome. A New York court found the most significant factor to be the state where the professional practiced and where the wrongful act occurred.[1]

Here are some basic principles in construing a dental malpractice policy. Interpretation of the contract usually raises a question of law; the contract is to be construed by its plain meaning.[2] If the language of the contract is ambiguous, it is construed to favor the insured because the courts view an insurance policy as a contract of adhesion, to be strictly construed against its author, the insurer.[3] Exclusions are narrowly construed against the insurer, whereas words of inclusion are liberally interpreted for the insured.[4] The courts construe a policy with the "reasonable expectations" of the insured in mind.[5] The court may determine coverage by considering who will benefit from the insurance proceedings, ie, the injured party.[6]

There are also general rules for deciding whether the insurer has a duty to defend. In analyzing allegations made in a complaint, the court will often interpret any factual allegations as requiring a defense. The duty to defend is deemed broader than the duty to indemnify because it can include groundless claims and excluded claims for which no obligation to pay will arise. The test is not whether the claimant has a viable cause of action against the insured but, rather, whether facts can be alleged that bring the injury within the coverage. The facts must still meet the basic requirements of the insuring agreement. For example, under an occurrence policy, allegations that conduct occurred within the policy period require a defense, but if it is determined that the acts did not occur during the policy period, the court will relieve the insurer from a duty to defend.[7]

Jurisdictions differ on the duty to defend if only some of the allegations come within the coverage. Some hold that if some of the causes of action are covered, then the duty to defend extends to all,[8] others that there is no duty to defend uncovered causes of action.[9]

If the claim is potentially within the scope of the policy, a refusal by the insurer to defend may be at its own peril.[10] Liability can include the cost of a reasonable settlement made by the insured,[11] or an estoppel or waiver of some or all of the carrier's rights.[12] Although an insurer should provide the insured with prompt notice of all coverage limitations, estoppel will only arise when the insurer's actions are detrimental or prejudicial to the rights of the insured.[13] Waiver is the intentional relinquishment of a known right.[14]

[1] 82 AD2d 790, 440 NYS 2d 660 (1981).

[2] 23 F3d 808 (3d Cir 1994).

[3] 821 F2d 216 (3d Cir 1987).

[4] 580 A2d 799 (Pa Super 1990).

[5] 435 NYS2d 900 (Sup Ct 1981).

[6] 186 NJSuper 347 (1980).

[7] 655 F2d 818 (7th Cir 1981).

[8] Ibid.

[9] 392 A2d 738 (1978).

[10] 655 F2d 818 (7th Cir 1981).

[11] Ibid.

[12] 692 FSupp 1181 (ND Cal 1988).

[13] 538 NYS2d 571 (App Div 1989).

[14] 692 FSupp 1181 (ND Cal 1988).

Policy Application and Declaration Page

19.4   The declaration page or face sheet identifies the named insureds, the policy limits, and the policy term. The policy or declarations page often incorporates provisions of the application. A written application usually asks the dentist many questions about his or her personal history and claims background and the characteristics of the practice. The representations that are of special concern to an insurance carrier are the nature of the practice and the dentist's knowledge of existing or potential claims. The typical claims-made policy will not afford coverage to a claim that, at the time of the effective date of the insurance, the dentist had a reasonable basis to believe might be made sometime in the future.[15]

[15]747 FSupp. 477 (ND Ill 1990).

The trend among insurance carriers is to integrate the application into the policy. Through this procedure, the dentist's statements in an application become a formal and integral part of the policy. This makes it easier for an insurance carrier to deny coverage on the basis of a material misrepresentation. Information regarding potential claims allows the underwriter to examine known risks and decide whether to issue the policy. Misrepresentations can give rise to a right of rescission or avoidance of the policy ab initio.[16]

[16]963 F2d 1023 (7th Cir 1992).

The typical claims-made policy provides in the insuring agreement or by exclusion that it does not apply to claims or known circumstances that preexisted the policy inception date, or retroactive date, that are likely to give rise to a claim. The disclosure in the application of circumstances likely to give rise to a claim can provide written and often conclusive evidence of why there is no coverage for the subsequent claim.[17]

[17]Ibid.

Amount of Coverage

19.5   The size of the policy limits required by a dentist depends on various circumstances. The most important are the risks that accompany the procedures the dentist performs, the form of the practice (corporation, partnership, or limited liability company [LLC]), the professional assets of the dentist, the personal assets of the dentist, the skills and experience of the dentists' employees, and the local law of recoverable damages. Dentists should make sure that there are adequate limits to protect their personal assets.

The amount of coverage is usually subject to two policy limits: *(1)* a per claim or per "dental incident" limit and *(2)* an annual aggregate limit for all claims or dental incidents. For example, the policy may specify limits to be $1,000,000 per dental incident and $3,000,000 aggregate for all claims ($1,000,000/$3,000,000). The per dental incident limit means that the company will pay no more than that sum as the total amount of all claims arising out of the same act, error, or omission. Continuous, repeated, or related acts, errors, or omissions are usually deemed to be a single dental incident.

The aggregate limit is usually defined as the total limit of the company's liability for all claims made within the policy year (plus any additional time provided for in an extended reporting endorsement).

Insuring Agreement: Who Is Insured?

19.6   There is wide divergence among insurers on how the policies define the *insured*. It always includes whoever is named in the declaration page; these are *named insureds*. Others who are afforded the benefits of coverage because of their relationship to the named insureds are described as either *additional insureds* or *insureds*. Most companies will not write a partnership unless all of the partners are insured on the same policy. Coverage for a professional corporation or LLC usually includes any officer, director, or shareholder.

Most companies require all employee dentists to be specifically insured under the partnership or corporation, or under their own insurance policies. The dentist should inquire whether coverage for employees (assistants, hygienists) or any new hire (dentists, too) are included, because some companies only insure such persons upon specific request and for payment of an additional premium.

The coverage for an insured usually includes any vicarious liability, that is, liability for another's acts, errors, or omissions for which the insured is legally liable. If an employee is negligent, the dentist will be entitled to a defense and indemnity for derivative liability. Some provisions may also include vicarious liability for nonemployed persons such as independent contractors.

Insuring Agreement: The Basic Provisions

19.7   Coverage is written for any act, error, or omission in the rendering or failure to render professional services as a dentist. What exactly are *professional services*? One court said that a professional act or service was one arising out of a vocation, calling, occupation, or employment involving specialized knowledge, labor, or skill, which is predominantly mental or intellectual, rather then physical or manual. The focus is not the title of the character performing the act, but the act itself.[18]

[18]183 Neb 12 (1968).

The insured must be obligated to pay damages because of an injury. Most policies define *injury* to mean bodily injury, sickness, or disease, including death. Thus, the duty to defend is triggered only if the action or claim involves an act, error, or omission in the rendering or failure to render professional services as a dentist that results in bodily injury, sickness, or disease, including death. Some policies now have a separate limit to reimburse the dentist for attorney fees while defending inquiries from formal accreditation standard review boards or an office of professional discipline, but none will indemnify a dentist for loss or a fine.

Occurrence Form

19.8   The occurrence policy was the form in which coverage was originally offered for professionals. The insurable event that triggers coverage is an *occurrence* during the policy period. The form arose from traditional general liability policies that focused on an *accident*. For the dentist, the insurable event became an act, error, or omission.

The coverage is for an act, error, or omission that occurs during the policy period regardless of when the claim is made. Thus, the occurrence form offers the advantage of coverage beyond the date of the policy's expiration, regardless of when the injury occurs or when the claimant's cause of action accrues, but only if an act, error, or omission occurred during the policy period. Because years may separate the wrongful conduct and the claim or suit, the dentist should permanently maintain all occurrence policies. A complication can arise if the occurrence falls over multiple policy periods, in which case the dentist may land in the middle of a dispute among insurers concerning who provides coverage and to what extent.

There are other disadvantages to the occurrence form. It does not cover acts or omissions committed before the policy period, even though the claim is made during the policy period. Occurrence policies are more difficult to find and more expensive than claims-made policies. When the claim is made in the distant future, a dentist may find that the policy limits are insufficient to cover the loss. Most importantly, especially at the present time, a dentist may find that the insurer who wrote the policy no longer exists or has severe financial difficulties.

Dental malpractice insurers also found the occurrence form unsatisfactory because of the difficulty of underwriting prospective losses for claims that would not be made until many years after the policy expired. The costs of defense and indemnity in the future are too difficult to predict and an appropriate premium therefore too difficult to set. Statutes of limitations further complicate such policies.

Claims-Made Form

19.9   The claims-made form offers more certainty in coverage interpretation and allows insurers to project their losses at the close of a policy year, especially if the claims-made form requires the claim to be made and reported during the policy period. The trigger of the coverage is when the claim is made rather than when the act, error, or omission occurred.

Insurers do not want to insure known claims or those reasonably likely to be made. A condition of claims-made coverage is that the insured did not know or had no reasonable basis to believe that an act, error, or omission had been committed. If at the time of the application the dentist knows of a claim or of circumstances that may reasonably give rise to a claim, this should be disclosed on the application.[19] There is also an express provision in the insuring agreement and the exclusions section that will preclude coverage for a known claim.

Today, most claims-made forms are written with a *retroactive date*. These require that a dental incident occur after the retroactive date and before the expiration date of the policy. The retroactive date is usually one of three dates:

[19]424 NW2d 189 (Wis 1988).

1. The date the insured began to practice
2. The date the insured converted from an occurrence form to a claims-made form (but watch out for carrier insolvency!)
3. The inception date of the insured's first occurrence policy

The policy typically defines *claim* to mean an assertion of the right to money or other benefits, including a suit or demand for arbitration.

The main disadvantage of the claims-made form is that it does not afford coverage after the policy expires. Therefore, a dentist must renew coverage each year so that there is no gap in coverage. For the retiring dentist, most companies offer a free extended reporting endorsement ("tail coverage") that extends the time for reporting a dental incident but applies only to acts, errors, or omissions that predate the policy expiration and are subsequent to the retroactive date. For others, tail coverage can be costly.

Notice Requirements

19.10   All policies require the insured to give prompt notice of a claim or suit, so that the insurer may effectively prepare a defense or, if possible, mitigate or avoid a loss. This is true even when reporting during the policy period is a condition of coverage. Most notice provisions are similar, requiring the insured to notify the carrier of any actual or alleged claim or suit. It also requires notice when the dentist becomes aware of an act, error, or omission that might reasonably be expected to be the basis of a claim or suit.

Courts have generally found the notice requirements in professional liability policies to be unambiguous.[20] Difficulties may arise in determining what type of information should be passed on to the insurance carrier. To determine whether a professional fulfilled the obligation imposed by the notice requirement, courts usually determine what a "reasonable professional" would have done.[21] In many states, the insurer must show that the delay in reporting prejudiced its rights; that is, it must show that the lack of proper notice prevented a viable defense from being asserted simply because it is out of the time allowed by court rules. However, some courts are willing to hold that late notice vitiates the policy and that the insurer need not show any prejudice at all.[22]

[20]472 NYS2d 635 (1985).

[21]461 SW2d 704 (Mo 1971).

[22]293 NE2d 76 (NY 1972).

Cooperation Clause

19.11   All liability policies state that the insured must cooperate with the company in the defense of a claim and suit or in any action for indemnity or contribution. It states that the insured will assist the company in effectuating a settlement and by attending hearings or trial. The policy usually states that the insured shall not, except at his or her own cost, voluntarily make any payment, assume any obligation, or incur any expense (except for first aid) without the consent of the company.

Subrogation

19.12   The policy contains a clause providing the company with the right of subrogation. The clause typically states, "In the event of any payment under this policy, the Company shall be subrogated to all the Insured's rights of recover." The same paragraph states the insured will cooperate to enforce such right and will do nothing to prejudice them. Subrogation is likely to occur when a patient sues only one of several treating dentists. For tactical reasons, it may be best for the dentist to resolve the entire case and seek reimbursement from the other dentists later by way of indemnification or contribution. The company would prosecute that case in the name of the dentist through the subrogation clause.

Defense and Settlement

19.13   The dentist's policy states that the company has an obligation to defend any claim to which the insurance applies. The defense of a claim can extend to any action, including one in small claims court. Because a dentist's reputation is considered to be an important professional asset and any settlement or judgment is reportable to the National Practitioner Data Base, the policy typically provides that the company will not settle without the written consent of the insured. To shift some of the financial risk, insurance companies sometimes include that consent to settle will not be "unreasonably withheld." If the dentist refuses to consent to a settlement recommended by the company, the insurer's liability can be limited to the amount of the proposed settlement plus the costs and expenses up to that date. The court has upheld such clauses.

Exclusions

19.14   Exclusions in dental professional liability policies vary considerably from company to company. A dentist must carefully examine the policy before its purchase. The following are the most common exclusions.

Contractual Liability. Most policies contain an exclusion barring coverage for liability assumed by a dentist under a specific contract or agreement. This leads to problems in today's managed care system because managed care companies require contractual indemnification agreements to be signed before a dentist is allowed to accept his patients. Most companies will simply name the managed care company as an additional insured, usually, but not always, at some cost.

Certain Dental Procedures. Many dental professional liability policies contain exclusions for certain treatment and procedures that pose high risks, such as the use of general anesthesia.

Uninsurable Exposures. These exclusions include intentional bodily injury, sexual assault, criminal acts, libel, slander, invasion of privacy, unlawful discrimination, and the unlawful dispensing of drugs.

Punitive Damages. Most policies exclude punitive or exemplary damages, as these are usually imposed for deliberately wrongful conduct, not negligence.

Injury to an Employee. Most policies exclude coverage for any injury to an employee or for workers compensation, unemployment compensation, or disability benefits.

Other Insurance Clauses

19.15 The dentist may have several professional liability policies that apply to the same dental incident, eg, if the present policy is of the claims-made form and past policies were of the occurrence form. Alternatively, multiple acts of negligence may trigger multiple occurrence policies.

Most policies provide for a contingency of "other insurance." There are typically three approaches to this case. The first is a "pro rata" clause, which has the policies respond based upon pro rata shares, using the policy limits as the basis for each carrier's responsibility. The second is an "excess" clause, which states that the insurance provided is excess insurance over any other valid and collectible insurance. The third, now rarely used, is a "no liability" clause that seeks to avoid any coverage for a loss if there is other insurance. Courts usually resolve "other insurance" clauses to provide coverage on a pro rata basis.[23]

[23]186 CalApp3d 545; 230 CalRptr 792 (1986).

Additional Coverage to Consider

19.16 *Property Coverage.* You will need coverage for your building or office for damage caused by fire, windstorm, etc. Dental offices have very costly equipment: office machines, dental chairs, X-ray machines, laboratory equipment, etc. Be sure that you get replacement cost coverage for all of your important equipment. In the event of a catastrophic loss such as a fire, you will be able to replace the equipment without absorbing depreciation.

General Liability Coverage. This provides coverage for accidents in your office or on your professional premises. If someone slips and falls in the foyer of your office, your professional liability policy will not apply; you need general liability coverage. One additional "add-on" coverage to look for here is for libel and slander.

The Business Office Policy. The BOP is a package that combines coverage for property and premises. Typically, it also contains a menu of other coverages available such as business automobile insurance, crime insurance, employment practices insurance, employee dishonesty insurance, and miscellaneous directors and officers coverage.

Employer Liability Coverage. Employment Practices Liability Insurance (EPLI) coverage has taken on a life of its own over the last few years and for good reason: The explosion of employment practices litigation. It covers all types of discrimination, wrongful termination, sexual harassment, and employment misrepresentation. Coverage often extends to Equal Employment Opportunity Commission (EEOC) investigations and even punitive damages.

Workers Compensation Coverage. This is mandatory in every state to cover you and your employees for work-related injuries.

Legal Terms
with Dental Applications

-A-

Adhesion Contract: These contracts are offered on a "take-it-or-leave-it" basis, providing the consumer no opportunity to negotiate the terms. For example, Dr. Smith is the only dentist in a wide geographic area that specializes in endodontics. To receive her services her patients are required to sign an agreement not to sue her if the treatment she provides is unsuccessful.

Administrator: Person appointed to oversee the handling of an estate when there is no will.

Affidavit: A written statement made under oath.

Age of Majority: The age when a person acquires all the rights and responsibilities of being an adult. In most states, the age is 18.

Alimony: Also called maintenance or spousal support. In a divorce or separation, the money paid by one spouse to the other in order to fulfill the financial obligation that comes with marriage.

Answer: In a civil case, the defendant's written response to the plaintiff's complaint. It must be filed within a specified period of time, and it either admits to or (more typically) denies the factual or legal basis for liability.

Appeal: A request to a supervisory jurisdictional court, usually composed of a panel of judges.

Arbitration: A method of alternative dispute resolution in which the disputing parties agree to abide by the decision of an arbitrator. In some states dental malpractice suits must go to arbitration, while in others it is voluntary.

Articles of Incorporation: A document that must be filed with a state in order to incorporate. Among the things it typically must include are the name and address of the corporation, its general purpose, and the number and type of shares of stock to be issued.

Assumption of Risk: A defense raised in personal injury lawsuits. Asserts that the plaintiff knew that a particular activity was dangerous and thus bears all responsibility for any injury that resulted. It might be considered an assumption of risk to have a generalist provide a surgical procedure despite the patient being told that the services should have been provided by a specialist.

At-Will Employment: An employment relationship where the employer has the right to fire a worker for any cause at any time—usually without any notice.

-B-

Bad Faith: Dishonesty or fraud in a transaction, such as entering into an agreement with no intention of ever living up to its terms, or knowingly misrepresenting the quality of something that is being bought or sold.

Bankruptcy: Insolvency; a process governed by federal law to help when people cannot or will not pay their debts.

Bench Trial: Also called court trial. A trial held before a judge and without a jury.

Beyond a Reasonable Doubt: The highest level of proof required to win a case. Necessary to get a guilty verdict in criminal cases. Said to be 95% certain to have taken place. Not applied to dental malpractice cases—these are civil suits.

Brief: A written document that outlines a party's legal arguments in a case.

Burden of Proof: The duty of a party in a lawsuit to persuade the judge or the jury that enough facts exist to prove the allegations of the case. Different levels of proof are required depending on the type of case. In dental malpractice suits the burden is on the patient-plaintiff to show the dentist-defendant was guilty of malpractice. In *res ipsa* cases, the burden shifts to the dentist-defendant to show he was not guilty of malpractice.

Buy-Sell Agreement: An agreement among business partners that specifies how shares in the business are to be transferred in the case of a co-owner's death.

Bylaws: A corporation's rules and regulations. They typically specify the number and respective duties of directors and officers and govern how the business is run.

-C-

Case Law: The law created by appellate courts when deciding individual disputes or cases.

Case of First Impression: A novel legal question that for the first time comes before a court. The first case in which the employer is held liable for the negligent acts of an employee.

Caveat Emptor: Latin for "buyer beware." This rule generally applies to all sales between individuals. It gives the buyer full responsibility for determining the quality of the goods in question. The seller generally has no duty to offer warranties or to disclose defects in the goods.

Challenge for Cause: Ask that a potential juror be rejected if it is revealed that for some reason he or she is unable or unwilling to set aside preconceptions and pay attention only to the evidence.

Change of Venue: A change in the location of a trial, usually granted to avoid prejudice against one of the parties.

Child Abuse: Defined by state statutes. Usually occurs when a parent or guardian purposely harms a child below the age of 18 years. In some states dentists are required to report suspected cases of child abuse to a government agency.

Child Neglect: Defined by state statutes. Usually arises from a parent's or guardian's passive indifference to a child's well-being, such as failing to feed a child or failing to provide health care, including dental care. Neglect of a child's dental needs may fall within the definition of child neglect.

Circumstantial Evidence: Indirect evidence that implies something occurred but doesn't directly prove it. If a man accused of embezzling money from his company had made several big-ticket purchases in cash around the time of the alleged embezzlement, that would be circumstantial evidence that he had stolen the money.

Class Action Suit: A lawsuit in which one or more parties file a complaint on behalf of themselves and all other people who are "similarly situated" (suffering from the same problem). Often used when a large number of people have comparable claims.

Clear and Convincing Evidence: The level of proof sometimes required in a civil case for the plaintiff to prevail. Is more than a preponderance of the evidence but less than beyond a reasonable doubt; somewhere between 51% and 95%.

Comity: A code of etiquette that governs the interactions of courts in different states, localities, and foreign countries. Courts generally agree to defer scheduling a trial if the same issues are being tried in a court in another jurisdiction. In addition, courts in this country agree to recognize and enforce the valid legal contracts and court orders of other countries.

Common Law: Common law is a system of jurisprudence that originated in England, and applied in the United States at the time of its independence. It is based upon principles of justice, reason, and common sense rather than on set laws. When applied to specific situations decided by a judicial body, it becomes case law.

Comparative Negligence: Also called *comparative fault*. A system that allows a party to recover some portion of the damages caused by another party's negligence even if the original person was also partially negligent and responsible for causing the injury. A patient who does not comply with a dentist's instructions related to home care may be guilty of comparative negligence that resulted in his own injury. Some states use the contributory negligence theory.

Compensatory Damages: Money awarded to reimburse actual costs, such as medical bills and lost wages. Also awarded for things that are harder to measure, such as pain and suffering.

Complaint: In a civil action, the document that initiates a lawsuit. The complaint outlines the alleged facts of the case and the basis for which a legal remedy is sought. In a criminal action, a complaint is the preliminary charge filed by the complaining party, usually with the police or a court.

Conflict of Interest: Refers to a situation when someone, such as a lawyer or public official, has competing professional or personal obligations or personal or financial interests that would make it difficult to fulfill her duties fairly.

Consideration: Something of value that is given in exchange for getting something from another person. For example, payment of a fee in exchange for dental care.

Contingency Fee: Also called a *contingent fee*. A fee arrangement in which the lawyer is paid out of any damages that are awarded. Typically, the lawyer gets between one fourth and one third. If no damages are awarded, there is no fee. Dental experts at trial are prohibited to participate in a contingency fee arrangement. Their fee is not dependent upon who prevails at trial.

Contract: An agreement between two or more parties in which an offer is made and accepted, and each party benefits. The agreement can be formal, informal, written, oral, or just plain understood. Some contracts are required to be in writing to be enforced. The dentist-patient relationship is a contractual one.

Contributory Negligence: Prevents a party from recovering for damages if he contributed in any way to the injury. Not applied to malpractice cases. See *comparative negligence.*

Copyright: A person's right to prevent others from copying works that she has written, authored, or otherwise created.

Corporation: An independent entity created to conduct a business. It is owned by shareholders. In dentistry it is called a professional corporation or professional association, depending upon in which state the entity is formed.

Creditor: A person (or institution) to whom money is owed.

Cross Examination: The questioning of an opposing party's witness about matters brought up during direct examination.

-D-

Damages: The financial compensation awarded to someone who suffered an injury or was harmed by someone else's wrongful act.

Special Damages: Reimbursement for out-of-pocket expenses

General Damages: Payment accessed for pain and suffering

Debtor: Person who owes money.

Decision: The judgment rendered by a court after a consideration of the facts and legal issues before it.

Defamation: The publication of a statement that injures a person's reputation. Dentist may be accused of defamation by patients or other health practitioners.

Libel: Written defamation

Slander: Oral defamation

Default: The failure to fulfill a legal obligation, such as neglecting to pay back a loan on schedule, or a fee when due.

Default Judgment: A ruling entered against a defendant who fails to answer a summons in a lawsuit.

Defendant: In criminal cases, the person accused of the crime. In civil matters, the person or organization that is being sued. It could be the individual dentist, a partnership, a professional corporation, a professional association, or a professional limited liability company.

Demonstrative Evidence: Physical evidence presented at trial, eg, dental casts, appliances, dentures, photographs, diagrams, illustrations, etc.

Dental Jurisprudence: The application of law to the practice of dentistry. Includes federal, state, and local laws that regulate dental practice and case law that affects dental practice.

Deposition: Part of the pre-trial discovery (fact-finding) process in which a witness testifies under oath. A deposition is held out of court with no judge present, but the answers often can be used as evidence in the trial. An examination before trial (EBT) is a deposition.

Direct Evidence: Evidence that stands on its own to prove an alleged fact, such as testimony of a witness who says she saw a defendant pointing a gun at a victim during a robbery.

Direct Examination: The initial questioning of a witness by the party that called the witness.

Directed Verdict: A judge's order to a jury to return a specified verdict, usually because one of the parties failed to prove its case.

Disbursements: Legal expenses that a lawyer passes on to a client, such as for photocopying, overnight mail and messenger services, payment for experts, etc.

Discovery: Part of the pre-trial litigation process during which each party requests relevant information and documents from the other side in an attempt to "discover" pertinent facts. The EBT is part of the discovery process as is the review by both sides of the patient's records.

Dismissal with Prejudice: When a case is dismissed for good reason and the plaintiff is barred from bringing an action on the same claim.

Dismissal Without Prejudice: When a case is dismissed but the plaintiff is allowed to bring a new suit on the same claim.

Due Process: The idea that laws and legal proceedings must be fair. The Constitution guarantees that the government cannot take away a person's basic rights to "life, liberty, or property, without due process of law." Courts have issued numerous rulings about what this means in particular cases.

Duty to Warn: The legal obligation to warn people of a danger. Typically, manufacturers of hazardous products have a duty to warn customers of a product's potential dangers and to advise users of any precautions they should take.

-E-

Emancipation: When a minor has achieved independence from her parents, often by getting married before reaching age 18 or by becoming fully self-supporting. It plays a large part in the issue of consent to dental care. An emancipated minor may consent to dental care without the consent of the parent or guardian.

Equal Protection Clause: Portion of the Fourteenth Amendment to the U.S. Constitution that prohibits discrimination by state government institutions. The clause grants all people "equal protection of the laws," which means that the states must apply the law equally and cannot give preference to one person or class of persons over another.

Equitable Estoppel: An individual is prevented (estopped) from benefitting from a situation in which he made a false representation or a concealment of material facts with knowledge of the facts to a party ignorant of the truth of the matter, with the intention that the party should act upon it, with the result that such party is induced to act upon it, to his damage.

Estate: All the property a person owns.

Evidence: The various things presented in court to prove an alleged fact. Includes testimony, documents, photographs, maps, and video tapes.

Expert Witness: A witness with a specialized knowledge of a subject who is allowed to discuss an event in court even though she was not present. For example, a dental expert could testify about the quality of care provided by a dentist defendant—whether or not it met the standard of care measured against the care provided by other dentists in the community.

Express Consent: Where both parties agree to the terms. May be written or oral.

Express Warranty (Guarantee): An assertion or promise concerning goods or services. Statements such as, "This denture will enable you to chew steaks without the denture becoming dislodged," or, "We will repair any problems with the dentures in the first year," are express warranties, as is, "You will be happy with these implants."

-F-

Felony: Serious crime punishable by incarceration for a year or more. Includes rape, murder, robbery, burglary, and arson.

Fiduciary Duty: An obligation to act in the best interest of another party. For instance, a corporation's board member has a fiduciary duty to the shareholders, a trustee has a fiduciary duty to the trust's beneficiaries, an attorney has a fiduciary duty to a client, and a dentist has a fiduciary duty to a patient—to always act in the best interest of his patient.

Forensic Odontology: The application of dentistry to the law, including criminal investigations, body identification, etc.

Foreseeability: A key issue in determining a person's liability. Some states require that for consent to be informed all risks that are *foreseeable* must be told to the patient. In others, the risks described need only be those that are *material* to the patient.

-G-

Garnishment: Also known as wage execution. A court-ordered method of debt collection in which a portion of a person's salary is paid to a creditor. Often used to collect child support payments.

General Partner: One of two kinds of partners in a limited partnership. A general partner has the right to participate in the management of the partnership and has unlimited personal liability for its debts.

Good Faith: Honestly and without deception. An agreement might be declared invalid if one of the parties entered with the intention of defrauding the other.

Gross Negligence: Failure to use even the slightest amount of care in a way that shows recklessness or willful disregard for the safety of others. In the Good Samaritan Laws, health providers covered under the law are immune from suit if found guilty of simple or ordinary negligence but not for gross negligence.

Guardian: Person assigned by the court to take care of minor children or incompetent adults. Sometimes called a conservator.

Guardian Ad Litem: Latin for "guardian at law." The person appointed by the court to look out for the best interests of the child during the course of legal proceedings.

-H-

Health Care Proxy: Someone designated to make a broad range of decisions for a person who is not able to give informed consent.

Hearsay: Secondhand information that a witness only heard about from someone else and did not see or hear herself. Hearsay is not admitted in court because it's not trustworthy, though there are many exceptions. Statements made in a text are hearsay.

Hostile Environment Sexual Harassment: Where a person is subject to unwelcome sexual advances, requests for sexual favors, or other verbal or physical conduct of a sexual nature to such an extent that it alters the conditions of the person's employment and creates an abusive working environment. Sexual harassment of employees is one of the risks to which dentists are exposed.

-I-

Immunity: Exemption from a legal duty, penalty, or prosecution.

Impairment: When a person's faculties are diminished so that her ability to see, hear, walk, talk, and judge distances is below the normal level as set by the state. Typically, impairment is caused by drug or alcohol use, but can also be caused by mental illness.

Implied Consent:
Consent Implied by Law: The law may grant consent to care in situations where the patient was unable to consent. For example at the scene of an accident where the person is unconscious.
Consent Implied by the Actions of the Party: When care is being provided and the patient permits it to continue without objection.

Implied Warranty: A guarantee imposed by law in a sale of goods or service. Even though the seller may not make any explicit promises, the buyer still gets some protection. Implied warranties are called implied duties in the doctor-patient relationship.

Implied Warranty of Fitness for a Particular Purpose: Warranty that exists when a seller should know that a buyer is relying on the seller's expertise. Has application in dentistry, particularly in the fabrication of dentures.

Implied Warranty of Merchantability: Warranty that guarantees that goods are reasonably fit for their ordinary purpose. Has application in dentistry, particularly in the fabrication of dentures.

Indictment: A formal accusation of a felony, issued by a grand jury after considering evidence presented by a prosecutor.

Indigent: Lacking in funds; poor.

Informed Consent: Except in the case of an emergency, a doctor must obtain a patient's agreement (informed consent) to any course of treatment. Doctors are required to tell the patient anything that would substantially affect the patient's decision. Such information typically includes the nature and purpose of the treatment, its risks and consequences, and alternative courses of treatment. There is both black letter law and case law on informed consent. Under common law, patients must be given enough information about the proposed procedure to enable them to make an intelligent decision as to whether to submit to the procedure, postpone it, or refuse it.

Interrogatories: Part of the pre-trial discovery (fact-finding) process in which a witness provides written answers to written questions under oath. The answers often can be used as evidence in the trial. In some states this is an alternative to the examination before trial.

-J-

Joint and Severable Liability: Cases in which a single person may be held liable or several persons may be held liable jointly for the same negligent act. Occurs in dental partnerships where each partner may be jointly or severably liable: partner A alone; partner B alone, or A and B together.

Joint Custody: When both parents share custody of a child after a divorce. There are two kinds of custody: legal custody and physical custody. Either or both may be joint.

Judgment: A court's official decision on the matters before it.

Judgment Non Obstante Veredicto: Known also as a judgment notwithstanding the verdict. A decision by a trial judge to rule in favor of a losing party even though the jury's verdict was in favor of the other side. Usually done when the facts or law do not support the jury's verdict. Although rare, it may apply in dental malpractice cases.

Jurisdiction: A court's authority to rule on the questions of law at issue in a dispute, typically determined by geographic location and the subject of the case.

Jury Charge: The judge's instructions to the jurors on the law that applies in a case and definitions of the relevant legal concepts. These instructions may be complex and are often pivotal in a jury's discussions.

Just Cause: A legitimate reason. Often used in the employment context to refer to the reasons why someone was fired.

-L-

Legal Custody: In a divorce, one of two types of child custody. A parent who has legal custody has the right to be involved in all the decision-making typically involved with being a parent, such as religious upbringing, education, and medical decisions. Legal custody can be either sole or joint. Compare with physical custody.

Liability: Any legal responsibility, duty, or obligation.

Libel: Defamatory (false and injurious) written statements or materials, including photographs or videos. Can be a risk to dentists.

Lien: A claim against someone's property. A lien is instituted in order to secure payment from the property owner in the event that the property is sold. A mortgage is a common lien.

Limited Liability Company: A business structure that is a hybrid of a partnership and a corporation. Its owners are shielded from personal liability and all profits and losses pass directly to the owners without taxation of the entity itself. May be organized by professionals, eg, physicians, dentists, attorneys, etc.

Limited Partner: One of two kinds of partners in a limited partnership. Is personally liable for the debts of the partnership only to the extent of her investment in it and has little to no voice in its management.

Limited Partnership: A partnership with two kinds of partners: limited partners, who provide financial backing and have little role in management and no personal liability, and general partners, who are responsible for managing the entity and have unlimited personal liability for its debts.

Liquidated Damages: The amount of money specified in a contract to be awarded in the event that the agreement is violated.

-M-

Malpractice: Improper or negligent behavior by a professional, such as a physician, dentist, or attorney. The failure of a professional to follow the accepted standards of practice of his profession.

Mediation: A method of alternative dispute resolution in which a neutral third party helps resolve a dispute. The mediator does not have the power to impose a decision on the parties. If a satisfactory resolution cannot be reached, the parties can pursue a lawsuit.

Minor: A person who does not have the legal rights of an adult. A minor is usually defined as someone who has not yet reached the age of majority. In most states, a person reaches majority and acquires all of the rights and responsibilities of an adult when he turns 18. See *emancipation*.

Misdemeanor: Crime that is punishable by less than one year in jail, such as minor theft and simple assault that does not result in substantial bodily injury.

Mitigating Factors: Information about a defendant or the circumstances of a crime that might tend to lessen the sentence or the crime with which the person is charged.

Motion: A request asking a judge to issue a ruling or order on a legal matter.

Motion for a New Trial: Request in which a losing party asserts that a trial was unfair due to legal errors that prejudiced his case.

Motion for Directed Verdict: A request made by the defendant in a civil case. Asserts that the plaintiff has raised no genuine issue to be tried and asks the judge to rule in favor of the defense. Typically made after the plaintiff is done presenting her case.

Motion for Summary Judgment: A request made by the defendant in a civil case. Asserts that the plaintiff has raised no genuine issue to be tried and asks the judge to rule in favor of the defense. Typically made before the trial.

Motion to Dismiss: In a civil case, a request to a judge by the defendant, asserting that even if all the allegations are true, the plaintiff is not entitled to any legal relief and thus the case should be dismissed.

Motion to Suppress Evidence: A request to a judge to keep out evidence at a trial or hearing, often made when a party believes the evidence was unlawfully obtained.

-N-

Named Plaintiffs: The originators of a class action suit.

Negligence: A failure to use the degree of care that a reasonable person would use under the same circumstances. Malpractice is a form of professional negligence.

Notary Public: A person authorized to witness the signing of documents.

Notice of Appeal: The document a person must file with the trial court in order to pursue an appeal.

-O-

Officers of a Corporation: Those people with day-to-day responsibility for running the corporation, such as the chief executive, chief financial officer, and treasurer.

-P-

Partnership: An association of two or more people who agree to share in the profits and losses of a business venture. The sharing of profits leads to the severable liability of an innocent partner for the negligent acts of a guilty partner.

Patent: A document issued to an inventor by the United States Patent and Trademark Office. Contains a detailed description of what the invention is and how to make or use it and provides rights against infringers.

Pension Plan: An employer's program for providing retirement income to eligible employees.

Peremptory Challenges: Limited number of challenges each side in a trial can use to eliminate potential jurors without stating a reason. May not be used to keep members of a particular race or sex off the jury.

Perjury: A crime in which a person knowingly makes a false statement while under oath in court. In some jurisdictions, making a false statement in a legal document can also be considered perjury.

Personal Guardian: Person appointed to take custody of children and provide for their care and upbringing. Distinguished from property guardian.

Plaintiff: The person who initiates a lawsuit.

Pleadings: In a civil case, the allegations by each party of their claims and defenses.

Precedent: A previously decided appellate case that is considered binding in the court where it was issued and in all lower courts in the same jurisdiction.

Preponderance of the Evidence: The level of proof required to prevail in most civil cases. The judge or jury must be persuaded that the facts are more probably one way (the plaintiff's way) than another (the defendant's). At least 50% certain to have taken place. Applies to dental malpractice cases.

Prima Facie: Latin for "at first view." Refers to the minimum amount of evidence a plaintiff must have to avoid having a case dismissed. It is said that the plaintiff must make a prima facie case.

Privileged Communication: Conversation that takes places within the context of a protected relationship, such as that between an attorney and client, a husband and wife, a priest and penitent, and a doctor and patient. The law often protects against forced disclosure of such conversations.

Punitive Damages: Money awarded to a victim that is intended to punish a defendant and stop the person or business from repeating the type of conduct that caused an injury. Also intended to deter others from similar conduct. Rarely imposed in dental malpractice cases, except if it is determined that the dentist intentionally lied to a patient about the treatment, or withheld information that caused an injury to the patient. Punitive damages are not covered in malpractice insurance policies.

-Q-

Quash: To nullify, void, or declare invalid.

Quid Pro Quo: Latin phrase that means what for what or something for something. The concept of getting something of value in return for giving something of value. For a contract to be binding, it usually must involve the exchange of something of value.

-R-

Real Property: Land and all the things that are attached to it. Anything that is not real property is personal property and personal property is anything that isn't nailed down, dug into or built onto the land. A house is real property, but a dining room set is not.

Reasonable Care: The level of care a typical person would use if faced with the same circumstances. The care provided by a dentist must be reasonable to be accepted by the courts as meeting a reasonable standard.

Reasonable Doubt: The level of certainty a juror must have to find a defendant guilty of a crime.

Re-cross Examination: Questioning a witness about matters brought up during re-direct examination.

Re-direct Examination: Questioning a witness about matters brought up during cross examination.

Remand: When an appellate court sends a case back to a lower court for further proceedings.

Res Ipsa Loquitur: A Latin phrase that means "the thing speaks for itself." Refers to situations when it's assumed that a person's injury was caused by the negligent action of another party because the accident was the sort that wouldn't occur unless someone was negligent. Has application to dentistry.

Retainer: Refers to the up-front payment a client gives a lawyer to accept a case. The client is paying to retain the lawyer's services.

-S-

Separation Agreement: In a marital breakup, a document that outlines the terms of the couple's separation.

Service of Process: The act of notifying the other parties that an action has begun and informing them of the steps they should take in order to respond—suit papers served to a dentist.

Settlement: The resolution or compromise by the parties in a civil lawsuit.

Settlement Agreement: In a civil lawsuit, the document that spells out the terms of an out-of-court compromise.

Shareholder: An owner or investor in a corporation.

Slander: Defamatory (false and injurious) oral statements or gestures. See defamation above.

Sole Proprietorship: A form of business organization in which an individual is fully and personally liable for all the obligations (including debts) of the business, is entitled to all of its profits and exercises complete managerial control. Applies to dentist in private solo practice.

Spoliate: Different jurisdictions have applied different definitions to the term, but it broadly refers to the intentional, reckless, or negligent destruction, loss, material alteration, or obstruction of evidence that is relevant to litigation. It is, however, still unclear if spoliation includes both negligent and intentional destruction of evidence, the loss of evidence, and/or evidence that was destroyed before litigation began. Applies to dental records that are changed or "lost."

Standard of Care: The degree of care a reasonable person would take to prevent an injury to another. In its application it is the degree of care a reasonable dentist would take to prevent an injury to a patient.

Standing: The legal right to initiate a lawsuit. To do so, a person must be sufficiently affected by the matter at hand, and there must be a case or controversy that can be resolved by legal action.

Stare Decisis: Latin for "to stand by that which is decided." Refers to the principle of adhering to precedent when deciding a case.

Statutes of Fraud: Laws in most states to protect against false claims for payment from contracts that were not agreed upon. The specific laws vary from state to state, but most require that certain contracts be in writing.

Statute of Limitations: Law setting deadlines for filing lawsuits within a certain time after events occur that are the source of a claim.

Strict Liability: Liability even when there is no proof of negligence. Often applicable in product liability cases against manufacturers, who are legally responsible for injuries caused by defects in their products, even if they were not negligent. Does not apply to dentistry.

Subpoena: An order compelling a person to appear to testify or produce documents.

Subpoena Duces Tecum: An order compelling a witness with a document under his control to produce it at trial. Applies to dental records.

Summation: The closing argument in a trial.

Summons: A legal document that notifies a party that a lawsuit has been initiated and states when and where the party must appear to answer the charges. Dentists being sued are served with a summons.

-T-

Tangible Personal Property: Anything other than real estate or money, including furniture, cars, jewelry, and china. The patient's dental records are tangible personal property as are dental equipment, instruments, office furniture, etc.

Title: Ownership of property. When a denture is given to the patient the title passes from the dentist to the patient. When a denture as handed from the patient to the dentist for an adjustment, the title does not pass to the dentist. She cannot withhold delivery to the patient to collect a prior fee.

Tort: A civil wrong that results in an injury to a person or property. Malpractice is a tort.

-U-

Uniform Commercial Code: A model statute covering things such as the sale of goods, credit, and bank transactions. All states have adopted and adapted the entire UCC, with the exception of Louisiana, which only adopted parts of it.

-V-

Valid Claim: A grievance that can be resolved by legal action.

Verdict: The formal decision issued by a jury on the issues of fact that were presented at trial.

Vicarious Liability: When one person is liable for the negligent actions of another person, even though the first person was not directly responsible for the injury. For instance, a parent sometimes can be vicariously liable for the harmful acts of a child and an employer sometimes can be vicariously liable for the acts of a worker.

-W-

Warranty: A promise about a product or service made by either a manufacturer, seller, or service provider.

Witness: Person who comes to court and swears under oath to give truthful evidence.

Worker's Compensation: A benefit paid to an employee who suffers a work-related injury or illness.

Writ: A judicial order.

Index